Karen Anand was born in Bombay in
London and Paris where she did vari
International Relations, and one in Fine Arts. After she returned
to India she did a diploma in Film Appreciation in the Film and
T.V. Institute, Pune. She has been a reporter and freelance writer
for many years and has contributed to many foreign and Indian
magazines.

She also did a diploma in Health and Nutrition from K.C. College,
Bombay, and ran a restaurant which specialized in European
gourmet food called the Salad Bar—the first of its kind in
Bombay—with Nelson Wang, the owner of China Garden. She went
on to start her own business and launched Bombay's first European
style Gourmet Cheese Shop and Delicatessen.

Karen Anand is married with two children.

*

Gul Anand is a well-known film producer and has many acclaimed
films to his credit. These include *Khatta Meetha* (1978), *Chasme
Buddoor* (1981), *The Guiding Light*, *Jalwa* (1986) for which he
wrote the screenplay, *Hero Hiralal*, *Chatran* (a wild life film),
Romancing the Taj which he directed, and a TV serial called
Farmaan.

Gul Anand is also a still photographer and has held several
one-man shows all over the world. He also contributes articles and
photo-features to many newspapers and magazines.

Gul Anand is married with two children.

THE PENGUIN

FOOD LOVER'S GUIDE TO INDIA & NEPAL

Karen & Gul Anand

PENGUIN BOOKS

Penguin Books India (P) Ltd., 210, Chiranjiv Tower, 43, Nehru Place, New Delhi 110 019, India
Penguin Books Ltd., 27 Wrights Lane, London W8 5TZ, UK
Penguin Books USA Inc., 375 Hudson Street, New York, NY 10014, USA
Penguin Books Australia Ltd., Ringwood, Victoria, Australia
Penguin Books Canada Ltd., 10 Alcorn Avenue, Suite 300, Toronto, Ontario M4V 3B2, Canada
Penguin Books (NZ) Ltd., 182-190 Wairau Road, Auckland 10, New Zealand

First published by Penguin Books India (P) Ltd. 1994

Typeset in New Century Schoolbook by Digital Technologies and Printing Solutions, New Delhi

The photograph of Vidana Soudha on page 17 is reproduced with the kind permission of Em Yes Studios, Bangalore. The photograph of a wedding feast on page 163 is courtesy Rono Mukherji; all other photographs by Gul Anand.

This book is dedicated to Pogo and Sasha, whom we hope will enjoy food as much as we do.

Contents

Introduction

This book is not a listing of all the restaurants in India. It is, we hope, and as the title suggests, an introduction to specialities, Indian or otherwise, which can be found in eleven major cities. In other words, a guide to the best places to eat good, wholesome, value for money food.

We cannot stress enough that this is a highly personalized and therefore subjective selection. We apologize if your favourite restaurant is not included. This could be for one of several reasons: it was not up to the mark; it was good, but not extraordinary in a city where there may have been hoards of other options; we simply ran out of time.

It took us two years, innumerable doses of Digene and many extended deadlines (thank you, Publisher), to research, update and compile this book. We are proud to say, though, that we tasted every single dish, the good, bad and ugly. The conclusions come straight from the heart, as well as from the stomach. Apart from having a great time, we also found some inspiring, committed foodies, as obsessed with good food as we are, and have made a lot of new friends in the bargain.

Even after such marathon efforts at authenticity, there are bound to be changes. Food is as fickle and as variable as the human condition. The quality may differ because the chef has changed, the supplier has let you down, or someone in the kitchen has quarrelled with his (or her) spouse before coming to work. There were times when we went gaga over a restaurant, and the next time we went there with friends to show off our discovery, it was not the same. Be wary of five-star restaurants too, since their menus tend to change every few months. On the whole, we found dishes and menus more consistent in the small chef-proprietor restaurants.

Restaurants are classified in three categories, according to the prices of the specialities we have recommended and cover a meal for one person, including dessert and a soft drink.

Inexpensive - under 100 rupees.
Moderate - 100 to 250 rupees
Expensive - over 250 rupees.

Remember, taxes and service are usually extra. In luxury hotels, you are charged a sales tax of fifteen per cent in addition to an expenditure tax of twenty per cent. In deluxe restaurants, a fifteen per cent sales tax usually applies, and in moderate priced restaurants, it is only eight per cent. Inexpensive places often do not levy any taxes or service charges.

We have, by and large, left out Coffee Shops, Bars and the new tribe of what we refer to as 'multi-cuisine' restaurants, i.e., the ones with over powerful air-conditioning, turbaned doormen and dishes from three continents which are rustled up in a matter of minutes. Very few of these fit into our definition of the book, which concentrates on speciality dishes.

Under each restaurant is the type of cuisine. This is only an indication to the speciality, and does not mean that other dishes are not served. The cuisines we have covered include North Indian or Moghlai, Muslim (mainly meaty), Chinese, Thai, Continental (with more of an emphasis on the British style), European (French, Italian, Spanish, etc.), Italian, Malvani (Maharashtrian Coastal, usually seafood), Goan (Christian), Goan (Hindu), Mangalorean, Bengali, Rajasthani, Tibetan, Andhra, Hyderabadi (Moghlai inspired), South Indian (usually dishes from Tamil Nadu, Karnataka and Kerala), and Maharashtrian.

This book would not have been possible without the help and guidance of many friends, including Rima Kayshap, Romu Sippy, Dimpy Sabarwal, Arunesh Mayyar, Dr Vijay Abbot, Daniel Yonzan, Munzurmal Amin, Sumitra Awchat, Kiran Arora, Rono Mukherji and the late Syed Sattar.

We hope you will have as much fun with the book, as we have had writing it.

Agra

There is very little to say about food in this sleepy, overgrown village, except that it should be better, given the number of tourists that flock here. Being just south of Delhi, the historical origins and influences in eating habits are practically the same as in the capital. But you are not likely to find authentic Moghlai food anywhere, despite the constant reminders of its glorious Mughal past.

Most tourists rarely spend more than a night here. Their priority is usually a comfortable bed for the night after a day of hectic sightseeing, and reasonable food, usually in that order. For this reason, speciality restaurants, outside the five-star hotels, have been slow to materialize.

For the street wise, most of the action takes place after five p.m. in the Sadar Bazaar area, where you can sample Agra's famous chaat and petha, a sweet type of halwa made from white pumpkin. If you are interested in a quick, satisfying street snack then Ram Babu Paratha Bhandar is the place. Watch out for the small, seedy restaurants which try to lure the innocent passer-by with promises of good, fast, cheap grub. Most of them are disaster areas where food is concerned. We found Dasaprakash, serving South Indian vegetarian food, excellent in terms of quality, cleanliness and comfort, and the best value for money in Agra.

If you are a five-star bird, then look no further than the Mughal Sheraton, with its extensive range of eating options, which range from Moghlai, Continental, and Chinese to buffets and barbecues.

Clearly not the place for a gourmet, but with careful planning, you could survive the trip here without 'Delhi Belly' or a similar ailment.

A meal for one person
Inexpensive: under 100 rupees Moderate: 100 to 250 rupees Expensive: over 250 rupees

Bagh-e-Bahar

Bagh-e-Bahar
Mughal Sheraton
Taj Ganj
Agra 282 001
Tel:361701
Fax:361730
Price:Expensive
Speciality:Continental
Timings:
  Breakfast: 6 to 11 a.m.
  Coffee Shop: 11 a.m. to
  7 p.m.
  Continental Restaurant:
  7.30 to 11 p.m.
Air-conditioned
Bar licence

An innovative idea in space efficiency, this elegant room is used for breakfast, as a coffee shop during the day, and is transformed into a highly recommended Continental restaurant, with a live band, in the evening.

Do not pass up the chef's homemade Pâté Maison, the soups, including a delicious Potage Saint Germain (peas and cream) and his excellent Chateaubriand, marinated in red wine and finished with mushrooms and a light hollandaise sauce. The Filet de Sole Grenobloise (river sole pan fried in butter with capers and lemon) and Canneloni Florentine, made with fresh pasta are also recommended.

During the day, the restaurant also has low calorie specials, accompanied by beautifully presented vegetables. These were innovative and light with an emphasis on vegetarian options, so often overlooked. The stuffed mushrooms (with spinach and cheese) were too small to make an impact. However, this was made up for by chef Anil Misri's creation, Mughal Cheese Steak, a masterpiece of culinary innovation. Three roundels of fresh paneer are sandwiched together with a non-spicy green chutney, and surrounded by a sweetish tomato and garlic sauce. The soya chicken roll with a stuffing of Chinese vegetables was wonderfully different and satisfying.

Between these two restaurants is a large dining-hall where a daily buffet is served for hotel guests only, in theory, but the management is flexible on this one. This is undoubtedly the best value in town. An array of Continental, Chinese, Indian, hot and cold desserts and ice cream, and a very good selection of cold cuts and salads, for around Rs 200 depending on the season.

Chimanlal Pooriwala

This shop has been redecorated 'contemporary' style, with plastic-top tables and metal chairs. It is also the size and shape of a railway bogie. However, it is one of the oldest eateries in Agra (1843), doing a roaring business selling just two items, puri (deep fried puffed bread) and bhaji (curried potato).

Chimanlal Pooriwala
Subash Bazaar
Next to Jamma Masjid
Agra
Price:Inexpensive
Speciality : North Indian
Vegetarian
Timings : 7 a.m. to 10 p.m.

The puris are served piping hot. The waiter keeps a watchful eye on your plate, and as soon as it is empty, a steaming puri reappears, as if by magic, and the bowl of bhaji is refilled. We found the bhaji a bit spicy, so a side dish of home-made dahi (yoghurt) helped put out the fire. We personally preferred to make a meal out of puri and dahi, with a sprinkling of salt and black pepper. The food is cheap, but you don't know when to stop—that's the catch.

The fourth generation of the Chimanlal family still cook and serve the food, to the fourth generation of loyal clients. The puris are fried in desi ghee, in a big kadai in front of the shop. The owner himself does the deed as he greets his familiar clients.

Dasaprakash

Dasaprakash
Meher Theatre Complex
1, Gwalior Road
Agra Cantt 282 001
Price:Inexpensive
Speciality:South Indian
Timings:12 to 3.30 p.m.;
6 to 11 p.m.
Air-conditioned

Queer decor of red gingham, mock tiffany lamps, white lattice work and stained glass, gives the impression of a nouveau fast food joint. But this is actually a franchisee of the popular South Indian chain we all know and love. One can't compare it with its parent operation in Madras, but it does serve the best South Indian food in the area. Rasam (spicy sour soup), idli (soft, fluffy rice cake), dosa (perfectly crisp rice pancake), vada (savoury doughnut), uttapam (thick rice and lentil pancake)—all come with silver sauceboats of sambar, chutney and potato bhaji, for slightly more than you would pay in the south. For those who don't need to watch their weight or their cholesterol levels, a generous pat of white butter wrapped in a piece of banana leaf accompanies the various dosas. A very good, unlimited vegetarian thali is also available for Rs 60 (plus taxes), which is very reasonable in this neck of the woods. Juices are freshly squeezed.

On the flip side of the familiar menu is an ice cream lover's dream: sundaes, floats, or just plain ice creams with a variety of toppings. The butterscotch and praline are particularly good.

A great idea for the often scorching Agra heat. Service is quick and quiet, and the restaurant, spotlessly clean.

Devi Ram Mithaiwala

A hole in the wall at the corner of Pratap Pura, this little dhaba turns out the most delicious kachori (deep fried, savoury patties) and potato vegetable in Agra. It is sold as fast as old, turbaned Umesh Chand, the partner-cum-chef, can physically turn them out. There is a perpetual rush and you have to elbow your way in, to catch the eye of the chef, if you want to be served promptly. No polite queues here. The hot kachoris,

Devi Ram Mithaiwala
Pratap Pura
Next to Ratanlal and Sons
  Photographer
Agra
Price:Inexpensive
Speciality : North Indian
  Vegetarian
Timings : 6 a.m. to 10 p.m.

stuffed plump with spicy channa dal, are overwhelming with home-made cold creamy yoghurt, all served in disposable clay pots.

There is no seating arrangement, nor are there any tables. You have to make do with a car bonnet, or the ledge of the nearby shop, which can be very uncomfortable, as the stall is bang in the middle of a regular, dusty Agra street. But a feast it is. Avoid the 'drinking water', and carry your own napkins or tissue boxes. The place is not very clean either, so don't come here if you have a weak stomach.

Umesh Chand makes wonderful sweets, especially imartis, a heavier cousin of the jalebi, at four rupees per 100 grams, but you should have a hefty sweet tooth to be able to appreciate them. In fact, everything here is sold at Rs 4. It probably saves accounting problems.

Joney's Place

Joney's Place
Kutta Park
Taj Ganj
Agra 282 001
Price:Inexpensive
Specialities:North Indian
  (non-spicy),
  Middle Eastern
Timings : 9 a.m. to 9 p.m.

Nicknamed the 'Yum Yum Food Restaurant', this tiny twenty-two seater is run by chef-cum-bearer-cum-cashier, Joney, whose large colour picture adorns one of the walls. The majority of his customers are foreigners looking for a place to eat simple, uncomplicated, non-spicy food, cheaply. There is also a black-and-white TV, connected to Star TV which seems to keep the customers happy.

The cuisine is a strange smattering of Middle Eastern food, including Humous (chick pea dip), Falafel (deep fried bean rissole) and Pitta (Lebanese flat, unleavened bread) bread, which, though poor imitations, seemed to be popular with Joney's clients. We personally felt the non-spicy Navratna curry (mildly spiced vegetables in a tomato gravy) and rice was well-cooked and good value. The cherry on the cake, however, was the banana lassi (buttermilk), served in a tall glass, which was absolutely delicious and so thick that we had to eat it with a spoon. 'No water is added,' said Joney proudly, 'besides, foreigners are suspicious of tap water.' The breakfast at Joney's Place is a real steal at Rs 10, for two toasts with butter, one egg cooked to order and freshly ground coffee or leaf tea.

It is tough passing time in Agra after you have had your fill of the Taj Mahal. Those fond of the bazaar scene gravitate towards Taj Ganj. Joney's is one place in Taj Ganj where you can have a lassi and watch the world go by, or watch Star TV, without burning a hole in your pocket.

Mughul Room

For comfortable, elegant dining in Agra, the Mughul Room is a front runner. It is a rooftop dining-hall with huge windows overlooking the Taj and the Agra Fort. The Tandoor section is magnificently displayed in a glass cubicle (open kitchen concept), where the chef can be seen in action. The burgundy carpet gives a very distinguished look to the dining-hall, which is clean and well-lit. There is a well-stocked bar next to the Mughul Room. The restaurant is multi-cuisine, but the focus is chiefly on Moghlai and Continental food. We are basically lovers of fish, so we were delighted when we tasted Poisson grill Del-Ray, which is a grilled fillet of fresh bekti, served with sautéed mushrooms, green peppers, tomatoes and the most delicious garlic spinach we have ever had. Another excellent speciality is the Kalmi Kabab (chicken legs grilled in the tandoor). The masala was light and the taste superb. Chateaubriand Steak (for two) and Steak Au Poivre (the chef's special) are good deals. Even though we tasted only a few of the dishes, it was apparent that the chef is skilled, and can turn out consistently good quality food.

A good place to make a beeline for when in Agra, especially if you miss fish.

Mughul Room
Clark Shiraz Agra
54 Taj Road
Agra 282 001
Tel : 361421-7.
Price:Expensive
Specialities: Moghlai,
   Continental
Timings:12.30 to 2.30 p.m.;
   7.30 to 11 p.m.
Credit cards accepted
Bar license

Navratna

Navratna
Mughal Sheraton
Taj Ganj
Agra 282 001
Tel:361701
Fax:361730
Price:Expensive
Specialities: North Indian,
  Moghlai
Timings: 12.30 to 2.45 p.m.;
  7.30 to 11.45 p.m.
Credit cards accepted
Bar licence
Air-conditioned

A wide choice of cuisines in one of Agra's oldest, and very contemporary five-star hotels, as chief chef Anil Misri, guides his chefs with great efficiency and innovation through the various sections of this sprawling hotel. The cuisine ranges from Indian and Chinese to Continental.

Navratna is the purple-and-white marbled Indian restaurant, serving a variety of Indian cuisines with some very interesting Kashmiri specialities, and some of chef Misri's own recipes. The Murg Tikka Achari (chicken tikka with pickle) is plump, juicy and mildly flavoured with achar spices, like methi and jeera. The Paneer Ke Soole Chutneywale (smoked paneer with green mint chutney) is a welcome change from the usual paneer in tomato gravy. The paneer is made by the hotel itself.

For the main course, Kashmiri Kalia Keser is a must. Ribs and shoulder pieces of mutton are stewed in a yoghurt-and-saffron curry, fragrant with dry ginger. Baoli Handi, boneless pieces of lamb cooked in an earthenware pot, is also delicious. For the vegetarians, the Khumb Pakeezah, stuffed mushrooms in a non-spicy tomato gravy, the chef's own version of Malai Kofta—cottage cheese with a stuffing of dry fruits, simmered in a cashewnut-and-cream sauce and Birbali Paneer (named after Akbar's grand wazir) which is cottage cheese coated with mint chutney and stewed in a butter and tomato gravy, should appeal.

Rotis and rice dishes are all excellent quality. The flaky Lachcha Paratha is a dream, and if that doesn't move you, the soothing sounds of the ghazals (evenings only) will. A great plus point is that there are no lingering smells of last night's dinner in this restaurant.

Barbecues of both Indian and Continental specialities can be arranged for small groups in the exquisite garden towards the back of the hotel.

Nazara

Like other Taj bars-cum-restaurants, Nazara is as warm and elegant as you would expect to find in the five-star category. This is probably the only place in Agra where you don't get fed up of seeing a painting of the Taj Mahal on the wall!

Nazara
Taj View Hotel
Fatehabad Road
Taj Ganj
Agra 282 001
Tel:361171-8.
Fax:361179
Price:Expensive
Speciality:North Indian
Timings:12.30 to 2.45 p.m.;
7 to 11.30 p.m.
Credit cards accepted
Bar license
Air-conditioned

Instead of a full dinner, what we would suggest, after a day of hectic sightseeing, is a long cool drink at the bar, accompanied by some tandoori items: Tandoori Chicken, Khaas Shahi Kabab, (an escalope of chicken is rolled out, flattened, coated with a marinade of cheese, yoghurt and spices, and then folded around its tiny bone), and Paneer Ke Soole Saunfwale, (chunks of cottage cheese are coated with a marinade of crushed fennel seeds and yoghurt and roasted in the tandoor). If you feel like a real regal treat (Rs 350 plus taxes), then opt for the Mayur Thali, which is Moghlai in inspiration and served on an exquisite silver thali. The silver cups overflow with an assortment of vegetables, curries, tandoori items, a variety of rotis, pickles papads and rice.

Definitely a very relaxing, luxurious way to end the day.

Ram Babu Paratha Bhandar

Ram Babu Paratha Bhandar
Belanganj
Agra
Speciality:North Indian
 Vegetarian
Timings:9 a.m. to 11 p.m.
Price:Inexpensive

Nicknamed 'King of Parathas', Harishankarbabu, son of Rambabu, carries on the glorious tradition of serving nine kinds of parathas, cooked in desi ghee, along with two vegetables, and three chutneys. Home-made full fat yoghurt is also available. The vegetables are free of onions and garlic, therefore ideal for Jains. But we, who are die hard garlic lovers, did not miss it. The aloo paratha, when eaten with the sweet-and-sour tamarind chutney, gave us a pleasantly different flavour, worth appreciating for its simplicity. The other two chutneys are mint and a sweet-and-sour tomato one. The assortment of parathas include plain, paneer, methi, gobi or aloo.

Two iron griddles are mounted on coal sigris (fires) bang on the pavement outside the shop, and the cooks are continuously frying parathas for the crowd seated inside. Among the vegetables, the aloo sabji is cooked everyday, the sookhi (dry) sabji is changed according to the season. We tasted kaddu bhaji (white pumpkin) and found it excellent. Those not used to spice could order a paratha stuffed with paneer (cottage cheese), or a vegetable of their choice, and have it with yoghurt. It makes a perfect combination, and a delicious meal. One paratha (especially the aloo, which was yummy) is more than enough, and in fact, in our case, we shared one and felt quite full.

The basic dining-hall seats fifty and is relatively clean. The permanent menu is painted on a blackboard inside.

Zorba the Buddha

By no means the ultimate in gourmet cuisine, Zorba provides welcome relief from the very average and often over spicy fare available in Agra. The restaurant is named after the owner's guru, Osho or Bhagwan Rajneesh, who called himself Zorba at the time the restaurant was opened.

> Zorba the Buddha
> E-13, Shopping Arcade
> Sadar Bazaar
> Agra
> **Price:Moderate**
> Specialities:Indian,
>   Continental Vegetarian
> Timings:12 to 3.30 p.m.;
>   6 to 9 p.m.
> No smoking
> Air-conditioned

As it is mainly aimed at the foreign budget traveller, the menu is extensive and very explicit for such a modest restaurant, and the food is relatively simple. Notes on the menu indicate which spices are used (no chilli, except on request), that they use no colour, that ice is made out of boiled water, and that the fruit and vegetables are 'nicely' washed. The Indian and European dishes taste broadly the same. Many contain nuts, raisins, cream and cheese, in keeping with what foreigners want, e.g., Bagh-e-Bahar, vegetables cooked in a sour cream sauce with nuts, Shan-e-Chaman, fruits, vegetables and nuts cooked in butter, and Shahi Kofta (described as 'mashed potato balls'), stuffed with cheese and cooked in a tomato sauce.

However, the Aloo Tamatar (boiled potatoes in a naturally thickened tomato sauce), without the usual spices, retained all its natural flavours. Naans come hot and fluffy and the paratha and Cheesy Chapatti were also first rate. The kofta and paneer (cottage cheese) items seemed very good. However, the Continental section lacked inspiration and the cheese sauces, especially in 'Humpty Dumpty' (vegetable bomb!), were a little bland.

Desserts and fruit crushes were tasty, clean, well presented and a great necessity in the Agra heat. Black Beauty, cold black coffee with ice cream was really delicious as was Honey Bunny, ice cream with sliced bananas, cream and nuts.

The restaurant is small, with simple white cane tables and chairs and a little vase of flowers on every table. The ceiling is blue with silver stars and the atmosphere quiet and meditative.

Service is pleasant and speedy. A cosy little place with uncomplicated healthy fare, caught in a sort of time warp.

Orange-seller at dawn

Bangalore

The name may mean 'boiled beans', but there is nothing farty about this growing city, which is rapidly becoming the Bombay of the south. With a growing corporate and 'silicon' clientele, in addition to the trendy and fashionable, it is not strange that the divergent backgrounds and tastes are reflected in the food. There are few places left in the city where you can still find traditional South Indian Tiffin and 'Meals' (full thali lunch or dinner). The exception is of course the legendary MTR (Mavalli Tiffin Room), and smaller establishments in the old part of town. Karavalli, at the Gateway Hotel, also serves an imaginative selection of South Indian cuisines, at extremely reasonable prices.

Visitors to Bangalore usually wander around the centre of town, in the area around Brigade and M. G. Road. Here, you'll find a takeover bid by the multi-cuisine restaurants, all trying to outdo each other in terms of decor, and all pinching each other's chefs with great regularity. The outcome is similar-tasting food in all of them.

Bangalore, being a cosmopolitan, busy city, has hit upon fast food, both indigenous and Western look alikes, to solve their mid-morning, mid-afternoon, and quick snacking problems. We found Darshinis, (South India's answer to fast food, serving local food in Western McDonalds-like surroundings), places like Amruth and Woody's, great answers. Bangalore was also a British Military Camp. Hangovers of the Raj are very evident in the architecture, the traffic policemen who wear white gloves and strange Daktari safari hats, bakeries and in certain places old-time eating habits. Go to the Breakfast Club, at the Victoria Hotel, if you would like a glimpse into the past. For the best contemporary Continental food, a half-an-hour drive out of Bangalore will take you to the Farmhouse, an enchanting, personalized, weekend restaurant.

Pubs are what Bangalore is known for these days. There are reportedly over three hundred of them in the city and everybody seems to have their favourite. They range from large, glitzy ones to simple meeting places. Most have a full bar licences but specialize in beer, usually draught beer. Most also serve a reasonable range of kababs and snacks. Recently however, many of them have expanded their repertoire to include pub lunches and exciting à la carte menus. We found the atmosphere in some of the newer pubs smoky and sleazy, to say the least, and attracting a weird tribe of young men who behave as if they have been seeing too many bad movies.

The top category (price wise) of pubs are actually revamped five-star hotel bars. They have been beautifully decorated and due to the competition from other pubs in the city, are surprisingly reasonably priced. We liked the Royal Derby at the Windsor Manor Hotel and the Polo Club at the Oberoi. From the originals, go for the classics, Pub World, Time and Again, Take 5 and Black Cadillac.

As a modern city, this is as pleasant as you can get, and the variety of eating places and restaurants at all price ranges, is somewhat staggering. However, you'll have to scratch real hard beneath the surface to find exceptional food, either local or Western.

A meal for one person

Inexpensive: under 100 rupees
Moderate: 100 to 250 rupees
Expensive: over 250 rupees

Amruth

This is a perfect example of the new South Indian fast food joints which have opened up all over the city, nicknamed 'Darshinis'. Amruth is situated in the basement of primarily a foodie complex, on the busy St Marks Road, in the heart of Bangalore. The interior, like American fast food places, is modern, and there are illuminated colour visuals of all the dishes. You pay the cashier, recieve your coupons, pick up your food, eat, either standing at a table outside or sitting on bar stools inside, and can be out in a matter of fifteen minutes. There is also a proper restaurant with upholstered furniture, waiter service and air-conditioning.

The food is remarkably fresh. Trays of idlis (soft, fluffy rice cakes) were popping in and out of the steamer every five minutes, and much faster than any American prototype. Upma (savoury semolina) and crisp vadas (tiffin) are all served with spicy coconut chutney, and Bisi Bele Bhath (a sambhar and rice mixture), with chilli wafers. The Thali, consisting of two parathas, a vegetable, sambhar, curd rice, pullav and pickles, is a total steal at Rs 11.

The whole restaurant is spotless, even the crowded stool area inside.

This is not only an indigenous answer to fast food, it goes much, much further, and is a perfect solution for busy urban life.

Amruth
14, St Mark's Plaza
St Mark's Road
Bangalore 560 001
Tel : 600088

Speciality : South Indian
 Vegetarian
Timings : 8.30 a.m. to 10 p.m.
Partly air-conditioned

Price : Inexpensive

Breakfast Club

Breakfast Club
Victoria Hotel
Residency Road
Bangalore
Price:Inexpensive
Speciality: South Indian
Timings: Sundays–9 a.m. to
  noon (Brunch);
  12.30 to 2.30 p.m.;
  7 to 11 p.m.

When you walk into the Breakfast Club at the Victoria Hotel, it is like walking back in time to the days of the British Empire. It is said that Sir Winston Churchill had breakfast here while he was in Bangalore playing polo. It was then an Officers' Mess and a dance hall. Nothing much has been changed, the stained glass windows, the high ceiling, the huge porthole ventilators through which the shaft of sunshine spotlights the dining-hall and the old wooden tables and comfortable cane chairs, occupied by the regulars.

Though the atmosphere is still unmistakably English, forget about eggs and bacon, and instead order idiappam and chicken stew, which is very well prepared. The chicken is stewed in coconut milk with bayleaf, cloves and diced potatoes. We also saw people tucking into paya masala with idiappam and, from the look on their faces, they appeared to be a satisfied lot.

You also have the option to brunch in the well-laid-out garden, where the Sunday newspapers are circulated for you to read at leisure. Nobody will rush you. It is an amazing oasis right in the nerve centre of Bangalore at Residency Road. Lunch and dinner are also served here but the place is famous for its Sunday breakfast and brunches. In fact, a five-star chef who is a fan of chicken stew and idiappam recommended that we try it here.

Casa Piccola

Although the location is hardly suited to a restaurant of this calibre (the basement of a commercial complex), it is the excellent food at Casa Piccola which draws the trendy folk of Bangalore.

Specialities are the pizzas, with their own wholewheat base, the Chicken Hot Pot and the Mexican Soup Pot. Fish and Chips and Burgers may sound ordinary, but the owner-chefs, Bhushan and Benjamin, managed to make them extra special with the addition of 'a touch of spice', they confessed.

Casa Piccola
Devatha Plaza
131, Residency Road
Bangalore 560 025
Tel : 212907
Price : Moderate
Speciality : Continental
Timings : 11 a.m. to 11 p.m.

Casa Piccola has an open kitchen, and a few cosy tables. The decor is homely, and the service, personalized. The restaurant scores where others fail, because of their consistent good quality and value for money food. It has now become a familiar meeting place in the city.

A touch of the Raj – Breakfast Club

Dum Pukht

Dum Pukht at the Wellington Windsor Manor Sheraton & Towers
25, Sankey Road
Bangalore 560 052
Tel:2269898; Fax: 2264941
Price:Expensive
Speciality:Avadhi (Lucknow) Indian
Timings:12.30 to 3 p.m.; 7.30 p.m. to midnight
Air-conditioned

Dum Pukht at the Windsor Manor, opened this year, under the personal supervision of master chef Imtiaz Qureshi, set in a regal style dining-room with a marble floor, mirrors and chandeliers. The cuisine is memorable for its intrinsic intensity of taste and flavour. The credit for digging up this almost extinct Avadhi cuisine goes to the dynamic Welcomgroup. Enormous containers used to be filled with foodstuffs and sealed. Hot charcoals were placed on top of the lids and fires lit underneath.

The starter, Harra Kabab, the vegetarian version of Shami Kabab came as a surprise, as it contained, besides spinach, channa dal, paneer and a bit of blood-purifying paan leaf. A strange combination. The Kakori Kabab, however, was superb. The raw papaya pickle with kishmish and spices in vinegar was an excellent tongue teaser to go with the kabab. A novel dish was Jhinga Dum Anari, another original creation (jumbo prawns cooked in fresh pomegranate juice, wrapped in silver leaf and dum cooked with select spices, till fluffy and soft).

The best was the traditional Kofta Handi Kabab: minced mutton koftas stuffed with desi egg-yolk and dried plum, spiced with nutmeg, saffron and cardamom and cooked till all the ingredients combine into an unusual *mélange* of flavours. Eaten with Gucchi Pullao or Lachchedar Paratha, the combination is heavenly. For the vegetarians we recommend Subz Purdah, a rich stew of fresh vegetables, mushrooms and pineapple cubes, cooked under a purdah of puffy pastry and Qureshi's delicious dal tempered with burnt garlic.

After such a heavy dinner, there was no logical reason to order dessert, but we did. Jaan E Azam, is a fancy sounding name for the delicious Shahi Tukra, wrapped in silver leaf, redolent with sinfully rich cream, sugar syrup and dry fruit.

Dum Pukht is an elegant cuisine, worth experiencing once.

Ebony

Barton Tower, with its magnificent, Manhatten-like facade and highly polished granite entrance, is a fitting introduction to the rooftop restaurant, Ebony, run by the young, enterprising Zubin Aria. The decor, as the name suggests, is black and smart with a good-looking bar inside. Though a little windy, we preferred to sit on the terrace, overlooking the city.

The Continental specialities were all exceptional, and well-flavoured with fresh herbs (the herbs used are indicated on the menu by a leaf). The Mushroom Florentine, fresh mushrooms on a bed of steamed leaf spinach, topped with hollandaise sauce, was superb. The spinach was perfectly cooked to retain its texture and colour, and the mushrooms, freshly sautéed. The Fish Bed Fort, simply grilled with butter, and served with rounds of toasts, topped with creamed mushrooms and spinach, was perfect.

For chicken lovers, go for the Chicken Marengo, in a tomato, cream and brandy sauce, flavoured with basil. All the Continental dishes are garnished with baby corn, baby carrots etc., in the French mode.

Aria, a Parsi himself, has introduced his own cuisine to the menu (the only Parsi food in Bangalore), with much success. Try the Khari Marghi Ma Salli, a typical Parsi chicken curry, topped with crisp potato straws, the Patra Ni Machhi (pomfret with green chutney, steamed in a banana leaf) and Tarella Bhinda (lady's fingers). We didn't try the North Indian food, but were told that the butter chicken here is the best in town.

By the time this book goes to press, Ebony will have started an evening barbecue on the terrace.

Ebony
Ivory Tower Hotel
Barton Centre
84 M.G. Road
Bangalore 560 001
Tel : 5589333, 5585164
Fax: 5588697
Price : Moderate
Specialities : Continental,
  Parsi
Timings : 12.30 to 3 p.m.;
  7.30 to 11.30 p.m.
Full bar licence
Credit cards accepted
Partly Air-conditioned

Hot Breads

Hot Breads
Copper Arch
Infantry Road
Bangalore 560 001
Tel : 5591848
Price : Inexpensive
Speciality : Snacks
Timings : 10 a.m. to 9 p.m.
Air-conditioned

Like most Military Cantonment towns (i.e., where the British army camped), Bangalore too has a distinct bakery culture. Koshy and Nilgiris were the pioneers in bread and cakes. Today, Hot Breads—a franchisee of the Madras Hot Breads, has taken their place, bringing European style pastries to Bangalore. On the lines of Croissants in Bombay in terms of decor and products. Hot Breads boasts of a variety of pastries with fillings, cakes, Danish pastries, Swiss rolls, pies and tarts, cookies, croissants, doughnuts, and, of course, their speciality—breads and buns.

There are thirty varieties of stuffed buns which are extremely popular snacks. They range from Chicken Satay and Cheese in the savoury to Raisin and Custard in the sweet section. Their Wheatgerm bread and Ginger bread are the most popular, but they also have Bloomers, French loaves and Choc Chip bread. From the extensive range of doughnuts, try the Chicken Curry one for a change! Most of the snacks cost between Rs 15 and Rs 20.

The restaurant is sparsly decorated with a few functional contemporary style tables and chairs and stark white walls. It seats around fifteen people. Most of their clients, however, prefer to take away. The open kitchen concept, a large window into the working kitchen itself where you can see the breads coming straight from the oven, assures the customer of fresh products. Although non-vegetarian fillings are popular, Hot Breads does not serve beef or pork. The restaurant as well as the take away section is entirely self-service. You take a basket and help yourself from the shelves. There is also a microwave if you want to eat right away.

There are franchisees of Hot Breads at Jayanagar, Bangalore Airport, Brigade Road and Koramangala. Anything leftover at the end of the day, is donated to an orphanage.

Hotel Cauvery

This modest but comfortable hotel in the centre of Bangalore, serves an excellent traditional Thali, a typical South Indian meal served in bowls on a steel platter in exceptionally clean and relaxed surroundings. Although the dining-hall is large, with huge windows overlooking the entrance to the hotel, the tables are well spaced, which makes the seating capacity around only fifty. The owners were having lunch at the next table, the day we were there.

Hotel Cauvery
11/37 Cunningham Road
Bangalore 560 052
Tel : 2266966, 2266967,
  2266968; Fax: 2260920
Price : Inexpensive
Speciality : South Indian
  Vegetarian
Timings : 6.30 a.m. to
  11.30 p.m.

Two thalis are available, one for Rs 21 which is limited in quantity (i.e., you don't get seconds), and an unlimited one, for Rs 40 which also includes soup and dessert. The former is quite enough, as the steel thalis are very large and accommodate large quantities and varieties of goodies. In addition to puris, chapattis, steaming hot rice, etc., we found the vegetables decidedly different—Kootu, a kind of Avial, made with pumpkin and channa, and South Indian Kurma (a white coconut-based curry). A dry vegetable is also served, along with the rasam (a thin hot-and-sour soup), sambhar (savoury dal with vegetables), and the day we ate there, a delicious creamy payasam (rice pudding) for dessert.

At Cauvery, the cooks go very easy on spice and oil, a welcome change. Service is done by waiters who have been with the restaurant since its inception in 1973.

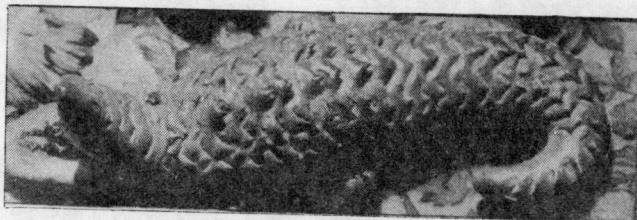

Crocodile bread at Hot Breads

Imperial Hotel

Imperial Hotel
93, Residency Road
Bangalore 560 025
Tel : 5883915
Price : Inexpensive
Speciality : Moghlai
Timings :12.30 to 3 p.m.;
   7 to 11 p.m.

A no-nonsense eatery, for people who are interested in generous portions of tasty, reasonably priced Moghlai food. We were told that people drive miles for the Chicken Kabab Special, pieces of chicken in tandoori masala, deep fried in egg. Butter Chicken, also a house speciality, is served with hot parathas. Other specialities include Kadai Mutton, Partridge Kabab and Partridge Biryani, served with extra gravy and kachumber. Once again, this was delicious, even though the rice used was not Basmati.

The menu has an extensive range of egg dishes, from egg curry to egg pakoda to omelettes, but the mainstay is tandoori. Just in case you need variation from the standard tandoori masala, they also have Chilli Chicken, Gobi Manchurian and Ginger Chicken which are all spicy and very filling. To enjoy this kind of food you should be really hungry. Whatever you do, don't come here if you are on a diet, as most of the dishes are either deep fried, or floating in thick gravies.

The place looks like a canteen, and has functional tables and chairs overlooking the street traffic. However, service is prompt and the food tasty.

Jockey Club

Situated in the Taj Residency hotel located in the busy business district of Bangalore, the Jockey Club is like an oasis for those seeking refuge after a hard day's work. The Jockey Club is a restaurant-cum-bar of an extremely distinctive pedigree. The sparkling silver, the polished brass, the gleaming chandeliers, warm Burma teak woodwork and etched mirrors add to an ambience that can only be described as infinitely gracious. Jockey Club has one of the few bars in the country with an extensive wine list.

Jockey Club
Taj Residency
41/3, M.G. Road
Bangalore 560 001
Tel : 584444 Ext No : 2077
Price : Expensive
Speciality : Continental
Timings : Noon to 3 p.m.;
   6.30 p.m. to midnight
Credit cards accepted
Air-conditioned

We dined on the smoked Chicken Verbier, a refreshing salad made with juliennes of smoked chicken, celery, apple and tomato in a creamy vinaigrette dressing, followed by Scampi Roselyn, sautéed prawns with red pimento, tomatoes, mushrooms and onions in a light wine sauce, flavoured with mustard and thyme. Both dishes were delightful. We ended off with Kahlua Mousse, a dangerously delicious dessert followed by black expresso coffee. Needless to say, wine was a natural companion to the meal, and our selection was a clean tasting, chilled Chablis. Some of the other specialities served here are Salad Angastura, Pearl Bisque (soup), Crevettes Diane (prawns in cream sauce), superb Grilled Tenderloin Steak with Béarnaise sauce.

Karavalli

Karavalli
Gateway Hotel
66, Residency Road
Bangalore 560 025
Tel: 5584545; Fax: 5584030
Price : Moderate
Speciality : South Indian
   (Non-vegetarian and
   Vegetarian)
Timings: 12.30 to 3.30 p.m.;
   7.30 p.m. to midnight
Credit cards accepted
Bar licence
Partly air-conditioned

Partly set in an informal aangan (courtyard) and partly air-conditioned, chic but simple styled dining-room, Karavalli is, according to us, perhaps the only restaurant in the five-star category in Bangalore that offers a superb range of South Indian specialities at very moderate prices. Vegetarians also have a wide range to choose from.

Thoroughly researched by a team of Taj chefs led by Ms Bernedette Pinto, and now under the supervision of executive chef A. V. Sriram and young restaurant chef Pramod Pillai, Karavalli offers a rich variety of traditional foods, the recipes of which were derived from the kitchens of traditional households from different parts of the south. Almost every dish on the menu is a sheer delight and quite different from anything else in the city.

The decor is a replica of a typical Keralite courtyard with comfortable cane tables and chairs. The service is attentive and the waiters extremely personable, unfailingly arriving at your elbow with a freshly cooked appam two or three seconds before you realize you need it. Before service begins, a basket of appetizers is left on the table which includes a variety of fried papads, karela (bitter gourd) rings, lotus root rings and banana chips. You could be tempted to stuff yourself silly with these titbits, specially the lotus root rings which are crisp, tasty and so different from anything else in the fried variety.

But we advise you to practise restraint since the chef has a number of new and exciting tricks up his sleeve for later courses.

For starters we recommend Hashale (an appetizer made from fresh coconut water, mint, honey and lemon) and Kane Bezule (delicate ladyfish marinated in freshly-ground Mangalorean spices and deep fried). Also try Meen Polichathu (the little fresh water fish from back waters of Kerala) marinated with Malabari masala wrapped in banana leaf and then pan fried, which took our breath away with its amazing taste and flavour. In the main dishes, Kori Gassi (chicken curry cooked in Mangalorean masala and coconut milk) was superb, eaten with Neer Dosa, a delicate handkerchief thin rice pancake. Next best at Karavalli was the Mutton Stew slow cooked in Malabar spices and eaten with steaming hot Appams (rice pancakes) served one at a time. Allow the foamy soft centre of the Appam to soak in the gravy before you tuck in.

For the vegetarians, we recommend Alambo Arepu—fresh mushrooms cooked in a special blend of masalas, to be eaten with rice and Bhindi Pepper Fry. For dessert we recommend Ada Payasam (a sort of rice pudding) which was unusually light and a perfect finish to a superb meal.

During lunch hours (only), Karavalli does special non-vegetarian and vegetarian thalis. From these we strongly recommend the vegetarian thali which is a fantastic deal for Rs 40 (plus taxes). You get unlimited quantities of superbly cooked vegetables including Bhindi Kitchadi (lady's fingers cooked in coconut masala and yoghurt), Vegetable Stew, Pineapple Patchali (diced pineapple cooked in grated coconut, mustard seeds, jeera and fresh yoghurt) Olan (slices of white pumkin cooked in fresh coconut milk), rich sambhar packed with drumsticks and pearl onions, delicious moong dal (goes with rice mixed with a teaspoonful of melted ghee) creamy yoghurt, tangy tomato rasam, assorted pickles, three chutneys, papads and appams not forgetting the basket of appetizers listed above and the light dessert Sevian (vermicelli in cream, flavoured with cardamom, kishmish and cashew nuts). Served on a green banana leaf the colourful spread evoked such a pungent prose, every morsel pleased the fundamental sense of sight, smell and taste. Light on the stomach as well as pocket, the vegetarian food at Karavalli was the best we have eaten in Bangalore.

Executive chef Sriram

K. C. Das Sweet Shop

K. C. Das Sweet Shop
3 St Mark's Road
Bangalore 560 001
Tel : 5587003, 5585672
Price : Inexpensive
Speciality : North Indian
  Vegetarian
Timings : 9 a.m. to 3 p.m.;
  3:30 to 9:30 p.m.

Ice Cream girl

K. C. Das, from Calcutta, is a neat, tidy shop, at the corner of St Mark's Road, with huge bay windows and a very long counter stretching the entire length of the shop. K. C. Das stocks over sixty different types of mithai (sweetmeats) at any one time. Although they are famous for their rossogollas and sondesh, K. C. Das also serves delicious, spicy snacks. Luchi Aloo Dum (a couple of puris with curried potatoes) and their namkeen kachoris, Khasta, Bela, Nimki and Hing (deep fried, layered bread) are mouth-watering.

For those not used to spice, you could simultaneously tuck into mishti doi (Bengali sweetened yoghurt), which is normally difficult to find outside Calcutta. From the extraordinary range of sweets, including several Bengali specialities, we strongly recommend the Rasmalai, Rajbhog, Kala Jamun and Malpoa. All these goodies are well under Rs 10 per piece. The only trouble is that you don't know when to stop.

Luchis are served at lunch, but you should try and make it by noon, as they start disappearing very quickly after that. K. C. Das makes them and the mishti doi only once a day.

Koshy's Bar & Restaurant

Koshy's is a landmark in Bangalore. Its large circa Fifties dining-hall is a popular meeting place. The fried fish and chips is excellent, and also recommended is their Baked Chicken (with spinach and mushroom) and Roast Mutton with mint sauce, all well below Rs 50 per dish. Another chef's special is Southern Fried Chicken, breast of chicken, crisp fried in batter and served with fluffy white mash potatoes, vegetables and brown sauce.

Koshy's Bar & Restaurant
39, St Mark's Road
Bangalore 560 001
Tel : 2213793, 2215030
Price : Moderate
Specialities : Continental,
  South Indian
Timings : 9:30 a.m. to
  midnight
Partly air-conditioned

Koshy's also has Tandoori and vegetarian dishes, as well as the usual Chinese. These are clearly there to appease the local palate, but could not be considered their specialities. The old-time British ambience demanded that we try out the good old Raj specials like the Mutton Broth, Roast Chicken with stuffing and Grilled Pork Chops, which we were happy with. On Sundays, Koshy's serve deliciously light Malayali Appams and stew (vegetarian and chicken), which along with other breakfast specials like Chicken Liver on toast, Bombay Toast (French Toast) and traditional Bacon and Eggs, make a very satisfying brunch.

The restaurant seats 120 in its non-air-conditioned hall which, though the upholstery is vinyl, still has a charm about it. The atmosphere reminded us of a New York 'deli'.

The sons of P. Koshy Oomman, P. O. Koshy and P. O. Matthew, look after the restaurant and one of them is always there.

Mavalli Tiffin Room (MTR)

Mavalli Tiffin Room (MTR)
14, Lalbagh Road
Bangalore 560 027
Tel : 2220022; Fax: 2239296
Price : Inexpensive
Speciality : South Indian
  Vegetarian
Timings : 7 a.m. to noon;
  4 to 8.30 p.m.
No tipping
No smoking

No visit to Bangalore is complete without a breakfast at this landmark of a restaurant, which has catered for many including chief ministers and chaiwallas for the last fifty years.

Though some of our friends discouraged us saying that the standards at MTR had gone down, we still have tremendous respect because they have neither succumbed to modernism nor have they compromised on their quality. They use natural ingredients and food is cooked fresh every day.

We started off with chilled Black Grape Juice, followed by a neatly piled up portion of Uppama (a semolina-based dish cooked with a rich mixture of chopped carrots, peas, cashewnuts, curry leaves, mustard seeds, ginger and garnished with slivers of ripe red tomato. Uppama is served with coconut chutney spiked with green chillies. The plump Masala Dosa, arranged in a triangular shape, arrived steaming hot along with a tiny steel katori (bowl) of pure ghee which was poured into the soft inside layer of the dosa. The belly of the dosa was pregnant with potato bhaji, garnished with fresh coriander leaves and green chillies, and absolutely ambrosial in taste. We could not resist the ubiquitous gulab jamun—the best we have ever eaten—followed by a superb coffee. Everything was perfect. The bill came to around Rs 70 for two.

MTR was founded in 1924 by a Yajnappa Maiya along with his brothers in a small shed in the same locality. Right from the beginning, the commitment to quality and taste has bred a loyal band of customers, and the name and the fame has spread throughout the country.

Today MTR is housed in a separate building. Innumerable black-and-white pictures of dignitaries who have visited are hung on the walls of the waiting rooms, which are as large as the dining-hall itself. You register as soon as you arrive and your name is called out when the table is free. Avoid Sundays, unless you are good at American football or wear a crash helmet.

Memories of China

The Taj Residency in Bangalore, despite its five-star status, is a homely place. The lunch-time buffets are extremely popular, especially the one in the Southern Comfort restaurant, where you can taste a variety of North and South Indian dishes, a large variety of salads and sweets for only Rs 100.

Across the corridor, Memories of China is considered one of Bangalore's best Chinese restaurants. Its buffet, a new concept, is the only Chinese buffet in town, and boasts of six vegetarian (aimed at the largely South Indian clientele) and five non-vegetarian dishes, including lamb, fish, chicken and pork. Soup is optional, and the sweets are several. The salads have an interesting selection of dressings, all trying hard to be Chinese. But the tea is authentic. Ask for the peppermints before you leave. At Rs 135 per head, you have an ideal lunch for that special treat. And that too, at the Taj.

Memories of China
Taj Residency
M. G. Road
Bangalore 560 001
Tel : 584444
Price : Expensive
Speciality : Chinese
Timings : Noon to 3 p.m.;
  7 p.m. to midnight
Air-conditioned

Nagarjuna

Hotel Nagarjuna Residency
44/1 Residency Road
Bangalore 560 025
Tel : 5585130, 5588222
Price : Inexpensive
Speciality : South Indian
(Vegetarian and
Non-vegetarian)
Timings : 11.30 to 3.30 p.m.;
6.30 to 10.30 p.m.

A clean, decent sort of place near Brigade Road, which serves typical, spicy Andhra food. The speciality here is the Thali, or 'Vegetarian Meals' for Rs 25 (plus taxes). Served on a banana leaf, you get all the South Indian staples—sambhar, rasam, dal, buttermilk, dahi, curry, with one typical dry Andhra vegetable. The Thali is unlimited, and hot refills do the rounds at regular intervals. The other specialities are the Mutton Biryani and the Chicken specials. The restaurant has eighteen different Chicken preparations, including Chicken 65 (the year the recipe was invented), Chicken Sixer, Garlic Chicken, etc. When we asked the owner to describe some of the chicken dishes, the three adjectives he most often used were 'masala', 'dry' (to describe the consistency of the dish) and 'gravy'.

Spicy food no doubt, but very good quality. Service is prompt and the large dining-hall (and bathroom), comfortable and clean.

Paradise Island

The West End Hotel is a very lush, tropical-looking place with Paradise Island, an Oriental-inspired eating house, with open verandas and an adjacent Cocktail Bar, Coconut Grove, in the most magical setting possible. Sit and sip a cocktail, gaze into the miniature lake which surrounds the restaurant or, if you must, go and savour the open buffet.

Paradise Island
West End Hotel
Race Course Road
Bangalore 560 001
Tel : 2269281; Fax: 2200010
Price : Moderate
Specialities : Oriental,
  Indian, Continental
Timings : 12.30 to 3 p.m.;
  7.30 to 11.30 p.m.
Credit cards accepted
Bar licence

The buffet (available only at lunch-time) is terrific value at Rs 165 (plus taxes) and offers a selection of six non-vegetarian and eight vegetarian hot dishes, soups, a salad bar, a dessert spread and very good griddle items, cooked while you wait. A different cuisine (Thai, Malaysian, Continental, Chinese) is featured every day in addition to regular Indian items. However, we were not overly impressed with the Oriental. The day we had lunch, it was Thai, and frankly we found the Thai dishes drowned in too much sauce, which diluted any attempt at authenticity. The Indian items being freshly prepared on the tawa and in the tandoor (tikkis, appams and tikkas) were excellent.

In the evening, Paradise Island is lit up like Fairyland and the ambience, with a live band, takes on a more glamorous tone. The menu includes Oriental with an emphasis on Thai, Indian and Continental. The Thai dishes were light years away from what had been served on the buffet for lunch, fragrant with Thai herbs and roots from the nearby herb garden. Go for Som Tam, a delicious salad of raw papaya, Tom Kha Hed, a fragrant coconut soup, and Kaeng Ped Gai, a Chicken Red Curry with Bamboo Shoots and Brinjal.

Also try the Poulet Marseilles, breasts of chicken stuffed with a mousse of pistachios, olives and chicken.

We felt that the number of varied cuisines here tends to dilute the impact of a single one. This is, however, a magical place to dine for the atmosphere alone. Choose your dishes carefully, or ask the very able chef Gautam Narayan, to guide you.

Queens Restaurant

Queens Restauramt
7, S. S. Centre
Facing Church Street
Bangalore 560 001
Price : Inexpensive
Speciality : North Indian
Timings : 11 a.m. to 10 p.m.

Recommended surprisingly by a five-star chef for its delicious chapattis and home-made bhajis, Queens Restaurant is housed in a garage in a lane off the famous Brigade Road. Ms Sonelam Sodha, a housewife, started off by supplying home cooked food in tiffins to office workers and later on expanded into a tiny twenty-four seater restaurant.

The menu is very small and select, and only slightly more elaborate than what you would cook at home. We recommend Peas Masala, Vegetable Kofta and Paneer Jalfarezi for the vegetarians and Butter Chicken and Chicken Bharta for the non-vegetarians. Everything is served with pullav and rotis hot off the tawa. Though a bit on the oily side, the dishes were nevertheless extremely tasty. Ms Sodha can adjust the spice according to your taste as you place your order, as everything is freshly cooked in an open kitchen.

During the afternoon, Queens also serves chaat (savoury snacks). The Raj Kachori Chaat is tasty, filling and cheap. On the dessert front, try their Shahi Tukra. It may not have the traditional, silver leaf, but it is delicious all the same.

Queens is furnished with simple tables and chairs, with an open kitchen where you can see the cooks working. A word of caution. Cooking fumes from the open kitchen permeate into the dining area, and may be uncomfortable for those prone to allergies.

Samrat Restaurant

Situated near the Race Course and the West End Hotel, Samrat or Chalukya, as it is more popularly known, is one of the most popular South Indian restaurants in Bangalore. Unfortunately, it has gone the way of other South Indian oldies, serving the genuine article with more than a smattering of North Indian and Chinese, a total concession to popular tastes.

> Samrat Restaurant
> Hotel Chalukya
> 44 Race Course Road
> Bangalore 560 001
> Tel : 2262287, 2261446,
>   2263444
> **Price : Moderate**
> Speciality : South Indian
>   Vegetarian
> Timings : 8 a.m. to 10 p.m.
> Partly air-conditioned

However, in the large hall on the ground floor (seats 150), you can still see most of the regulars tucking into the unlimited Thali, South Indian snacks and the popular pullav and gravy. The standard Thali is Rs 22, and comprises of three vegetables, sambhar, soup, rasam, dahi, buttermilk, rice, puris, papad, etc. The special one at Rs 46 includes ice cream and pullav. In the air-conditioned section on the first floor, Ganapati Prabhu, the manager, said that Mushroom Manchurian, Vegetable Do Piaza and Paneer Bhurji, were the most popular dishes. Chalukya also has breakfast specials—upma, known here as Khara Bhath; hot, moist Seera (Kesari Bhath), Pongal and Bisi Bele Bhath.

Service is swift, and waiters will also serve you in your car if you park in their car park, which you often have to do, as the restaurant is chock-a-block at lunch-time.

Sana

Sana
26, Haines Road (Egyptian Block)
Behind Cantonment Bamboo Bazaar
Bangalore 560 051
Tel : 569416; Fax: 569268
Price : Inexpensive
Speciality : Middle Eastern
Timings : 1 to 3 p.m.;
6 to 11 p.m.
No alchohol served or permitted

Sana serves some of the finest Middle Eastern food in India, in the grottiest of surroundings. The restaurant is run by Nabeel Gani, whose family owns the run down tenement block in which Sana is situated. The area itself is dark and dingy, and it doesn't get much better as you walk up the three flights of narrow stairs to the terrace. Here, makeshift tables, plastic chairs and potted plants have been thrown around to create the basic requirements for a restaurant.

However, the food is surprisingly authentic. Plates of Humous (chick pea dip), Moutabel (aubergine, dahi and tahini dip), Foul (mashed beans), and Baba Ganoush (aubergine dip with parsley and spring onions), all arrive with a generous drizzle of olive oil. The Falafel is, however, disappointing. 'I bring the olive oil myself, from Dubai,' said the rotund and robust third generation Syrian. Continue with the Fatoosh, a salad of mixed vegetables with bits of crisp roti and olive oil, and the deliciously succulent Grilled Chicken. The Shwarma, a stack of prepared lamb, was rotating on a spit nearby. Don't leave without trying it, either plain or in a roomali roti, served with salad and onion.

The family children came and played with us partly, we suspect, to mop up the leftover dips. This is apparently a daily ritual. As dips are not part of the menu at home, the children sneak upstairs for them.

After dinner, enjoy a Turkish Coffee, Mint Tea or a puff at the hookah. Service and decor are very basic, but Nabeel's entertaining family and the food, makes this well worth the trip.

The Farmhouse

Ashrafa and Saeed Sattar,[*] have the ideal set up on their delightful farm, half an hour from Bangalore. While Ashrafa concentrates on producing her Farmhouse Breakfast Cereal with Waheeda Rehman, Saeed sets his passion for food to work. On weekends only, he enamours you with both his large, joyful persona and his excellent Continental cuisine. Bear in mind that nothing is standardized here and there is no printed menu. Saeed will serve you what is seasonal, what he happened to stumble across at Russel Market that morning, or simply what takes

The Farmhouse
45 Kalena Agrahara
Mt St Joseph P.O.
Bannerghatta Road
Bangalore 560 083
Tel: 6631401
Price : Moderate
Speciality : Continental
(European)
Timings : Fridays : 8 p.m. to
midnight
Sat/Sun : 1to 4 p.m.;
8 p.m. to midnight

his fancy. You can be assured that everything is fresh and prepared with love.

For Rs 200 (all inclusive) you are served around seven courses, one after the other, at a leisurely pace. Don't come if you are in a rush: dining in courses, with well-spaced-out intervals, takes time. You may start with Shrimp and Avocado cocktail (Mushroom and Avocado for the vegetarians), followed by Baby Quiches, a vegetable soup and Saeed's speciality, Fish braised in dill and lemon. By braising, the fish retains its juices and texture, without being overcooked. A vegetarian Lasagne or Pizza is usually featured somewhere along the line. The main course could be Lamb Chops with mint sauce, or the more daring Stuffed Veal Loaf. A tossed Green Salad refreshes the senses before dessert, which is either Cheesecake, Chocolate Mousse or fruit, and coffee.

If, like us, you simply can't saunter through Saeed's culinary

---

[*]   Saeed Sattar died in May 1994, just as this book was going to the Publishers. His spirit lives on and the Farmouse restaurant is open for business as usual.

generosity, you can request fewer courses but larger portions (although the normal portions are large enough as it is) of your favourite things.

Total vegetarian meals can be organized, if you inform the Farmhouse in advance. They stock wine and beer, but you can bring your own, for a nominal cover charge.

The set up, although basic, is charming. Simple tables and chairs are set outside, right next to the Sattars' beautiful house, surrounded by greenery (although you can't see it at night).

An outdoor dining experience, not to be missed if you are in Bangalore over the weekend.

The Only Place

As the very charming owner of this American style café, Haroon Sulaiman Sait, will tell you, OP's was originally 'the' meeting place in Bangalore. The original restaurant was an old, ramshackle bungalow, surrounded by bougainvillaea, trees and monkeys. Today, right near the entrance to the fashionable Mota Arcade on Brigade Road (which occupies the old plot of land), the magic has gone, but both the food and Haroon live on. In keeping with the times, the decor is pine and green, light, bright and airy. Brunch, breakfast and snacks come first—waffles, quiches, sandwiches, chicken wings, etc. The mainstay is the Italian food and, of course, the steaks. We recommend the Chateaubriand Regular (two hunky slices off the main fillet) and the Hamburger Steak. The accompaniments are traditional—boiled vegetables, fries and mashed potatoes. We personally didn't go overboard on the fried onions. Whatever you do, don't leave, even if you are full to the gills, without trying either Haroon's Apple Pie with cream, Strawberry Pie or Chocolate Gateau topped with marshmallow. All the desserts are displayed at the entrance to the restaurant, near the cash til. The Apple Pie has thick chunks of apple with a glazed, lattice pastry and the strawberry pie is made with whole, ripe strawberries from the hill stations of Panchgani and Mahabaleshwar. Portions are generous, as is the hospitality. No booze is served, but you can bring your own.

The Only Place
Mota Arcade
Brigade Road
Bangalore
Tel: 5588678
Price : Moderate
Speciality : Continental
Timings : 10.30 a.m. to
3.30 p.m.; 6.30 to 11 p.m.
Credit cards accepted

The Tamarind Tree

The Tamarind Tree
Avalahalli
Anjanapura P.O.
Off Kanakapura Road
Bangalore 560 062
Tel (farm) : 8435234;
   (reservation) 5533321,
   5533324
Price:Moderate
Speciality : Cuban/Mexican
Timings :Fridays: 7.30 to
   midnight
Sat/Sun: Noon to 4 p.m.
   7.30 p.m. to midnight
Reservation essential

The second weekend restaurant to open outside Bangalore as recently as August 1993, on Venkataram Reddy's farm. Venkataram himself is a dealer in colonial, antique furniture and his wife Namratha and friend Vasantha Krishnaswamy handle the restaurant. The setting is perfect. A large pond around which are niches, filled with antique chairs, benches, and marble-topped tables where you can relax and gently drift into the mood of things. There is a bar (bring your own) which serves beer and soft drinks only, a bonfire and a quaint dining area. The place is spacious, well-designed and stylish, with purpose and effect in mind.

The food however was a little disappointing. Good home food it certainly was, but lacking, we felt, any particular Cuban or Mexican identity. Mrs Krishnaswamy, whose husband worked for the United Nations, lived in Cuba and countries of Central and South America for many years. What she serves here are lots of fairly ordinary dishes. Let's hope that it is just teething troubles. Starters come in the form of Stuffed Eggs, Platanito Golpiado (raw banana fritters) and Mini Pizzas. Dinner started with a salad of cucumber and radish, followed by rather good Fried Brinjals, delicious Grilled Chicken, Macaroni with Spinach, Black Eyed Beans, Spanish Rice and Lamb Stew.

Unfortunately, everything was served at the same time and on the same plate. The apple crumble with cream was yummy.

A wonderful ambience, but can get a bit noisy. Don't expect gourmet fare. At best, this is simple home cooking.

The Schezwan Court

Pale blue decor and priceless prints set the scene for this fiery Chinese cuisine. The night we dined here the restaurant was packed not with business executives on expense accounts as you often see in five-star hotels but local families, savouring what is probably the nearest foreign cuisine, in terms of spice, to their own.

The Schezwan Court
The Oberoi Hotel
37-39 M.G. Road
Bangalore 560 001
Tel : 5585858
Price : Expensive
Speciality : Chinese Schezwan
Timings : 12.30 to 2.30 p.m.
    7.30 to 11.30 p.m.
Credit cards accepted

The starters were superb. The Honey Glazed Spare Ribs, Golden Shrimp Rolls (rather like a sesame prawn toast rolled up) and Salt & Pepper Prawns, with a hint of fragrant five-spice, are all highly recommended. Wash this down with chinese tea (plenty of it) and prepare yourself for the spice of a lifetime. Roll gently into things, with Steamed Spinach, topped with fresh mushrooms and oyster sauce. Follow this with Shredded Pork with Hoisin sauce. We tried the Diced Chicken, with cashew nuts and dry chillies, which though tasty, was more like something Andhra. Sweat wiped off the forehead and glasses steamed up, we ploughed on through the Sliced Lamb with hot sesame sauce and Malaysian Noodles. By this time we thought our taste buds had been numbed for life.

If you like your Chinese food fully flavoured, but not doused with chilli, for Heaven's sake don't order anything marked with a chilli, however tempting it sounds. Alternatively, ask the chef to tone down the spice. We found the 'schezwan' sauce overpowering, not only because of the effect it had on our sinus, but also because it masked all the wonderful flavours and sauces, which the restaurant has gone to great lengths to make and procure.

The dishes are well-presented in traditional pretty floral crockery and the service is exemplary.

Tycoons

Tycoons
1 Copper Arch
83-83/1, Infantry Road
Bangalore 560 001
Tel : 5591745, 5591356
Price : Moderate
Specialities : Continental,
   Indian
Timings : 11.30 a.m. to
   3 p.m.; 7 to 11.30 p.m.
Full bar licence
Reservation recommended
Credit cards accepted
Partly air-conditioned

Of all the many multi-cuisine restaurants which have sprung up in Bangalore in the last few years, Tycoons, in terms of decor, service, style and food, must rank among the best. You can dine outdoors in the very pleasant waterfall garden (can get a bit hot at lunch-time) which reminded us of the south of France, or in the air-conditioned restaurant which is certainly comfortable but more conventional in terms of style and decor. The director Desmond Rice is always on hand to answer any queries or see to personal requests.

We noticed that more than half the clientele (the restaurant was packed at lunch-time on a weekday) was eating Continental, which is unusual when Indian food is available too. The Chicken Canneloni, is made with home-made pasta and is very creamy. The Grilled Fish (surmai or seer as it is known in the south) was fresh, Chicken à la Kiev, mouth-watering, but the steaks, though very tender, may be a little too well marinated. The American Salad, though not extraordinary, makes a good accompaniment.

The Indian dishes are more standard. A variety of kababs, like Reshmi Kabab (non-spicy boneless chicken roasted in the tandoor), Paneer Tikka (cottage cheese) and Murg Lassan kabab (chicken marinated in garlic and light spices) to start with, followed by the usual gravy dishes. The Murg Kali Mirch, hot with roughly crushed fresh black pepper and the very tender Bhoona Gosht, are worth trying with the cocktail Kulchas (baby naans). For dessert, the Caramel Soufflé filled with nuts, is a must.

Tycoons has a full and adventurous bar serving all the traditional cocktails and imported Scotch, Cognac and wines.

Woody's

Woody's is another popular South Indian fast food joint. The restaurant is a large (it looks larger than it actually is, because of the mirrored walls), modern, fun place. We would describe it as 'Roy Rogers goes East', i.e., the ambience is distinctly Western, with illuminated photos of all the dishes displayed above the long service counter. The food is a mish-mash of traditional South Indian staples, to Chinese, North Indian, shakes and ice creams.

Woody's
177/178 Commercial Street
Bangalore 560 001
Tel : 5582714
Price : Inexpensive
Speciality : South Indian
Vegetarian
Timings : 8 a.m. to 11 p.m.
Partly air-conditioned

Try the Rice Kadubu, a breakfast speciality of idli rice mixture, which has been set in a glass and is then taken out and served steaming hot accompanied by coconut chutney, green chutney and pickle. We preferred the more unusual items, like Mangalore Pathrode, arbi leaves rolled and stuffed with rice paste, tamarind, jaggery and spices. Other things to try are Sajjige (sujee) Roti (on Mondays only), the Ragi (Nachni) Masala Dosa, Pesarattu (a dosa made from moong dal), Cabbage Pathrode (cabbage stuffed dosa) and Semige Balahar Bhath, (a sevian).

Downstairs is self-service, with seating on high bar stools, or you can stand. There is waiter service in the small, air-conditioned section upstairs.

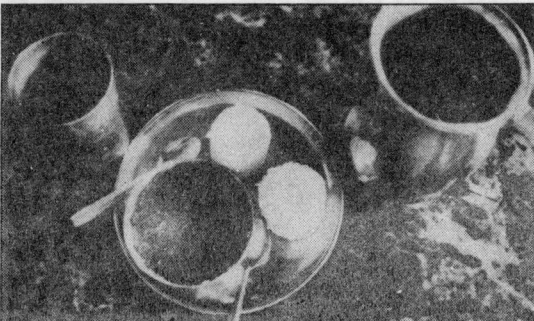

Rice Kadubu

Bombay

Bombay, of all the cities in India, offers undoubtedly the most cosmopolitan, culinary adventure. Although it is the capital of the state of Maharashtra, there is no particular local cuisine. Bombay attracts people from all walks of life, the rich, the poor and the beggar, and from every conceivable community in the country. They all come here for one purpose only, to seek their pot of gold. In this quest, many leave behind a little of their homeland, making this a city of a fantastic number of varied and different eating places. It is also a trading city and a port, so hard cash always seems to be floating around, waiting to be spent. And, as many Bombayites living on this overcrowded island have been forced to move way out of the centre of town to live, it automatically means that there is a large floating population, working and eating in the city every day.

Despite the constant changes which are inevitable in a busy business-orientated city, certain areas still remain relatively unchanged. The Muslim area around Mohamedali Road houses wholesalers and some of the most delicious street food in the city. During festivals like Id, the whole area is transformed at night into one gigantic circus of activity and non-stop eating.

However, one of the most reliable restaurants for Muslim food is still Olympia, on Colaba Causeway.

For vegetarians, Thaker Club in the traditionally Gujarati area of town, Bhuleshwar, offers one of the most authentic and most reasonable thalis in the city.

Another popular, inexpensive cuisine is coastal seafood, prepared either by Mangaloreans, Goan Christians, Goan Hindus or Maharashtrians, who traditionally come from the coastal areas of the state. Gajalee, in Juhu, which serves the most divine Bombay Duck (not the quacking variety) and Anantashram, hidden in the lanes of the sleepy little microcosm of Goa, Kotachi Wadi, near Opera House, are both perfect examples.

There is no area in town which is known for its North Indian specialities, although the cuisine, as with the rest of India, has invaded just about every multi-cuisine restaurant. For great, inexpensive Tandoori food, Pal's in Bandra is the place.

While we are at street level, we cannot overlook the many snack and juice centres in the city. The Haji Ali Juice Centre, is open almost round the clock, and in addition to juices and milk shakes, has the most delicious fresh seasonal fruit and cream. The Bharatiya Vidya Bhavan Juicewalla specializes in hand-churned ice cream and Rajasthani lassi, and you'll get the best paan in town right opposite. Parsi Dairy kulfi is legendary, but the flavours of New Kulfi house, at the corner of Chowpatty are more adventurous. For ice creams, old Yankee Doodle on Marine Drive, Natural Ice Cream, which serves hand churned 'real' ice cream and the newly-opened Baskin and Robbins in Juhu, are by far the trend-setters.

Chaat, Bombay style, must be the most widely eaten street food in the city. Everybody has their favourite Panipuri and Bhelpuri walla. We find the chaat outside Elco Arcade, in Bandra, and Kailash Parbat, have maintained their quality and standards.

For those with a sweet tooth, the places to head for are Chhappan Bhog, selling Bengali mithai, Tewari at Opera House for their scrumptious pure ghee, Boondi laddoos, and the very traditional Tharu, Sindhi mithaiwalla in Khar.

Snacking is a popular pastime in this city. We could write endlessly about everybody's favourite places. The above are just some of the ones we like. Another problem with street food is hygiene. It is very easy to fantasize about the 'good old days' when you got the best fish in Koliwada, the best paya in Nul Bazaar, or the best kababs on Grant Road. We tried all these out but found it impossible to recommend them purely on the grounds of hygiene. However, Crawford Market, Grant Road Bazaar, Linking Road in Bandra, etc., are still great places to browse, people-watch and feel the famous heart beat of the city.

In the moderate price range, you are spoilt for choice. Our favourites include Under the Over, Rahul Akerkar's Bistro at Kemps Corner, Trishna, with superb Mangalorean food, Sheetal in Bandra and the ever faithful, Nanking in Colaba. In the space of no more than a year, Pubs and Pizzas are the new buzz words in the city. By far the most innovative of the new lot is the very recently opened Pizzeria Uno on Marine Drive. Karla and Sevi Singh pioneered the popular American concept of home delivery pizzas with their enormously successful Pizza Express which has been a trail blazer for several other such operations.

Bombay has a very definite élite who travel, know good food and love entertaining in five-star hotels. And with an increasing number of foreign businessmen in the city nowadays, the five-stars have responded favourably. Of all that is on offer, Zodiac Grill at the Taj, undoubtedly beats all the rest for creative European cuisine. Nelson Wang's China Garden is simply the most authentic, flamboyant Chinese restaurant in India. The newly opened Thai Pavillion at the President Hotel is extraordinary, and you'll always get great Italian food at the Trattoria.

Bombay, in a nutshell, has a soul, usually a hungry one. It really can be a gourmet's nirvana, without spending a great deal of money.

A meal for one person

Inexpensive: under 100 rupees
Moderate: 100 to 250 rupees
Expensive: over 250 rupees

Amritsari Fry Centre

Amritsari Fry Centre
Linking Road
Near Telephone Exchange
Khar Pali Road
Bombay
Tel : 542244.
Price : Inexpensive
Speciality : North Indian
Timings : 7 p.m. to midnight

Basic and not terribly pristine or clean, Amritsari Fry Centre is manna for late night carnivorous foodies, who prowl the streets for some substantial satisfying food, after attending boring functions (as often happens with us), or simply for pigging.

'Tak Taka Tak' is the sound of Sardar Gurdish Singh's kurpi, as he hammers away with one hand at the huge tava (griddle), pushing, turning and tossing away at the Gurda Kapura (kidney and offal), while the other hand quietly throws in spoonfuls of delicious paya (trotter) gravy. Meanwhile, steadfast foodies crowd around the stall for a whiff of the goodies.

The ingredients could not be fresher; gleaming platters of fresh offal—gurda, kapura, brain, liver and chicken tikka, are arranged around the tava, behind which Sardar Gurdish Singh presides. What joy it is to be able to drool over the magnificent display of food, while waiting in anticipation for your dish to get ready. The gravies are made from a combination of paya soup and fresh green masalas, with heaps of coriander. It requires massive will power to prevent yourself salivating like a hungry cocker spaniel, while the 'Tak-Tak' is going on.

You can sit on one of the half-a-dozen or so makeshift, roadside seats, or simply stand and eat (we prefer this as we can watch Gurdish's performance at the tava). If you have a car, then you have that option too. All the dishes are approximately Rs 30, and come with freshly-baked pau (soft spongy bread). For a late night snack, this place is sensational. Amritsari Fry Centre now has a branch in Jackson Heights, Queens, New York!

Anantashram

Tucked away in Kotachi Wadi, a bypath of Girgaum, where time seems to have stood still, Anantashram continues to serve delicious Coastal food, cooked on charcoal sigris, as it was done when it first started over sixty years ago.

Anantashram
46, Khotachi Wadi
Girgaum
Bombay 400 004
Price : Inexpensive
Speciality : Malvani (Coastal)
Timings : 11 a.m. to 2 p.m.;
  7 to 9 p.m.

It is an amazing place to visit. There are two rooms where about twenty single (yes, single) marble-topped tables and uncomfortable steel chairs are laid out facing each other. If you need privacy, there is also a family room, which frankly is not big enough to swing a cat. Eating at Anantashram is a singularly serious and selfish business. The waiters, all cooks as well as co-owners, are led by Baba Khadpe. Anantashram does not believe in formality, so they serve food in their home attire of striped pyjamas and vests. The walls are full of black-and-white pictures of their ancestors and of Hindu gods. The service is abrupt to the point of rudeness. But all this is compensated by the food which is out of this world.

Our favourite dishes are Crab Masala, Prawn Masala, Teesra (shellfish) masala with a portion of Mandeli (small crisp fried fish). The masala dishes are thick with coconut, and not red with chilli. Rotis done first on a tava and then tossed on the red hot charcoals, get puffed up and are served one by one. Steaming rice is served with their special ussal (sprouted) dal. Finally, we drink the solkadi, a wicked sour-and-spicy drink made with thin coconut milk, green chillies and kokum, which helps the digestion. Seafood is the basic focus of a meal, but mutton and chicken are also on the menu. There is hardly anything for vegetarians. The menu changes constantly, according to the availability and season of the fish. You get a basic thali, and then order your add ons. The prices have gone up recently, but you can still eat like a king (two non-vegetarian dishes, rice, two rotis, yogurt, solkadi) for less than Rs 50 per person (all inclusive). A word of warning: the spice level seems to fluctuate in this eatery, from happily bearable to excruciatingly hot.

Apoorva Restaurant & Bar

Apoorva Restaurant & Bar
Noble Chambers (Vasta
  House)
S.V. Brelvi Road
Fort
Bombay 400 001
Tel : 2870335
Price : Moderate
Speciality : Mangalorean
Timings :11.30 to 4 p.m.; 6 to
  11 p.m.
Sundays: 11.30 a.m. to 4 p.m.
Credit cards accepted
Partly air-conditioned

With an entrance resembling the Parthenon in Athens, and a typically 'synthetic' interior, with formica top tables, stainless steel chairs and Rexine plastic seating, it is difficult to believe that Apoorva serves some of the best coastal food in the city. Do not be misled by the extensive menu, which includes Chinese too. Zero in straightaway on its seafood specialities, for which people drive miles.

Start off with the ladyfish, which got its name because of its delicate flesh and flavour. It has a unique taste, said Apoorva's owner, since it comes from sweet water estuaries, which are mixed with salt water from the sea. Jamnagar and Mangalore are two sources of this delectable fish. After this, opt for Crab Curry or Fish (pomfret) Gassi, both cooked with coconut and freshly ground masalas, to be eaten with plain boiled rice or tandoori roti. Both dishes are excellent. But the cherry on the cake at Apoorva is the Kolhiwada prawns—marinated in typical Punjabi masalas, without any dreadful batter, and deep fried. They go down very well with a glass of chilled draught beer. We even ended the meal with prawns (our major weakness), and left the restaurant with their remarkable taste lingering on our taste buds.

A. Ramnaik's Udipi Shri Krishna Boarding

Situated bang opposite Matunga Railway Station (Central), the first Udipi Restaurant in Bombay has been serving superb South Indian food, at incredibly low prices for the past fifty years.

For Rs 10, you get a wonderful thali, with two bowls of rice, puris, sambhar, rasam, three vegetables, papad, pickle, yoghurt and buttermilk. All freshly made, all superbly cooked. For Rs 26 you can eat unlimited quantities of the same thali, plus a choice of home-made desserts: basundi, rossogolla or kheer. The buttermilk was seasoned with a hint of ginger. It makes a light, satisfying meal, made even more appetizing by the banana leaf on which it is served.

A. Ramnaik's Udipi Shri
   Krishna Boarding
1st floor, Mun Market
   Building
Matunga (Central Railway)
Bombay 400 019
Tel : 4142422, 4143863
Price : Inexpensive
Speciality : South Indian
   Vegetarian Thali
Timings : 10.30 a.m. to
2.30 p.m.; 7 to 10 p.m.
Mondays closed

The spotlessly clean restaurant is on the first floor, and the decor is functional. In fact, there is a notice outside the kitchen saying THOSE WHO WISH TO SEE OUR KITCHEN MAY DO SO. Service is prompt and polite. Dressed in shorts and aprons, the waiters are eager to please. There is no tipping. The place is always full, so go early.

Bade Mian

Bade Mian
Tulloch Road
Colaba
Bombay 400 039
Price : Inexpensive
Speciality : Muslim kababs
Timings : 7 p.m. to 2 a.m.

By now, everybody who loves good Muslim kababs knows the white bearded man who presides over his pavement restaurant. You may get better Muslim food in various quarters of Mohamadali Road, but none as accessible or as legendary as this one. Situated conveniently behind the Taj Hotel, it is not uncommon to see the trendy youth of the city drive up after boogeying the night away next door and Arabs coming for a nibble before taking on Colaba Causeway. The lane itself has deteriorated in the last few years and has now taken on a sleazy tone. This does not seem to interfere with Bade Mian's roaring business.

We know people who will insist on coming here as soon as they land at Sahar Airport. If you have never tried the Baida Roti (an egg roti stuffed with kheema) here, you haven't lived! Other items worth drooling over are the Chicken Tikkas, Chicken Tangri (leg), Mutton Boti Kabab and Kheeri Kalegi (udder and liver). Have them with a dash of lime or wrapped with raw onion in a roti. Avoid the chutney if you have a sensitive stomach. Soft drinks are brought to you by the service boys. Most people take away, eat in their cars or on the bonnet.

A landmark in the city.

Bagdadi

As you enter this nondescript-looking restaurant on Tulloch Road, you are bombarded with notices all over the wall which read, PLEASE DO NOT ARGUE WITH THE WAITERS, and ANY PERSON MISBEHAVING SHALL BE HANDED OVER TO THE POLICE, which makes you wonder whether you have come to the place which serves the famous Bagdadi chicken. When we asked our waiter, Shakti, whether the notices were serious he shrugged and said, 'Lots of people come here tight (drunk) and fight with the waiters on any count.' As he was speaking, there seemed to be a commotion at the cash counter which proved the point.

Bagdadi
Tulloch Road
Near Regal Cinema
Appolo Bunder
Bombay 400 039
Tel : 2028027
Price : Inexpensive
Speciality : Persian
Timings : 10 a.m. to midnight

The Bagdadi special, Chicken Fry, is well worth enduring the queue, the crowded benches you have to sit on, and maybe the occasional scuffle you will have to witness. The boy sitting on the same bench as us had come all the way from Ghatkopar for the chicken. The specials are the Chicken Barbecue, tandoori, or pot roasted (boiled). A large leg of chicken, moist, tender and tasty, is marinated in a sauce (made with freshly-ground masalas), the ingredients of which are kept secret by the fourth generation of owners, Shakil Ahmed and his son, Samir. 'Iranis and Iraqis eat two full chickens at a time,' Shakti proudly informed us. The same Chicken Fry also comes with gravy, which is highly avoidable, as it is watery and tasteless. The large tandoori roti, enough for two, is crisp and tasty.

Other specialities include the Beef Stew, Chicken Chilli Fry, Biryani, etc. but we would recommend the chicken. It is undoubtedly the best value for money in town for a quick chicken dinner. A word of advice, unless you are a staunch feminist or out to prove a point: women would be better off dragging a male friend along. Try and avoid peak meal times too.

Bharat

Bharat
317 Arun Chambers
Shahid Bhagat Singh Road
Bombay 400 001
Price : Moderate
Speciality : Mangalorean
  seafood
Timings : 11.30 a.m. to 3.30
p.m.; 5.30 to 11.30 p.m.
Bar licence
Credit cards accepted
Air-conditioned first floor

Bharat is a new coastal restaurant situated diagonally opposite Grindlays Bank on Shahid Bhagat Singh Road. This was previously a vegetarian Udipi restaurant which the owners decided to transform completely early in 1994 noticing the growing popularity of Mangalorean seafood restaurants.

Unlike other Mangalorean restaurants, though, this one is larger and has been brightened up, with an air-conditioned section on the first floor and a more spacious 126-seater downstairs. Both areas have marble flooring and steel tubed chairs with brown Rexine upholstery. The whole place tries very hard to be up-market, with glass bubbles full of fish (first floor) and a glass wall waterfall (ground floor). The service, though friendly, has not been upgraded and the place is always full of a mixed bunch who come here primarily to eat. We would frankly stick to the ground floor which we feel is more honest, homely and where you are more likely to find somewhere to sit.

The menu at Bharat is small, but all the specialities we tried were excellent. We were quite worried about trying the crab in green masala, Crab Harialy, mainly because we thought the masala would swamp the taste of the crab. But the fresh crab done in a slightly spicy, 'wet' masala made from spinach, green chillies and cothmir (and, we suspect, a touch of green colour) was quite exotic and certainly worth recommending. The fish tikka (Barbecue Fish), chunks of rawas in a dry Mangalorean masala, devoid of the familiar red colouring, was superbly cooked. Idli and Neer Dosa served with Prawn Gassi, a thick coconut-based curry was intriguing. However, you must try the Bangda Chilli, cooked in an earthenware pot and the Lady Fish Fry. Don't, whatever you do, let the over zealous young Turk, Sharath Salian (the owner's son who now runs the place) talk you into having the tandoori items, especially the tandoori crab. Stick to the Mangalorean specialities, and we guarantee you'll have a feast to remember.

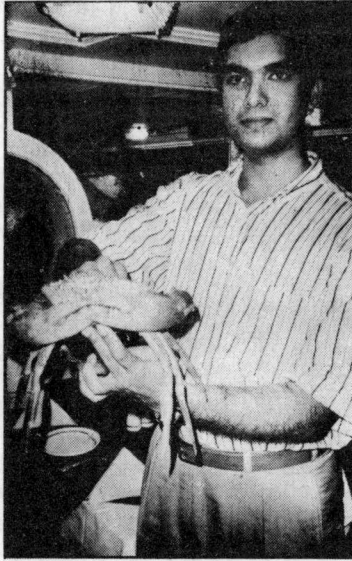

The speciality at Bharat

Bombay A-1 Restaurant

Bombay A-1 Restaurant
Grant Road Junction
7, Procter Road
Bombay 400 007
Tel : 3889808, 3881146
Price : Inexpensive
Speciality : North Indian
Timings : 7 a.m. to 11 p.m.

Located under the Grant Road bridge, Bombay A-1 Restaurant is a down to earth, simply-furnished place, where the focus is on food.

The specialities change every day, but their daily menu is extensive enough with a decent vegetarian section, Parsi dishes and mutton. If you can manage to go on a Friday, then you can try out their superb Kadai Mutton and Paya Masala in a thick, delectable gravy. Both dishes have pungent, assertive flavours, a unique blending of spices and are, fortunately, easy on the red chilli. We started with a portion of Tandoori Chicken (mercifully without the red colour) of good size, and well cooked with the juices intact and, finally, half a plate of Mutton Biryani, which was excellent. The rice was fluffy, each grain separate and the meat steamed pink. The secret of enjoying a good Kachche Gosht ki Biryani is really very simple. Go early, preferably at 11.30 a.m. when the pateela (special utensil) of biryani is first unsealed. Try and get the first plate and you will see the difference. There is nothing much for vegetarians here. Avoid the Chinese and Parsi items. The rotis, flaky and crisp were excellent accompaniment.

The decor is modern, with a wood and glass ceiling. The seating is comfortable with cushioned chairs and formica tables, cramped together to accommodate the maximum number of customers. The napkins were torn and the service a bit slow.

Candies

Despite there being an amazing number of fast food and snack places in the suburb of Bandra, this unpretentious, hole in the wall leads the pack. The specialities, in order of popularity, range from soft bread, chicken sandwiches (kept temptingly on a large, round platter at the counter), which the regulars help themselves to, while ordering from the rest of the simple menu. Pereira makes his own mayonnaise which is light and not glutinous. Other favourites include Chicken Biryani, Chicken Noodles, Mutton Roll and Fried whole leg of chicken.

Candies
Ashok Apartments
Opposite Petit School
Union Park
Bandra
Bombay
Tel : 6045058, 6423326
Price : Moderate
Speciality : Snacks
Timings : 8.30 a.m. to
  9.30 p.m.

Mr Allan Pereira (Ex Macronell, the famous Bandra Bakery and Caterer), the unassuming owner, has found the magic balance between price and quality. No wonder Candies has become the refilling station for Bandra's teenagers and hungry film wallas working in the busy sound studios nearby. The service by Menino and Nicholas Fernandes, is fast and friendly, but the place can hardly take ten hungry customers. The best thing to do is take away.

Although Candies is open till a very convenient 9.30 p.m., the 'Sold out' sign often appears before closing time. Another great selling gimmick, which ensures that nothing is carried forward, is a twenty-five per cent discount on anything remaining between 8 p.m. and 9 p.m.

Chawla's

Chawla's
15th & 33rd Road
Bandra West
Bombay
Tel : 6443313
Price : Moderate
Speciality : North Indian
Timings : Lunch and dinner

If you are ravenously hungry and can afford calories, then make a beeline for Chawla's, and order their famous Special Cream Chicken. Says Ronnie Singh, the owner who personally supervises the kitchen, 'We use the freshest double cream and home ground masalas to prepare our chicken, and the secret recipe (now a closely-guarded family secret) of our great-grandfather from Punjab.'

One plate of half a chicken is enough for two. Though cooked in double cream, the moist and tender chicken is far from bland. The thick gravy contains the right blend of finely-ground, fresh spices. Eaten with hot tandoori roti, (served to you one at a time, crisp and piping hot), it becomes truly a magnificent experience! There are other treats too: Tandoori Chicken, Seekh Kababs, Bhoona Gosht, Tandoori Fish and some vegetable dishes, but it is best to stick to the Cream Chicken. The vegetarian dishes here include Special Palak Paneer, Vegetarian Biryani, Channa Pindi and Dal which are frankly only there to 'garnish' the chicken items.

Tables and chairs are laid out in the patio, which is the main restaurant. The shop-cum-kitchen services the take away orders. Being outdoors, it is best for dinner when the evening is cool and the ambience, lively.

Chawla's also has branches in Ludhiana, Moradabad, Patiala, Mandi, Govindgarh, Chandigarh, Amritsar, Delhi, Jallandhar, and Haldwani.

They also do free home delivery.

China Garden

One of the greatest compliments one can credit Nelson Wang with (the brain behind China Garden) was paid by a fellow restauranteur, who, when asked which his five favourite restaurants were said, 'I give all first five places to China Garden.'

Winner of the Best Restaurant of the Year (1991 and 1992), China Garden lives up to its reputation.

Truly a gourmet restaurant of high calibre, China Garden is a must for all those who visit Bombay. The interior, for a start, is more international than Chinese, with white and green as the predominant colours, a miniature waterfall, gold leaf urn and original screens. Though some of Parmeshwar Godrej and Sunita Pitamber's original decor has been changed, it is still an elegant and awe-inspiring place to dine.

China Garden
Om Chambers
123 August Kranti Marg
Kemp's Corner
Bombay 400 036
Tel : 3630842; Fax: 3630706
Price : Expensive
Speciality : Chinese
Timings : 12.30 to 3 p.m.;
   7 p.m. to midnight
Reservation recommended

Before dinner, have a drink at Nelson's Piano Bar next door, or at your table. You'll get the finest Margharitas and Strawberry Daiquiris in the city here. With the drinks, try the delectable Steamed Mushroom Wontons or the deep fried Corn Curd, a sort of solidified version of sweet corn soup.

You have 300 unique recipes, many of which Nelson has created, to choose from. This can be confusing and time consuming. Our advice is to glance at the gourmet menu but eventually have a chat with the mâitre d'hôtel or Nelson himself. Constantly improvising, Nelson has also added other Oriental dishes to his Chinese menu, like the fiery and fragrant Thai Tom Yum soup and Korean Barbecue, served with an imported sweet bean paste, which are both excellent. For those who like something out of the ordinary, Nelson also serves Frogs Legs and the most divine Steamed Oysters on the half shell with burnt ginger and light soya. From the soups, try Fun Sei Thong, bean thread noodles, pickled vegetables and a meat of your choice, in a clear broth and the Barbecue Wonton soup, stuffed wontons in a clear soup garnished with Barbecue pork.

Whatever else we may order, we never miss the prawns here. It requires an extraordinary sense of timing and technique to retain the texture of a Tiger Prawn, without causing it to turn to rubber, and Nelson has done it. Initially, one gigantic tiger prawn (it can be prepared to your choice, but we preferred it with burnt ginger) seems enough to feed the whole table, but once you start, you just can't put it down. We also recommend the Vietnamese Barbecue, which requires your active participation and can be quite therapeutic. Succulent (only undercut is used) slices of beef (marinated in magic herbs and sesame oil) or chicken along with an electric grill are organized on the table. Spring onions, rice pancakes and Vietnamese sauce are the traditional accompaniments. It takes less than a minute for the meat to be cooked to a 'melt in the mouth' consistency. Meanwhile, prepare a pancake by dipping it into a bowl of water to soften it, coat it slightly with the sauce, place a few sprigs of spring onions and finally the cooked meat. You then roll up the pancakes yourself.

If you are in the mood for fish, try the Steamed Pomfret, with spring onion and ginger. Another favourite, and a complete meal, is the Mongolian Steamboat. You have a cauldron of steaming hot stock, in which you cook your own vegetables and tiny, prepared cuts of meat, fish and poultry, in a small, wire fishing net. Vegetarians love China Garden for their Pattaya Baby corn (in a Thai green curry paste), Asparagus with Pepper and Nelson's special potato recipes, using Chinese ingredients.

Whatever you eat at China Garden, finish off with a sizzling Teppan dish. We usually choose the Teppan Soba, soft fried noodles that sizzle.

The only problem sometimes with China Garden is the noise level, which tends to echo. This is a high profile restaurant and is therefore always packed, so don't go without a reservation.

Empty plates at China Garden

City Kitchen

A visit to City Kitchen is a must for all those who are fond of honest to goodness, no frills, home cooking. There is no compromise on ingredients, quality or quantity, and yet the restaurant maintains reasonable prices. The credit for this goes completely to the chef-proprietor, Sacru Menezes, whose signature is evident on each dish served here, whether it is fish curry with fluffy rice or the melt-in-the-mouth mince cutlets, served with fiery curry sauce. The menu is chalked up daily on a blackboard, according to what is fresh at the market, but you can always be sure that Chicken and Pork Vindaloo and Mutton Masala will be there. If you are lucky, you may even get a portion of Tongue Chilli Fry, as it normally gets sold very quickly. The portions are generous, and nothing seemed to be more than Rs 20. We also strongly recommend the soup. The stock was strong and flavourful, mixed with diced spinach, carrots and potato.

> City Kitchen
> 301, Frere Road
> Fort Market
> Bombay 400 001
> Tel : 2610002
> **Price : Inexpensive**
> Speciality : Goan
> Timings : 11.30 a.m. to
>   3:30 p.m.; 7 to 10 p.m.

The service is a bit sloppy, and the cutlery and crockery plastic and ordinary. But don't let that deter you from trying out some honest, flavoursome food.

The restaurant has an old, high ceiling with ancient fans and big windows, overlooking the busy Frere Road. The seating is basic but comfortable and not cramped. No music, no noise. The focus is on good food.

Copper Chimney

Copper Chimney
Dr Annie Besant Road
Worli
Bombay 400 018
Tel : 4924488, 4924499,
   4920208
Price : Moderate
Speciality : Moghlai
Timings : Noon to 4 p.m.; 7 to
   12.30 p.m.
Reservation recommended
Valet parking
Air-conditioned

Established in 1972, Copper Chimney is still the best place in town for Tandoori food. The restaurant is large with a bamboo ceiling, marble flooring with thick pile carpets, pictures of birds on the walls and the circa Sixties furniture on slightly raised flooring.

We go to Copper Chimney for Reshmi Kababs (succulent, generous, boneless, cubes of chicken, marinated in masala, and cooked to perfection in the tandoor). We also order a plate of plain palak (spinach) stewed in garlic and butter, and a couple of roomali rotis. The chicken pieces are juicy, the palak tasty and the roomali (which you can see being tossed in the air like a handkerchief in the open kitchen), worth dying for. The Tandoori Jumbo Prawns are also superb. Besides palak, vegetarians can bank on Paneer Tikka and Paneer Musselum (in fresh tomato sauce). There is a wide range of rotis, including Jumbo Kabuli Naan (for the family). Good desserts include small Gulab Jamuns, doused in thick, warm, rose-flavoured syrup, Malai Kulfi (Indian ice cream made with full cream) and Kulfi with Falooda (with cream and vermicelli), all home-made and excellent quality.

One word of advice: insist that all your tandoori items are freshly made, not reheated from the batches of half-cooked meats displayed on the hooks. This may mean a wait of thirty minutes or so, but definitely worth it. All the tandoor items are prepared in the glass fronted kitchen, one of the first restaurants in Bombay to start the trend.

There is a plaque at the entrance which says THE OWNERS EAT HERE. We doubt if the owner, J. K. Kapoor has any time on his hands, busy as he is running the more up-market Bombay Brasserie, a few doors away. Copper Chimney has branches in Bandra, London and Bahrain.

Delhi Darbar

A sprawling old restaurant at the junction of Falkland Road Delhi Darbar has been serving some of the finest Moghlai food in Bombay for the last twenty-two years. The chef-proprietor has created dishes which have been copied by other fashionable restaurants. But many keep coming back to this simple old place for their fill of Bheja Masala, Gurda Kaleji Fry and Khichda available only on Wednesdays and Fridays. The food is 'spicy' due to the use of whole masalas. We recommend the White Mutton, slow cooked with white boiled onions and cream sauce, flavoured with cardamom. Try the Dabba Gosht, (meat slow-cooked with onion, tomato, ginger and garlic), Mutton Kheema Special and the Palak Gosht. The best way to eat these is with Reshmi Roti. Not the place for vegetarians.

Delhi Darbar
197, Corner of Grant Road
Opp New Roshan Cinema
Bombay 400 004
Tel : 3882589, 3875656
Price : Inexpensive
Speciality : Moghlai
Timings : 10 a.m. to midnight

City slickers

The restaurant is huge, with a labyrinth of rooms and corridors with tables and chairs everywhere. We somehow preferred the corridor near the kitchen, or the veranda, to the air-conditioned section for we could enjoy the hustle and bustle of the place and also see what everyone else was eating. There is no decor to speak of but who cares if the food is good. This is definitely not the place to bring the boss and his wife for dinner. For those who are uncomfortable about the area, or about who they might be sitting next to, there is a smart, air-conditioned branch of Delhi Darbar located at Holland House, (Shaheed Bhagat Singh Road, Near Regal Cinema, Colaba), which serves almost the same food at higher prices.

Fountain Inn

Fountain Inn
Nanabhai Lane
Halima Building
Building No-7
Flora Fountain
(Near the American dry fruits store)
Bombay 400 001
Tel : 2834167
Price : Inexpensive
Speciality : Mangalorean
 Seafood
Timings : 11.30 a.m. to
 2.30 p.m.; 7 p.m. to 10 p.m.
Credit cards accepted

Fountain Inn serves seafood and is worth mentioning because of its fresh fish and chicken, at unbelievably low prices.

Besides the usual range of seafood in curries and masalas, Fountain Inn serves idlis (four) with Chicken Masala, a wonderful combination popular with most of the customers. The coconut gravy was thick and velvety. Though delicious, we found the portion too big and had to get the rest doggy bagged. Try the Ladyfish Fry which was delicious. Chicken Chilli is yet another popular speciality. Most dishes cost around Rs 20. The place is packed most of the time and the fast turnover assures that the food is fresh.

The restaurant is about forty feet long, narrow in width with tables cramped together. Tables are usually shared, as a lot of people come here alone. The decor is grey and white with steel chairs. Worth a visit.

Gajalee

Though we love trying out all manner of creatures from the sea, we were somehow never tempted by the popular but slimy, shapeless Bombil, or Bombay Duck.

We were introduced to Gajalee and to the famous Bombil, by film director and foodie, Sai Paranjpaye. We kicked off with Kokum Solkadi, an excellent hot-and-sour appetizer made with coconut milk, kokum, ginger, garlic and green chillies, all strained to look like a pinkish pina colada. The cheerful waiter, Gurunath Patil, then brought us the Bombil (four on a plate), fried crisp and fluffy, rather like Japanese Tempura. As soon as we bit into it, our taste buds went mad trying to cope with the luxury of crunchiness and buttery softness, in the same mouthful.

Gajalee
Hanuman Road
Vile Parle (East)
Bombay 400 057
Tel : 8388093
Price : Inexpensive
Speciality : Malvani
Timings : 11 a.m. to 3.30 p.m.;
 7 p.m. to 11 p.m.
Partly air-conditioned

The other dishes we recommend are: Clam Masala, Mori (shark) Masala and Fish Koshimber. The masala for each preparation is ground separately, therefore each dish retains its flavour. Vade (puris made with ground rice, urad and channa dals) are served with the gravy dishes.

Gajalee has now added an air-conditioned section seating forty, complete with fancy upholstered furniture and silver service. In here the Bombil tends to arrive rather deflated compared with the outside where they are literally dropped on the table from the frying pan. The prices are also fifty per cent higher and no thalis are served. We prefer the slightly larger, more modest original section.

The kitchen is spotless and quality control maintained by Chandrakant Shetty, the chef-owner. This has no doubt contributed to the success of Gajalee, which has grown from a hole-in-the-wall dhaba, to a proper restaurant, with drooling customers often waiting outside.

Gaylord Restaurant & Bar

Gaylord Restaurant & Bar
New Narina Road
Churchgate
Bombay
Tel : 221376, 220985
Price : Moderate
Speciality : Continental,
   Indian
Timings : 9.30 a.m. to
   11.30 p.m.
Credit cards accepted
Air-conditioned

As soon as you enter the arched portals of Gaylord, you get a feeling of comfort and elegance, typical of the Fifties. The tables are neatly laid out, with crisp, pink linen. The burgundy chairs are luxuriously cushioned, the chandelier, the mirrored walls, etc., all create a relaxed ambience. You can sit either on the ground floor, the first floor or, in fine weather, on the veranda outside next to the new bakery. The bakery has become very popular, turning out over 200 bread and pastry items.

The menu is extensive (six pages!), but Gaylord is best enjoyed at non-peak hours, when they serve some of the freshest sandwiches (Club and Ham and Cheese), hot breads and cakes in town. Or you could try some of their Continental specialities, like the Roast Lamb with mint sauce (succulent slices of lamb cooked in its own juice), Chicken Chasseur, sautéed with fresh mushrooms and green peppers, and for vegetarians, Cannelloni Indiana (a pancake stuffed with spinach and braised in tomato broth). They are accompanied by boiled vegetables and mashed potatoes.

For those with a sweet tooth, there's the ubiquitous Creme Caramel, which was excellent. As you go out, you will invariably be seen off graciously by a charming old man, Shakeel Khan, the oldest employee of Gaylord, reflecting the charm and grace that was and is the hallmark of this restaurant.

Goa Portuguesa

A great deal of hype and publicity surrounds this small, but smart Goan eatery. The decor is pleasant enough, service friendly and the food is somewhere between five-star finesse and rustic home cooking. All the ingredients are, however, brought from Goa, along with the cooks.

Goa Portuguesa
Opp Mahim H.P.O.
Near Hinduja Hospital
Kataria Road
Mahim
Bombay 400 016
Tel : 4440202, 4440707
Price : Moderate
Speciality : Goan
Timings : Noon to 3 p.m.;
  7 p.m. to 12.30
Air-conditioned

The Lobster Masala was tremendous. Stick to one 'masala' dish, as all the masalas taste similar after a while, and they are pretty pungent. The Stuffed Crabs make a good starter, followed by Pomfret Reichade, and finish with the Goan Prawn or Fish curry and Goan red rice. For those who are not fond of seafood, there is the Chicken Xacuti or Pork Sorpotel, both good but nothing on the seafood. Frankly, this restaurant is more suited to fishy people who enjoy a swig of feni or a glass of wine to the strumming of a guitar. The restaurant has a full liquor licence, with some unusual cocktails—we'll leave you to discover them for yourself.

By the time this book is out the restaurant will have a separate vegetarian section.

The Golden Dragon

Golden Dragon
The Taj Mahal Hotel
Apollo Bunder
Colaba
Bombay 400 039
Tel : 2023366
Price : Expensive
Speciality : Chinese
Timings : Noon to 3 p.m.;
   7 to 11.30 p.m.
Credit cards accepted
Air-conditioned
Reservation essential

The Golden Dragon is a restaurant full of surprises. The food, clearly depending on how busy they are (and it is often packed), varies from good to amazing. Near Christmas, they called us up about a speciality they were introducing, the famous Peking Duck.

The duck in question took about an hour to prepare. While waiting, we nibbled on a portion of Har Sui Mai, wafer-thin wrappers filled with prawns, crab meat, bamboo shoots and mushrooms mildly spiced and delicate scallops, pan fried with pink rain ginger and onion.

Finally the *pièce de résistance* arrived in full glory, served by a team of well-trained waiters. The Peking Duck, golden, crisp, succulent and glowing with a coating of honey. So often when a classic dish is introduced from one country to another, it loses its identity in the voyage. The Peking Duck in the Golden Dragon proved to be the real McCoy. It is served, traditionally, in three stages. First the crisp golden skin, to be eaten with pancakes smeared with Hoisin sauce and a sprig of spring onion, rolled together like a roti. The first course, in fact, is the best part of the duck. Then comes the meat of the duck stewed with bean sprouts and juices of the duck and the last course is the soup made from the duck stock. The palate quivers at the memory of each course.

Later on, chef Sandeep explained the secret behind the authenticity of the dish. The duck was imported from Beijing and so was the special oven for roasting. With this, the Golden Dragon has a new one over the rest of the Chinese restaurants in Bombay.

The other specialities pale before the above dish but we will mention them anyway for those who want variety.

For those who like spicy food, the lobsters in chillies and mustard sauce are wonderful. For the adventurous vegetarians, we recommend asparagus pancakes, lightly spiced with soya, and garnished with scallions and fresh coriander. Also try the delicious crisp fried Morrel Mushrooms pan fried with green pepper.

The decor is Chinese but conservative. The walls are covered with beige China Silk. The Chinese lanterns are golden beige. The seating is comfortable, and the service impeccable.

Gomantak

Gomantak
301, Miranda Chawl
N.C. Kelkar Road
Bombay 400 028
Tel : 4305631
Price : Inexpensive
Speciality : Malvani
Timings : 11.30 a.m. to 3 p.m.;
    7.30 to 10.30 p.m.
Mondays closed

Located near Plaza Cinema in Dadar, Gomantak is a small forty-seater restaurant serving some of the finest Malvani food at very reasonable prices. It is so popular that you have to arrive by noon for lunch and by 7.30 in the evening for dinner to ensure that you get a table. You will then have to queue, as there is no system of reservation.

Unlike other Malvani restaurants, the top-selling specialities here are not seafood, but meat based. The Mutton Sukha (dry) or Mutton Masala, are scrumptious. Succulent pieces are simmered in a coconut-based masala curry (on a coal fire) and served with thin, hot chapattis. Their Liver Masala was also superb. From the seafood brigade, Shell Fish Masala, Shark Masala and Crab Curry were delightful. The best seafood dish was their Fish Curry (more like a French bouillabaisse, a stew made with different kinds of fish). The other items on the menu are Dal and Special Bhaji, but in all honesty we would not recommend this place for vegetarians. All dishes are priced well below Rs 20. No desserts are served.

The decor is modern but without any character. The furniture is functional. The restaurant and the kitchen (which is partly visible) is kept spotlessly clean. Service is faultless.

Gupta Restaurant

Established in 1954, Gupta
Restaurant owned by Gurpal Singh
Gandhi alias Kaka, serves, perhaps,
the most authentic Punjabi food in
the Dadar area in the inexpensive
category. What is striking about
Gupta's is that though most of the old
North Indian restaurants have
changed over to cooking over a gas
fire, it still uses coal sigris to cook the
food which invariably runs out by the
evening.

Gupta Restaurant
Gokuldas Pasta Road
Dadar (East)
Bombay 400 014
Tel : 4141002, 4143532
Price : Inexpensive
Speciality : North Indian
Timings : 11:30 a.m. to 4 p.m.;
   7 to 11 p.m.
Sundays closed

Even though the Tandoori
chicken and other non-vegetarian dishes are quite popular here, we
strongly recommend the vegetarian dishes which are exceptionally
good, e.g., Mooli Ka Saag (radish vegetable), Aloo Methi, (potato and
fresh fenugreek), Karela Piyaz (a dry dish of bitter gourd and onions),
Sukha Urad Dal Dry (lentils), Vadi Aloo (potato and gram flour
dumplings), Sarson Ka Saag (fresh mustard greens) and Makki Ki Roti
(fresh corn roti), when in season.

We were especially besotted by the daily special, Baingan Ka
Bartha. Brinjals are first roasted on a coal fire, meat removed and then
soaked in yoghurt. This is then toss fried along with red onions, ginger,
garlic, and home-ground masalas in a kadai and then garnished with
fresh coriander. The smoky flavour, the texture and the tartness of
yoghurt, all combine to produce a mind-blowing dish. There are also
other regular excellent dishes like Gobi Aloo (a dry dish of potato and
cauliflower), Palak Paneer (spinach and cottage cheese curry) and
Chole Masala (spicy bean stew). All the dals here are superb: it may be
a wonderful yellow chana-urad mix, kali dal or rajma. However, make
it a point to tell the waiter to avoid the oil tarka, which makes it too
heavy and, we feel, dilutes the original flavours. The tandoori rotis are
made from 100 per cent whole wheat flour and have extraordinary
texture and the smoky flavour of the coal fire. Most of the vegetable
dishes are priced below Rs 15 and together with two rotis at Rs 2 each
the bill is never over Rs 20 for a hearty and tasty meal. We also

recommend the Punjabi Lassi, a house speciality made from full cream yogurt. A complimentary plate of superb Tamarind Chutney and fresh onion rings are served with each meal.

Though housed in a garage with ordinary tables and chairs, Gupta's has built up a loyal band of clients who eat here regularly. Gupta's is also known for catering to film units. Film stars shooting at studios across the street are often seen here for a true taste of Punjab.

Dishing out biryani

Haji Tikka Corner

If you like to feel the heartbeat of a busy bazaar, then Khara Tank, off Mohammad Ali Road, is the perfect place. The bustle of activity is simply electrifying. It also houses the biggest assortment of lip smacking, Muslim dishes in a tiny space, measuring no more than a hundred square yards.

Haji Tikka Corner
76, Raudat Tahera street
Opp Evan-E-Hussaini Hall
Bombay 400 003
Tel : 3781938, 3733865
Price : Inexpensive
Speciality : Muslim
Timings : 5 to 11 p.m.

The problem with eating in places like this is usually the hygiene. The rule of thumb seems to be that if there is a speedy turnover (which in this case, there is), and the kababs are cooked right in front of you on red hot coals, you are probably quite safe. However, please avoid the 'drinking' water. Carry your own or order a soda.

The Haji Tikka Corner, tucked away on the Raudat Tahera Street, is like an oasis in the hyperactive Khara tank, where one can sit in peace, under an efficient fan, and eat some of the finest Muslim food in South Bombay, for an unbeatable price. The decor is 'modern', with a big laminated picture of the Brooklyn Bridge and the Manhattan skyline! The menu is scribbled on a signboard. A portion of Chicken Biryani, cooked on a coal fire, costs a mere Rs 14. The mutton koftas (three in a plate for Rs 11) are absolutely delicious. The Tandoori chicken, grilled on coal, is a sure shot, as is the sheekh (beef) kababs at Rs 5.50. Avoid the seafood, even if it is a daily special. For one of the finest desserts in the area, hop next door to Jawakal Sweets for their Phirni (rice pudding fragrant with rose), made in individual earthenware saucers.

The service is good. Try to visit this area during Id or any Muslim holiday. Although crowded, you will have the time of your life.

Ideal Corner

Ideal Corner
12 F/G Hornby View
Gunbow Street
Fort
Bombay 400 001
Tel: 2621930
Price : Inexpensive
Speciality : Parsi
Timings : 11 a.m. to 4 p.m.
Sundays closed

As we are always on the lookout for the perfect biryani, so are we for the perfect Dhansak—the delicious combination of mutton, dal and vegetables—the signature dish of the Parsis. One of the best Dhansaks we have so far discovered, is at Ideal Corner, an unpretentious place, at the corner of Gunbow street. Open only for lunch, it serves an exquisite range of Parsi dishes. We tasted the Dhansak, both vegetarian and non-vegetarian and they were truly satisfying. The mixture was thick and aromatic, with the prominent taste of cardamom. The kababs, both vegetarian and non-vegetarian, were delectable, and the brown onion rice, cooked just right.

Dhansak is served on Tuesdays, Wednesdays and Fridays. The delicious Chicken Farcha (chicken deep fried with a crisp coating of egg) came with French fries. We also recommend Kheema 'n' Dill, mince cooked with dill which is served on Tuesdays. The other Parsi dishes served daily are Sali Boti (a light mutton curry served with potato chips) and excellent Mutton Cutlets with or without gravy. Avoid the Chinese and fast food snacks and leave some place for dessert, especially the Bread Pudding and the Lagan Nu Custard (creme caramel).

The restaurant is circular-shaped. The tables are covered with green tablecloths under glass tops. The walls are a strange combination of green and pink. The general upkeep of the place is good. It is difficult to find a place to sit during lunch hours, because of the office crowds.

Definitely worth a visit, if you are fond of Parsi food.

Indian Summer

On the face of it, Indian Summer appears to be yet another multi-cuisine restaurant. We found it a cut above the rest of the Tandoori Brigade. Working within the parameters of North Indian food, the chef has turned out some very interesting dishes like Badalon Ke Beech, delicious mince flavoured with cinnamon and cloves, served on a bed of basmati rice. The Chello Kabab, though nowhere near the original Irani version, is the best we have found in Bombay. Basmati rice is steamed with butter, cream and milk, and mixed together with succulent pieces of charcoal-grilled boneless mutton. The vegetarians have a good choice here, with Sham Savera (a combination of cottage cheese and vegetables, stuffed in a basket of spinach) and Lahsooni Taus Dingri (fresh mushrooms cooked with corn and garnished heavily with coriander). The chick pea dip, Humous makes a good starter.

Indian Summer
80 Veer Nariman Road
Churchgate
Bombay 400 020
Tel : 2835445, 2835650
Price : Moderate
Speciality : North Indian
Timings : 11.30 a.m. to
3.30 p.m.; 7 p.m. to midnight
Air-conditioned

Indian Summer has a well-stocked bar and an imaginative Barman, Bhim Rao, who does excellent cocktails. We recommend the special 'mocktail', a non-alcoholic combination of buttermilk, crushed almonds, mint and strawberries.

A new restaurant designed by a glass work specialist, the decor is unique because of its mirror-work ceiling, walls and pillars. The seating is extremely comfortable, and the service superlative.

Indian Summer is an excellent place to dine in style, on food which is a cut above the rest.

Jeff Caterers

Jeff Caterers
143, A, End of Bazaar Road
Bandra
Bombay 400 005
Tel : 6421493, 6421856,
  6426518
Price : Inexpensive
Speciality : Bohra Muslim
Timings : 5 to 8 p.m.

Our search for the perfect biryani finally ended at this stall-cum-takeaway, which does roaring business catering to parties and weddings. The stall is open from five to eight every evening. Everything usually gets sold out by 7 p.m., especially the Mutton Biryani. Jeff (short for Jaffarbhai) also does excellent Mutton Cutlets which, placed between two slices of bread, would beat any hamburger hollow. Also try the Kichda, a superb wholesome dish, made from cracked wheat, three dals (tuvar, moong and masoor), select pieces of meat and freshly-ground masala. A variety of daily specialities are available, and any dish can be ordered in advance. Though well-known for biryani and Stuffed Bakra (whole goat), Jeff also does wonderful Dal Chawal Palida, a simple dish of dal cooked with vegetables and served with rice, and Baingan Bhartha for the vegetarians.

There is no seating, just a takeaway, backed by superb service and extraordinary food. The only catch is that you either have to book your requirement in advance, or go early, before the biryani finishes.

Kailash Parbat

Kailash Parbat has gone through a lot a changes since it opened as a panipuri-cum-chaat (spicy snacks) place in 1952. Now, besides its old stand and eat-n-run service on the ground floor, it has also introduced an air-conditioned restaurant on the first floor. A pretty ceiling with fibre glass panels of attractive floral designs lit up, comfortable chairs, clean granite tables and big sunny windows overlooking the busy Colaba causeway. Punjabi and Chinese dishes have been added to the menu, but the good old snacks, Panipuri, Dahi Batata Puri, assorted Pakora and Pav Bhaji are still the hot favourites! The prices are higher in the air-conditioned section, but reasonable, compared to other air-conditioned restaurants in Colaba. What urged us to review Kailash Parbat is the consistent good quality of the snacks, the home-made tasty food. The tava chapatti, Sindhi curry (made with gram flour, kokum and pakodis), Alu Palak, Channa Bature are delicious and served in generous quantities. We also noticed that half the restaurant was full of young girls who, for some reason, feel secure enough to come here on their own. Indeed a rare sight outside five-star hotels and hats off to Kailash Parbat for maintaining this.

Though simple, combinations like Koki (a thick Sindhi roti made with whole wheat, onions, pomegranate seeds, coriander and green chillies) eaten with fresh yogurt, and channa dal garnished with freshly made mint chutney eaten with Pakwan (a crisp flat deep fried bread) are popular. Other interesting dishes are Sai Bhaji (every Tuesday and Friday) and Bhee (lotus stem) in a light tomato gravy. From the Punjabi dishes, Special Gobi was quite delicious, made with freshly-ground

Kailash Parbat
1st Pasta Lane
Colaba
Bombay 400 005
Tel : 241972, 2045281,
2874823
Price: Inexpensive
Timings : 7.30 a.m. to 11 p.m.
Specialities: Sindhi, Punjabi
Partly air-conditioned

masala tempered with fresh cream. A portion of cabbage and tomato salad was laid on the table along with fresh cut lemons and home-made sun-dried lemon pickle, without masala, a typical Sindhi speciality.

The service was excellent—our waiter, Shakti, was anxious to please. From the desserts, Kailash's Sindhi 'Pyalo', a cupful of kulfi (Indian ice cream), Falooda (sweet vermicelli), Rabdi (thick cream) and rose syrup makes an ideal finale to a meal difficult to match elsewhere at the price.

Panipuri at Kailash Parbat

Kamling Chinese Restaurant

Kamling was recently refurbished with a modern granite floor, tasteful Chinese paintings of flora and fauna on the walls and comfortable upholstered seating. It is one of the oldest Chinese restaurants in Bombay and is very popular with foreigners, especially the Japanese who come here regularly for the Chimney Soup, a real value for money dish normally shared by two. The soup is kept hot by live charcoals within the chimney pot which contains boiling Chicken broth, packed to the brim with goodies like fish and meat balls, prawns, beancurd, mushrooms, Chinese greens (bakchoy) and bean thread noodles. This can make a complete meal. If you are still hungry, try their Dimsum (Chinese samosas stuffed with meat, chicken and prawns) and the Crab Fuyong (crab omelette).

Kamling Chinese Restaurant
Nagin Mahal
82, Veer Nariman Road
Churchgate
Bombay 400 020
Tel : 2042618, 2045643,
    2853137
Price : Expensive
Speciality:Chinese
Timings : Noon to 11 p.m.
Air-conditioned

Another perfect combination is Shark Fin Crab Meat Soup as a starter followed by Stir Fried Beef in black mushrooms and oyster sauce eaten with white rice along with a plate of Chinese greens to balance the meal.

Vegetarians have a big choice here. The Singapore rice noodles were superb with Stir Fried Broccoli with baby corn, or Beancurd in black bean sauce.

One of the few places in Bombay where you can still get authentic Chinese food.

A good place to go if you are in the area.

Khyber Restaurant

Khyber Restaurant
145, M. G. Road
Bombay 400 023
Tel : 273227, 273228, 273229
Price : Expensive
Speciality : Moghlai
Timings: 12.30 to 4 p.m.;
    7.30 p.m. to midnight
Credit cards accepted
Bar licence
Air-conditioned

We used to visit Khyber almost once a month for their succulent kababs and the inimitable, Brain in Green (mint and coriander) Masala till it was refurbished with a new up-market image, Casbah-like decor and prices almost doubled. Though the food is as good as it was, the place is designed more for entertaining than for an evening with friends.

On our recent visit, we were disappointed with the Sheekh, but the Reshmi Kabab (chicken), Tandoori Pomfret and Pomfret in Green Masala were very good. They still do the best Bheja (brain) Green Masala and Gurda Kapura Sheekh Kabab (a superb combination of perfectly cooked kidney and other offal minced and barbecued on a skewer). If you are a confirmed carnivore, then opt for the Kabab platter, an assortment of kababs, chicken liver, chicken sheekh, mutton chops, etc.

On the vegetarian front, the paneer selection is superb mainly due to the good quality of paneer. Start with Paneer Shashlik, generous lightly spiced cubes of paneer alternated with slices of capsicum on a skewer, and grilled. Palak Paneer and Paneer Khorma (cottage cheese in a creamy coconut and cashew gravy) do well as main dishes. Also recommended is Tuvar Dal, which is lighter than the usual Maa Ki Dal. Simple Tandoori or Khasta rotis are ideal to mop up the rich gravies. Sign off with Gajar Halwa, carrot halwa made with pure ghee and garnished with pistachios and almonds or the home-made Kulfi. All said and done, if you order only the grilled and tandoori dishes, Khyber will delight you. We found the gravy dishes too rich and overpowering.

The second floor, actually called Casbah, is now a disco, with 'translite' blow ups of Amitabh Bachchan, Michael Jackson, Madonna and Elvis. Somehow the idea of shaking a leg after eating Leg Barra, doesn't seem physically possible, at least not to us. Nor is the pungent aroma of Moghlai food conducive to a romantic shuffle on the dance floor, but then, it takes all sorts.

Kobe Sizzlers

Known for its beef and chicken specialities, Kobe is very popular with the younger crowd. The menu has everything on it, including soups, salads, chaat, snacks, juices and ice creams. But we can honestly only recommend the sizzlers. If you are allergic to fumes, ask for an ordinary plate, instead of the specially designed one for 'sizzling'.

Kobe Sizzlers
12/13, Sukh Sagar
Hughes Road
Bombay 400 007
Tel : 3632174
Price : Moderate
Speciality : Steaks and
  Hamburgers
Timings : 9.30 a.m. to
  11.30 p.m.
Credit cards accepted
Air-conditioned

We found the steaks good. Among the sauces, the garlic sauce was excellent, redolent with chopped as well as mashed garlic. But the black pepper sauce was too strong for our comfort. The Chicken Sizzler was a bit of a disappointment, as the chicken was tough, but that may not always be the case. The dishes come piled with a selection of boiled vegetables (beans, carrots, cabbage) and French fries. You can ask for mashed potatoes, if you wish.

For the vegetarians there is Paneer Shashlik. The soups were average and so was the Vegetable Burger.

Kobe, then, is really good for steaks, but nothing else.

The restaurant is divided into two sections and seats sixty downstairs and thirty upstairs. The decor is modern, with simple dark furniture. The waiters are young and enthusiastic.

Kool Corner

Kool Corner
Jeroo Building
137, M.G. Road
Opp University
Bombay 400 001
Tel: 271674
Price : Inexpensive
Speciality : Parsi
Timings : 7 a.m. to 7 p.m.
Sundays closed

Run by Mr and Mrs K. B. Irani, a husband and wife team, this tiny restaurant with seating for about twelve, serves the best Kheema/Potato Patties in town. Generous in size, it makes a wonderful snack-cum-meal if eaten with slices of bread and kachumber. Tuesday is a sell out at Kool Corner, as the regulars turn up en masse for their Mutton Biryani, quite different from Muslim Biryani, and yet with a clear, defined identity. Monday is Curry Chicken, Wednesday, Dhun Dal Patia, Thursday, Sali Boti, and Saturday the regular Kheema Patties, snacks, Samosas, Masala Bread, etc.

Good quality ingredients brought daily from the market, home-ground masalas and the superb taste, makes this unassuming place worth a visit, if you are somewhere in the Fort area. The best time to go for Biryani is around noon. Simple wooden tables and chairs, no decor but warm and affectionate service by the Iranis does the trick.

La Rotisserie

This is another one of those superb dining experiences that defies description. Chef Dominique Viger, a charming down to earth fellow, follows the principle of 'purist' French cuisine—he does not drown a good thing with heavy sauces and unnecessary garnishes. The Rotisserie has recently added a large number of imported items to their menu, including salmon (both smoked and fresh), Dover Sole, T bone and Rib-eye steaks and New Zealand Lamb Chops, which gives the chef more scope and the menu a more dependable flavour.

La Rotisserie
The Oberoi
Nariman Point
Bombay 400 021
Tel : 2025757
Price : Expensive
Speciality : French Grills
(Table d' Hote for lunch)
Timings : 12.30 to 2.45 p.m.;
7 to 10.45 p.m.
Credit cards accepted
Air-conditioned

We kicked off with a Lobster Salad, with mustard sauce, flecked with a tomato and vodka sorbet. The portion of smoked salmon was the largest we have ever had in India. No roses or fancy envelopes, the three large slices of this delectable smoked fish, were simply placed on a plate, surrounded by the traditional accompaniment of capers, onions and wedges of lemon, nothing more. It went down even better with the complimentary glass of chilled champagne. Of the hot starters, the Morrel Mushrooms stuffed with Lamb's Brain were exotically different and very creamy. You could actually call it a day at this point. We, of course, did not. We decided to try something different, and we were not disappointed. The fillets of Dover sole stuffed with an extremely good mousse (more like a terrine) rich with lobster, were amazingly rich. Back to the Rib-eye, yes it is undoubtedly the best steak served in India today. Tender, juicy, soft like butter, and served with a Béarnaise or Green Pepper Sauce, it is the perfect answer to the perennial quest for great red meat.

The Rotisserie also serves a reasonably priced business lunch, four elegant courses, for the price of a sandwich and beer in a coffee shop.

If you, like us, very occasionally hanker after perfect accompaniments, to the tune of a glass of robust Burgundy, then look no further.

Leopold Café

Leopold Café
Colaba Causeway
Bombay 400 0039
Tel : 2020131
Prices : Moderate
Speciality : Irani,
Continental, Indian, Chinese
Timings : 8 a.m. to midnight
Credit car accepted
Beer licence
Partly air-conditioned

'. . . where East meets West'

'It's the only place in Bombay where East meets West,' said young Farzan Sherian, one of the partners of the now over 100-year-old café. The crowd was made up of largely foreign budget travellers, students and trendy folk. Draught beer flows as freely as the young folk.

The extensive menu (267 items) spans Irani, Indian, European and mainly Chinese cuisine. All are competent and very little or no spice is used. Everyone had his own Leopold favourite. One German swore by the Chicken Fried Me Fan. An Australian freaked out on the Iranian chicken and rice, Chello Morge. Our particular temptation was the Chicken Tikka and naan, juicy, chunky pieces of grilled chicken on a bed of beet roots, with tinted slivers of onions. From the Chinese menu, go for the regulars like the Sweet and Sour Chicken, Me Fan noodles and any of the fried rice dishes.

Another Leopold attraction is fresh juices. It has one of the biggest fresh juice bars in Bombay and the servings are generous.

The age-old high ceiling, fans and old posters give the restaurant a distinguished look. There is an air-conditioned pub on the first floor where the action shifts after 10 p.m. What makes Leopold complete is the atmosphere—unpretentious.

Ling's Pavilion

Lings's, now three years old, takes up where the legendary Nanking (closed for renovation), the family's first restaurant, has left off. It is an up-market eatery specializing in well-executed gourmet dishes to tempt the most discerning palate. Exquisite specialities are deftly prepared here to produce sublime sensations.

Start with Dimsums, Chinese snacks or starters, also available from 3 p.m. to 7 p.m., as they are in China and most Chinatowns the world over. We recommend Vegetable Momo, a giant wonton stuffed with mushrooms for the

Ling's Pavilion
K.C.College Hostel Building
19/21, Landsdowne Road
Bombay 400 039
Tel : 2850023, 2850024,
224533
Price : Expensive
Speciality : Chinese
Timings : Noon to 3 p.m.;
6 to 11.30 p.m.
Credit cards accepted
Air-conditioned
Bar licence
Reservation recommended

vegetarians and Stuffed Crab Claws and Stewed Meatballs for the non-vegetarians. Next, order their delicious Stewed Spare Ribs and Stuffed Chicken Wings in oyster sauce or Spicy Barbecue Chicken Wings. The Shellfish (clams, squid, oysters and mussels) are also perfectly cooked here in spring onion, soya and green chilli. The starters at Ling's are so good that it would not be foolish to make a meal of them.

But we come here for the King Crab, either in spring onion and ginger, or in black bean sauce, or just plain steamed. King Crabs are available throughout the year at this restaurant and if you need proof of their freshness, Baba, (who runs the place) will send the live specimen to your table for you to inspect. It is surprising why no other restaurant in Bombay can match the quality of crabs at Nanking and Ling's. It must be largely due to big Baba, who we have seen at Grant Road Fish Market at the crack of dawn, personally selecting his crabs for the day.

You must also try the Baked Salty Chicken, Ling's version of Begger's Chicken and the fabulous fragrant Supreme Rice, cooked in an earthenware pot. Ling's do some unusual soups. We were pleasantly surprised with their delicious and quite different Snow White Soup, semi-thick fish stock with shark fin and egg drop, and surprisingly no fishy smell. Their exotic Steamed Coconut soup, with chicken and shark fin is served in a coconut shell, but needs a day's notice.

The vegetarians can start off with Steamed Mushroom Wontons and then graduate to bean curd in black bean sauce and Ling's stir fried Broccoli or Saucy Okra (lady's fingers toss fried in soya and chilli sauce), with steamed white rice. The names at Ling's are gems, Buddha's Delight, Hidden Jewels in the Cave, Harvest of the Flourishing and Cross the Bridge Soup, which make interesting reading while you are waiting.

Ling's Pavilion is an elegant 100-seater restaurant, with all the trappings of a Chinese film set. The waiters are dressed in uniforms which look like kung fu costumes and the whole setup is straight out of a Wang Yu movie (a grand staircase, moulded ceiling, a pond with goldfish and two tiers), where the action could erupt any minute. Unfortunately or fortunately, it never does. The ambience at Ling's is understated, low key and quiet. People come here to enjoy their food and to show it off to others. Although this is a mecca for the city's gourmets, they don't make a noise about it. All the ingredients are fresh, and it is left to you to order the preparation and spice you would like. The crockery and food presentation are not very exciting for this calibre of restaurant but the service is excellent.

Mahesh Lunch Home

Mahesh Lunch Home (which, incidentally, serves dinner and has a bar as well) is known for its Mangalorean specialities. So just plum for crisp fried ladyfish as a starter and then move on to the superb Crab Masala, in a light coconut curry. Those who like chicken can try the Chicken Sookha (in a dry masala) and finally take in the tangy Fish Curry and Rice. Do not waste money and space on dessert. If you are still hungry, Prawn Masala should make you happy. The seafood at Mahesh is the daily catch and is therefore as fresh as can be.

Mahesh Lunch Home
8B Cawasji Patel Street
Fort
Bombay 400 001
Tel : 2870938
Price : Moderate
Speciality : Mangalorean
Timings : 11 a.m. to 3 p.m.;
   6 to 11.30 p.m.
Partly air-conditioned

The decor is functional, and furnishing simple Rexine, cushioned chairs and ordinary tables. The air-conditioned section on the first floor is dingy and dimly lit, like a shady gambling den, and best avoided, unless it is unbearably hot. The ceiling on the first floor is so low that even short people tend to stoop. The service is prompt and very polite. Definitely worth a visit.

Mela

Mela
Phirki Corner
Worli
Bombay 400 018
Tel : 4945656, 4946956
Price : Expensive
Speciality : North Indian
Timings : Noon to 3 p.m.;
    6 p.m. to midnight
Credit cards accepted
Bar licence
Air-conditioned
Reservation essential

As soon as you enter this restaurant, you find yourself in Dhami Sabarwal's fantasy world, where all the stops are pulled out to give you an entertaining evening. Astrologers, mehendi, portrait artists, film hoardings, posters and the Caroussel Bar all vie for your attention.

Our first trip to Mela was on invitation. We therefore had little say in the ordering and were subjected to the gourmet platters (Rs 200), which included a full range of kababs, seafood (not a speciality here), dal and rotis. We found it too heavy and did not appreciate the mix of flavours.

Left on our own, we parked ourselves at the Caroussel Bar, ordered a drink and a plate of Mela's famous Galoti Kababs (patties of finely-ground kheema) and Kakori Kababs (well pounded soft minced kababs on skewers). No rice, no dal, no rotis. We left the restaurant feeling great.

The other delightful alternative at Mela is to join the gourmets at the Akhada (Tournament Ring), a special section of the restaurant where marinated meats are leisurely cooked over glowing embers of charcoal. All this is done right in front of you by the Akhada chefs.

The menu is long and adventurous, but the above specialities alone are enough to justify a visit to Mela. An ideal place to entertain.

Ménage à Trois

It was a marvellous idea, and quite a coup, to get Anthony Worrel Thompson to recreate and adapt the menu of his famous restaurant (serving starters and desserts only) in Knightsbridge, London.

The Apollo Bar today may not be Beauchamp Place, but it still does its best to present beautifully turned out little courses, ideal for that 'special' lunch.

Don't come here to hog. Ménage à Trois is designed for those who love nouvelle cuisine, i.e., the quality and presentation is outstanding, but the portions are small.

Ménage à Trois
Taj Mahal Hotel
Apollo Bunder
Colaba
Bombay 400 039
Tel : 2023366
Price : Expensive
Speciality : European
Timings : 12.30 p.m. to 3 p.m.
Credit cards accepted
Bar licence

Start off with a cocktail or a drink from the bar. The Apollo bar still shakes and stirs the best cocktails in town and, if Victor is there, don't pass up the opportunity to try his Dry Martini, which has uplifted our souls and spirits after many a bad day at the office. Wine by the glass, both foreign and Indian, is also available.

The menu changes seasonally, but you can always request something off the menu, which you may have previously enjoyed. From the current offerings, try the Pâté of Cheese and Pimento, or the Warm Chicken and Cheese Mousse. The cold starters go wonderfully with the baby rolls, which we tended to stuff ourselves with, as they come warm and inviting. Vegetarians need not worry. There are a host of options, including a delicious pastry envelope of asparagus and artichoke on a saffron cream. Of the main courses, or the 'warm starters', the Baby Lobster and Fricasse of seafood are as tempting as the pinwheels of tenderloin and walnuts in a Burgundy *jus*.

The peak of lunch was undoubtedly the desserts. Whatever you choose will be visually poetic and taste pretty special too. The Chocoholics Anonymous has weathered several changed menus, which is testimony to its popularity. It's all sinful and wicked, and features chocolate in all its most tempting forms—mousse, terrine, sorbet, ice cream and truffles. Don't pass up the ice creams and sorbets, they are all made by the chef especially for this restaurant.

Covers are few, so the service is extra attentive. Courses are well spaced as each dish is prepared to order, so don't come here expecting large portions or a quick lunch. We love this restaurant because of its leisurely pace, beautifully presented food, and great view of the Gateway of India and the Arabian Sea to one side and South Bombay to the other. Although Ménage à Trois is a restaurant in its own right, it is situated in the rather conservative setting of the Apollo Bar, with its wood panelling and pink colour scheme. Service is outstanding. 'Small and Beautiful' has to be your philosophy of food to appreciate Ménage à trois.

Nanking

Nanking is one of the oldest Chinese restaurants in Bombay (over fifty years old) and one of our favourites. It is a mid-market eatery, a no-nonsense kind of place and great value for money. We go there basically for the fabulous seafood, especially the jumbo sized crabs. The preparation of the scavenger is according to the wish of the customer, but the old man Yick Sai Ling and his sons, will advise you to try it simply steamed, or lightly fried, with spring onion and ginger.

Nanking
Pheroz Building
Chhatrapati Shivaji Marg
Close to Taj Mahal Hotel
Bombay 400 039
Tel : 2020594
Price : Moderate
Speciality : Chinese
(Cantonese)
Timings : Noon to 3 p.m.;
6 to 10.30 p.m.
Beer licence
Credit cards accepted
Air-conditioned

The Cantonese dishes here are wonderful. Fresh fish and meats are treated with respect and not doused with heavy sauces or numbed with chillies, unless, of course, you want it that way. Our favourite starter is the Bean Thread with Meat Ball Soup (a superb combination of delicate noodles with minced pork balls, in a flavourful, clear chicken soup). Follow this with delicious Spare Ribs in soya sauce, or Tofu (bean curd), stuffed with minced pork.

We also recommend Steamed Fish (whole pomfret) with black bean sauce, yet another masterpiece, unmatched by any other restaurant. Often the best thing to do with fresh fish is as little as possible. At Nanking they have perfected this art.

For the vegetarians, we recommend the Asparagus and Egg Cream Soup and the Vegetable Wontons, which come with a dip of tangy sweet-and-sour sauce. For the main dish, Tofu is a good bet. Ask them to cook it with vegetables of your choice. Do not forget to order one Chinese green (spinach, water vegetable or broccoli) with a tempering of garlic. Fresh fruit is always served after the meal, so you can avoid dessert.

The decor, with the red latticework staircase leading to the first floor, simple tables and chairs and calendars with Chinese nymphets adorning the walls, has not changed for years. Now that their big sister restaurant, Ling's, around the corner, is well and truly established, Nanking is closing for renovation. In a way, we'll be a little sorry. Along with Gourdon, Little Hut and Bombelli (which no longer exist), it is one of the last reminders of the rip roaring Fifties in Bombay and a true landmark in this city. Service is good but a bit slow during peak hours. For the best and biggest crabs, go early or book.

Baba – the man behind the crabs

Nish

A low profile Chinese restaurant with an unusual name, Nish has, in its two years of existence, stealthily created a niche for itself as a family restaurant serving superb food at bearable prices. What is also unique about Nish is that for once you have a high street Chinese restaurant without the word 'Manchurian' on the menu. The food here is way above your usual chop suey routine, due to both the quality of the raw materials, and of course the chef.

Nish
Nidhi
76, August Kranti Marg
Kemps Corner
Bombay 400 036
Tel : 3878484, 3871949
Price : Expensive
Speciality : Chinese
Timings : 11.30 a.m. to
  3 p.m.; 7 p.m. to midnight
Credit cards accepted
Bar licence
Air-conditioned

Their Shark Fin Crab Meat Soup, rich with generous quantities of both, was the best we have eaten in Bombay. We had heard from friends about their speciality, Squid, and it turned out better than we had expected. The stir fried baby squid arrived, steaming hot, in black bean and ginger sauce. Bacon wrapped prawn is an ideal accompaniment to the soup. Prawns on toast was average.

Next was the Beef in Oyster sauce. The chef deserves a medal for this one. Succulent slices of beef, toss fried with spring onions, ginger, garlic, tiny pea sized peppers, and doused gently with oyster sauce, bowled us over with its fragrance and taste.

For chicken lovers, we recommend Crispy Chicken Chilli with spring onions. You also have a choice of fresh crab (kept live in the kitchen so couldn't be fresher), jumbo prawns, lobsters, cooked to customers' specifications. It is an amazing menu with lots of delicacies and would require a few trips to be able to appreciate them.

For the vegetarians, we recommend Bean Curd in Tomato. Superbly cooked, it came garnished with diced tomatoes and a light, delightfully spicy but not overbearing gravy. The mushroom rice that accompanied it was perfect.

The 100-seater restaurant is situated on two levels and is decorated tastefully with black granite and marble flooring. The layout is elegant with clean lines. The walls have niches with stained glass. There is a separate party room and a well-stocked bar seating around forty people. 'I want to cater to the family crowd,' said owner Chandrakant Shetye, an ex-race course bookie. It was therefore amusing to read the cocktail menu with raunchy names like Blow Job, Between the Sheets, Slow Comfortable Screw and so on.

The Chinese restaurant has mostly young Indian waiters out of which Cedric, the young captain is most helpful.

The restaurant, surprisingly, does not smell of the typical soya and chilli sauce and is kept superbly clean as is the large kitchen where non-vegetarian dishes are cooked separately from the vegetarian ones.

'Please don't sit for too long'–
Olympia

Olympia

Ever since most people around us can remember, and that spans many decades, nothing has changed in this Muslim restaurant near the Electric House, on Colaba Causeway. Our favourite Chicken Butter Fry, soft tava rotis, Brain Masala, Mutton Biryani and the Chicken Liver Masala, are always delicious, and always great value, and the two-levelled eatery is always packed, no matter when you go.

Olympia
39, Colaba Causeway
Shahid Bhagat Singh Road
Bombay 400 039
Tel : 2021043
Price : Inexpensive
Speciality : Muslim
Timings : 7 a.m. to midnight

Rasoolbhai, the old patriarch of the family, still runs the place, and refuses to change a thing. He is not interested in the world outside. He does not read the papers or watch TV (in fact, he doesn't even own one), or go to movies. His food, therefore, has remained traditional. While almost every other restaurant serves 'conveyer belt' broiler chickens, he serves desi, free range ones. Though pathetically small, they do actually taste better. The masalas are still ground on the premises and lots and lots of fresh coriander is used in his gravies, which is what gives the dishes at Olympia their unique flavour. Even the dal and vegetables are extraordinary.

Vegetarians should take note that even the dal is cooked with fresh mutton stock and a notice on the wall actually tells you that you may also find the odd mutton bone in there too!

The decor, like the food, has not changed. It is such a pleasure to find rare old Irani marble tables and chairs, well-kept and still in use. The old-fashioned portholes for cross ventilation, the ancient fans, the original Coco Cola signboard, the notice telling you not to comb your hair in the sink, the age-old aluminium basin and jug of warm water, brought by the waiter after you have finished. It is as if time has stood still.

Only Fish

Only Fish
229 Om Geeta Nivas
L.G. Road
Mahim
Bombay 400 016
Tel:4373821; Fax: 4440566
Price : Expensive
Speciality : Bengali (Seafood)
Timings : Noon to 3 p.m.
  7:30 p.m. to midnight
Reservation recommended
Credit cards accepted
Air-conditioned

Only Fish is a designer restaurant, decorated with fish nets, concave mirrors, a fish-shaped menu and service on clay plates. The walls are mirrored to give a spacious look, but the restaurant is in fact tiny. Only Fish is the brain child of admen, the Chatterji brothers and food is their passion. This is Bombay's first exclusive seafood restaurant, serving bekti, pomfret, hilsa, rohu, gol and prawns. The sublime Bengali, the fiery Chettinad, the flavours of Goa and robust Punjabi dishes, are conjured up by the three Bengali cooks who have manged to coax remarkable flavours out of local ingredients, leaving you feeling satisfied and delighted.

We would recommend that you stay with the exquisite Bengali dishes as the other regional fish specialities pale in comparison. The Bengalis have mastered the art of skillfully blending mustard with other spices, which seems to work wonders with seafood. The starters, Fish Missile, known in the kitchen as Saddam Hussein, is a fillet of bekti stuffed with a mince of prawns and rawas. We were so happy with this that we didn't venture to try the Flat and Furious nor the Karate Fish. Malai Chingdi, known here as Suburban Cream Prawn, was truly a masterpiece. Prawns, deveined, but with the shells intact, are broiled in a heavenly sauce of mustard, black cumin, green chillies and coconut milk. The sweetwater fish, hilsa, in a spicy sauce of mustard, black cumin and green chillies and hot steamed rice, is frankly all you need. 'We fly in the hilsa from Calcutta. It is only the Hooghly which can give hilsa this particular flavour,' claimed Anil Chatterji. The Shorshay Bata Mach, river fish in a fiery mustard and green chilli sauce is also tremendous. Other Bengali specialities are Dal with Carp and Dahi Rohu.

A word of warning—the servings here are small, especially the hilsa, so order a dish or two more than usual.

Pal's Chicken Corner

Although the seating is limited to a few makeshift benches, or your car, if you are a fresh fish freak then Pal's is the place for you. Every day tons of fresh rawas (still breathing) are personally purchased by owner T. S. Sabarwal straight from Sassoon docks. The firm fish is then cut into thick boneless chunks and marinated in a secret blend of 'Koliwada' spices created by Sabarwal. It is then deep fried in a smoking hot kadai, and served piping hot, with a sprinkling of amchur masala. For some reason, there is neither a trace of grease or that all-too-familiar fish smell. Koliwada fish was originally invented by Sabarwal's partner, Badalsingh, who introduced it at the Mini Punjab at Koliwada. The rest is history. Here the fish is sold by weight. 250 grams (Rs 25 all-inclusive) would be enough for one hungry soul.

Pal's Chicken Corner
Kailash Centre
Shop No-8, 16th Road
Bandra
Bombay 400 050
Tel : 6407995
Price : Inexpensive/
  Moderate
Speciality : North Indian
Timings : 7 to 11 p.m.

Pal's is also famous for its chicken specialities, especially the Barbecue Chicken Wings and Chicken Legs. The only reservation we have is the all-too-familiar red colouring in the masala. Once again the special masala sprinkled on the chicken does wonders. Pal's is miles ahead of other tandoori places in terms of quality and value. The place is no doubt a little dingy and always packed, but the food is absolutely delicious.

Pancham Puriwala

Pancham Puriwala
8-10, Bazaar Gate Street
Opp V. T. Station
Fort
Bombay 400 001
Tel : 2618750, 2622719
Price : Inexpensive
Speciality : North Indian
 Vegetarian
Timings : 8 a.m. to midnight

Over 125 years in business, Pancham Puriwala existed long before even the horse-drawn carts plied the streets of Bombay. It has been feeding the rich and the poor alike, with its own delicious version of North Indian vegetarian food. For a fixed price, now a princely sum of Rs 10 (all inclusive), five puris and two vegetables are served with unlimited helpings of the delicious home-made lime and chilli pickle. The yogurt, made of full cream milk, is extra.

There is no decor to speak of. This is just another small retaurant, with functional wooden tables and chairs. There is an open kitchen, where you can see fresh hot puris being rolled and fried.

No frills, no fancy service, but good, tasty, satisfying food, with no after effects. Explained V. N. Sharma, the present fourth generation owner, 'We use the best quality hing and Rainbow brand masalas, and the frying is done in hot vegetable oil.'

Abhishek Sharma, the fifth generation, has decided to spruce up the place and instal water purifiers, etc., but he has no intention of tampering with the speciality of the house, Puri and Bhaji, because, he says, 'That's our bread and butter!'

Paradise

Paradise served fast food as far back as the Fifties. Today, the menu has expanded to include Chinese, North Indian and Parsi dishes. The Parsi dishes are a welcome addition and worth trying out. Mr and Mrs Irani manage the kitchen while their daughter sits at the cash counter.

Our favourites at Paradise are Sali Murghi to be eaten either with bread, rice or hot tandoori naan; Kid Gosht; Sali Boti, and the ubiquitous Patra Ni Machhi.

Daily specials include an excellent mutton Dhansak on Wednesdays and a chicken one on Saturdays and Sali Boti on Sundays. Yet one more hot selling speciality at Paradise is something called Temptation. Mutton and chicken slices are stacked between slices of bread which is then dipped in egg batter and fried. Ideally this should be shared. We also recommend the Scotch Broth, a hearty barley chicken stock broth, with chunks of chicken and croutons, followed by Temptation and finish off with Creme Caramel. A perfect meal at an affordable price.

The price per main dish is well below Rs 50 (all inclusive) and around Rs 70 with roti or rice and pudding. All the servings are generous. The restaurant seats about thirty. Service is excellent, but avoid peak hours. The owners of Paradise have thoughtfully kept a weighing scale at the entrance!

Paradise
Sindh Chambers
Colaba Causeway
Bombay 400 005
Tel : 232874
Price : Moderate
Speciality : Parsi, Continental
Timings : 11 a.m. to 11 p.m.
Mondays closed

Waiting patiently

Pizzeria Uno

Pizzeria Uno
143, Marine Drive
Bombay 400 020
Tel : 2856115, 2851876
Price : Moderate
Speciality : Italian Pizzas
Timings : Noon to 11 p.m.
Air-conditioned

It seems that the more qualified you are, the deeper the desire to get your hands dirty, especially in the business of food. So we were not surprised when we saw the young, good-looking husband and wife team of Hemant (a computer whiz kid) and Rashmi (fashion designer) Mehta personally managing the kitchen of their newly-opened restaurant. It is as if the city has been crying out for Pizzeria Uno which, incidentally, serves some of the finest pizzas in Bombay. The dough is freshly made, so is the pizza sauce. The toppings, starting from basic tomato, cheese and basil lead up to exotic combinations called Bombay Masala, with ajwain and garam masala, and Makai Delight, with corn. Our favourite, with tangy Jalapeno peppers, came piping hot and tasted wonderful. The mixture of cheddar and mozzarella cheeses used hit the perfect balance of taste and stretchability, and the Jalapeno peppers, spicy but not 'burning', the best in India.

Pizzeria Uno is centrally located, on the corner of Marine Drive and Churchgate, and seats about sixty. The decor is modern, comfortable and casually elegant, with large bay windows, bamboo chicks and checkered tablecloths. The open kitchen has a brick wall look. The waiters wear casual white T-shirts and black trousers. The service is good.

Pradeep Gomantak Bhojanalaya

If you are on a tight budget and want fresh food at rock bottom prices, then this is the place.

The non-vegetarian Thali contains katoris of Kokum Saar (a sour, appetizing drink), Ussal (sprouted) dal, one roti, two cups of rice, fish curry and your choice of fried fish. Two boys go around giving refills of the delicious curry. All this for around Rs 16 (all inclusive), which must surely make it the cheapest non-vegetarian Thali in town. The range of fried fish includes rawas, pomfret, halwa, surmai, mandeli, etc. There is also Dry Mutton and Liver. Popular fish like pomfret and rawas run out by noon.

Pradeep Gomantak
Bhojanalaya
15, Gunbow Street
Fort
Bombay 400 001
Tel : 2665906
Price : Inexpensive
Speciality : Goan
Timings : 11 a.m. to 3 p.m.;
    7 to 10:30 p.m.
Sundays closed

The eatery is now twenty-five years old. It charged ninety paise when it first opened, for the same non-vegetarian Thali, reminisced D. P. Amonkar, the owner.

Tables and chairs are simple, and the seating capacity about twenty. The only problem with this tiny place is that it is always full. Prepare yourself for a wait or get there very early.

Purohit

Purohit
Veer Nariman Road
Churchgate
Bombay 400 020
Tel : 2049231, 2046241
Price : Inexpensive
Speciality : Gujarati
  Vegetarian Thali
Timings : 11 a.m. to 11p.m.
Partly air-conditioned

Puris in the making

Established in 1939, Purohit is one of the oldest thali restaurants in Bombay, serving, strangely enough, a mix of Punjabi and Gujarati vegetables. Originally they served in silver thalis only, but today farsan, two vegetables, one dal, one kadi, boondi raita, rice and rotis are served in a stainless steel one.

The dal was comparatively less sweet than the normal Gujarati one, and the Punjabi vegetable (mixed) was mercifully not oily. The flaky samosa was delicious. Overall, the food was wholesome and tasty, though not really the best in town. There is an air-conditioned section on the first floor, which costs about twenty per cent more. The Deluxe Thali (Rs 56, all inclusive) includes an appetizer, pullav (instead of plain rice) and unlimited helpings of dessert. Even those with a healthy appetite should be satisfied, though, with the simple Thali (Rs 40, all inclusive). For the more hep crowd, there is also a Western Thali, with tomato soup, bread and butter, cutlet, salad, pullav and curry jelly! In case you are not all that hungry, all the thali vegetables (and many more) are available as individual items on the menu.

The place looks a bit run down, with the usual basic furniture and waiters going around with buckets of dal. Service is prompt.

Rajdhani

Situated near Crawford Market, Rajdhani serves an excellent vegetarian thali, which includes four vegetables, rice, roti, snacks, pickles, papads, lassi, curd and perhaps the best Gujarati Dal we have ever tasted. The evening menu is changed to include an assortment of exotic rotis and khichdi or pullav with Dahi Kadi. Their doodi vegetable and the farsan (steamed dokhlas and samosas) were delicious. The thali is under Rs 50 (all inclusive) with unlimited helpings. Dessert costs an extra Rs 10.

Rajdhani
361, Sheikh Menon Street
Bombay 400 002
Opp Mangaldas Market
Near Crawford Market
Tel : 3449014, 3426919
Price : Inexpensive
Speciality : Gujarati
   Vegetarian Thali
Timings : 11 a.m. to 3 p.m.;
   7 to 10 p.m.
Sundays: Lunch only
Air-conditioned

The quality of the food is consistently good, and one can see a tremendous effort to please the customer. As soon as you sit down, a team of young, enthusiastic waiters hover around and quickly pile on the steaming food. They seem to control the frantic pace of your eating by setting into motion a super fast speed of service. Hot puris and rotis appear on your plate, before you realize you need them, and they keep on appearing till you finally cross your hands over your thali to indicate that you have finished.

The restaurant is one long corridor, tiled grey, with tables cramped together. The seating is definitely uncomfortable, with one elbow tucked into your side while you are eating, but the food and the service are efficient. The water is filtered.

Revival

Revival
Chowpaty Sea face
Bombay 400 007
Tel : 3619206
Price : Moderate
Speciality : Indian,
 Continental Vegetarian
Timings : Noon to 3 p.m.;
 7 to 12 p.m.
Reservation recommended
Credit cards accepted
Bar licence
Air-conditioned

Revival has, since it opened two years ago, established a niche by identifying itself as a pure vegetarian restaurant, serving traditional Indian as well as Continental vegetarian food. There are also special dishes for Jains and Marwaris. In fact, Revival also intends to introduce a full fledged Salad Bar by the time this book is out.

On the food front, the Bhindi Rajasthani, crisp-fried lady's fingers, stuffed with dry spices, makes an excellent, unusual starter. Sabzi Lazeez (cottage cheese cooked with dry fruits in a rich tomato-and-cream gravy) and Kesri Khorma (mixed vegetables cooked in saffron cream gravy) are the hottest selling dishes, but a little rich for us. Golden Chop was interesting. It is made from coarsely chopped carrots, peas, cottage cheese and dates, covered with cornflakes (yes, cornflakes) and then deep fried. The Ravioli Italian, made from home-made pasta, fresh spinach and thick broth, makes a wonderful main dish, for those looking for healthier alternatives.

The decor is tastefully 'art deco'. Try and sit at the tables overlooking Chowpatty Beach. The restaurant has a full fledged bar serving exotic cocktails and beers, which you can enjoy even if you don't intend to eat here. Service is attentive.

Ritz

Dining at the Ritz can be nostalgic if, that is, you are old enough to remember the band which played at their old night club, the Little Hut, and the wonderful Italian food which Mario, the temperamental Italian chef, used to rustle up. You can now get a whiff of all this at the recently refurbished Lido restaurant-cum-bar. Chef Ranjit Biswas, who trained under Mario, now carries the torch with the help of S. Solomen at the bar, a man of all seasons and veteran of the 'Mario' epoch too.

As, unfortunately, the menu has been compromised with the inclusion of Chinese, Indian and

Ritz
5, Jamshedji Tata Road
Churchgate
Bombay 400 020
Tel:220141, 2850500
Price : Expensive
Speciality : Italian
Timings : 11 a.m. to midnight
Credit cards accepted
Bar licence
Air-conditioned

Italian dishes, it is wise to stick to the Italian ones. The home-made pastas, Lasagnes (stuffed with spinach and chicken mince), Chili Con Carne, and the Tagliatelli (al dente) are all perfectly prepared and melt in the mouth. We also recommend the Chateaubriand for two. The home-made puddings and gateaux are easy on the stomach. The selection of wines is limited but acceptable, and Solomen's cocktails, especially the Margharitas, make a good aperitif. Price wise, Lido costs about a third less than five-star hotels, but is equal in quality and service.

Saayba Hotel

Saayba Hotel
Shop No. 1 & 2
Zarina Co-operative Service
Society
Bhatiya Building
S. V. Road
Bandra (West)
Bombay 400 050
Tel : 6436620
Price : Inexpensive
Speciality : Mangalorean
  Seafood
Timings : 11:30 a.m. to
  3:30 p.m.; 7:30 to 11p.m.
Mondays closed

You have to keep your eyes peeled to locate the green bamboo door, indicating the entrance to this small thirty-seater restaurant, on the left hand side of Mahim Causeway. The effort is worth it, as Saayba serves some of the freshest seafood in town.

If coconut curries are not up your street, we suggest you try the Fried Fish. You have a choice of Rawas (Indian salmon), Surmai (kingfish) and Pomfret—all fresh and juicy, fried to perfection without any sign of grease. Order Usal Dal, rice and/or rotis and you have a perfect meal, well within Rs 50 (all inclusive). The Oyster Curry, Bombay Duck, vegetable and dal were very average and quite avoidable.

The seating and decor is functional (formica-topped tables and folding chairs) in this small, garage-like space, but it is perpetually full of people who look like regulars (they know what to order and just tuck in, as opposed to first timers who ask for a menu and gaze around aimlessly). The kitchen is minuscule but clean and the service is prompt. Basic fresh food and good value.

Sabar Dining Hall

Sabar restaurant, a part of the Nrisinha Lodge, has been serving simple satvic (home type) thalis since 1903, when the price was only six annas. Now, even at Rs 30 (all inclusive), the mind-boggling variety of bhajhis, rotis, dals, rice and snacks, is definitely worth every penny.

The tamarind-based rasam was simply delicious and so was the dahi kadi (a thin yoghurt-based curry) flavoured with curry leaves. The vegetables served to us were tendli, Besan Vadi (Rajasthani dish) in dry masala, plain moong dal with jeera tadka. All eaten with piping hot rotis, Bakhri, or bajra rotis. Later on in the meal, rice is served with a teaspoonful of pure ghee to be mixed with dal. The menu changes from day to day, but the total number of dishes remain the same except that khichdi is added to the evening menu.

Sabar Dining Hall
Deokripa 1st floor
177, Dadabhai Naoroji Road
Fort
Bombay
Tel : 2612604, 2612605,
2612606
Price : Inexpensive
Speciality : Gujarati
Vegetarian
Timings : 11 a.m. to
2.45 p.m.; 7 to 9.30 p.m.

The restaurant is on the first floor. The furniture is basic. The decor non-existent. The ceiling is low, so you have to watch your head. The food and service, however, are consistently good. It's home away from home. The lodge is also a dormitory with beds which are let out at Rs 80 each. The customers are all regulars and the kind of food served could be eaten often, as some in that area do, without any after effects.

Samovar

Samovar
Jehangir Art Gallery
Kala Godha
Fort
Bombay 400 023
Tel : 244580, 2047276
Price : Inexpensive
Speciality : North Indian
 Snacks
Timings : 10.30 a.m. to
 7.30 p.m.
Sundays closed
Beer licence

Located in Jehangir Art Gallery, Samovar is a convenient meeting point for artists, those who browse, or simply for those who are in the area and feel like a good snack. It overlooks an unkempt garden and has two long lines of cane tables and chairs with no decor to speak of except multicolour lamps overhanging. Yet the place is perpetually full as it serves excellent snacks, sandwiches, juices and coffee, at very reasonable prices.

The daily specials are chalked up on a blackboard in addition to a simple printed menu which has basic snacks like stuffed rolls, sandwiches, Sam's Roti Pizza (which has a wholewheat chapatti as a base instead of pizza bread) and delicious drinks like Fresh G, chilled guava juice and kala khatta (kokum) squash. We love to go there for a simple Aloo Paratha. The other popular specialities are Chaat (bhelpuri, aloo chaat, etc.) as well as the hot pakoras, deep fried savoury snacks made with chick pea flour, a must during the rainy season. More substantial lunches include Prawn Curry or Vindaloo, Mutton Hyderabadi, Vegetable Pullav and Rajma (kidney beans). Beer is also served. The desserts are very interesting and well done. Try the home-made Apple Pie with ice cream or the Chocolate Brownie with ice cream.

Sardar Refreshment

Sardar Refreshment, at the Tardeo Bus Stop, serves the best Pao Bhaji in Bombay. At night, the stall is surrounded by people either waiting for or relishing this snack. The theatricals are entertaining too. The mountain of vegetables is bashed almost to a pulp, on a huge tawa with home-ground masalas, and finally smothered with dollops of butter. Meanwhile, the assistant warms the soft bread (pau), and dips that into another pool of melted butter. Finally, when the Bhaji is served, the chef places a fresh sliver of butter on each plate and then places the butter-soaked pao next to it! Toasted papads can be ordered to neutralize the extra butter.

Sardar Refreshment
166, A Tardeo Road Junction
Bombay 400 034
Tel : 4940208, 4940211
Price : Inexpensive
Speciality : Pau Bhaji
(Vegetarian)
Timings : 10 a.m. to 1 a.m.

Service is good and fast. We were told that the filmstar Amitabh Bachchan comes here often. His Pao Bhaji is served to him in an air-conditioned van, parked discreetly away from the shop to avoid a riot.

Sardar claims to have created this popular Bombay snack twenty-five years ago. All the others are imitations.

Plain tables and chairs are arranged inside the shop, as well as out on the patio, where you risk taking in the exhaust fumes of the buses from the depot just across the road.

Sarvi

Sarvi
184/196, Dimtimkar Road
Nagpada
Bombay 400 008
Price : Inexpensive
Speciality : Muslim
Timings : 7 a.m. to midnight

Mr Naan

Sarvi has, for many years, been our favourite haunt for beef kababs. Despite the seedy location, opposite the Police Station in down-town Nagpada, we were told that the great Raj Kapoor used to come to Sarvi at least once a month and shout, 'Salaam Alekum, Kabab Lagao.' Ali Azgar, alias Jumbo, rattled off a string of film stars and other celebrities who frequent Sarvi, adding, 'even the doctors in the Dawood Nursing Home across the road recommend our Aab Gosht to their patients in their diet!' This ramshackle mess has clearly not been touched since it was founded by Haji Ghulam Ali Sarvi, ninety years ago. Jamaluddin, the hairy head waiter, makes sure the hot rotis reach the customers almost as soon as they come out of the tandoor.

At Sarvi you simply hog. Start with the deliciously light Paya Soup, then the famous Kababs, grilled on coal. There are other fabulous items like Kheema Pav, which is best for breakfast. Not forgetting the Aab Gosht, which is broiled in water with kabuli channa (chick peas). Fresh masalas are ground daily on the premises and my best efforts to get the recipe of the Kababs and the roti failed. Said Jumbo, 'It is our family secret.'

So if you are a Kabab and Paya fan, and are not too fussy about the surroundings, then this is the place for you.

Sea Lounge

This is a veritable institution in the five-star circuit. Sea Lounge, overlooking the Gateway of India and the Arabian Sea, has probably played host to more pre-nuptial meetings and secret rendezvous, than any of its well-trained, staunchly loyal staff may care to remember.

It is the perfect place to sit, snack and browse in comfortable elegance, without fear of being asked to leave if you have overstayed your coffee. Although the menu changes fairly often, regulars swear by the Crepe Fantasy, bean sprouts, spinach and onion in a light pancake, overflowing with silky white sauce, the Chilli Cheese Toast, and all the items on the Chaat Corner. We always go for the desserts, especially the Viennoise, their home-made mocca ice cream set in a wine glass, and their Chocolate Truffle Pastry.

Sea Lounge, with the soothing sounds of the grand piano, is undoubtedly one of the nicest, most relaxing places you can treat yourself to in the city. The bay view window seats are always the most sought after, but you can always indicate this to the Captain on duty if they are occupied, and he or she will call you when one is free.

Sea Lounge
Taj Mahal Hotel
Apollo Bunder
Colaba
Bombay 400 039
Tel : 2023366
Price : Expensive
Speciality : Snacks
Timings : 10 a.m. to 1a.m.
Credit cards accepted
Air-conditioned

Sheetal Restaurant And Bar

Sheetal Restaurant And Bar
648, Rajasthan Building
Khar Pali Road
Bombay 400 052
Tel : 6497938, 6460643
Price : Moderate
Specialities : North Indian,
  Chinese
Timings : Noon to 3 p.m.;
  7.30 p.m. to midnight
Credit cards accepted
Bar licence
Air-conditioned

One of the finest restaurants for fresh seafood and North Indian Tandoori dishes, Sheetal is perpetually packed with foodies from tinsel world and has recently become an up-market restaurant. The food has also gone up a couple of notches. The bottom line with this restaurant is high quality: fresh Pomfret is brought in daily, crabs are kept alive in tanks, lobsters are fleshy and the prawns, Jumbo. Munna Singh, the son of the founder Kartar Singh, offers a wide variety—Tandoori, Szechwan and Continental.

For those who do not like spicy food, we recommend Pomfret Steak in Crab Sauce which is absolutely ambrosial and the Jumbo Crab in a ginger lemon butter. For those who like spice, try the Fish Steak Szechwan. Sheetal's Szechwan sauce is mind-blowing: a very light translucent sauce, that, though spicy, raises the flavour of the fresh pomfret. Try the Crab Chilli (without shell) with a tandoori roti or mini naans. Also recommended are Tandoori Crab, Lobster Afghani, Prawns Lasooni and Paneer Punjabi. To suggest chicken dishes would be a waste of time as we only eat seafood here.

For the vegetarians, we recommend Peas Methi Malai. We normally ask Kastar Singh to go easy on the malai in order to bring out the flavour of the methi. The prices are high, but few complain.

Sheetal Samudra

Managed by the effervescent Bunto Singh, Sheetal Samudra, although an affiliate of Sheetal in Bandra, has a personality of its own. Besides the seafood, which is equal if not better, than Sheetal's, we went crazy over the Tandoori kababs and Chicken Tikkas. They had that extra something, indicating that the Management and the cooks know what they are doing.

Sheetal Samudra
Unity Compound
Juhu Tara Road
Juhu
Bombay 400 054
Tel : 6122973, 6126218, 6460643
Price : Moderate
Specialities : Seafood and Tandoori Specialities
Timings : Noon to 4 p.m.; 7 p.m. to midnight
Credit cards accepted
Bar licence

The dishes to try out here are the amazing Tandoori Crab, always full of flesh and spiced just right. The Lobster Afghani in a cream sauce, and the Sheekh and Reshmi Kababs are all freshly-cooked and elegantly served. To go along with them, try the Khasta (crisp) and Misi (gram flour and wheat) rotis. Vegetarians should try the Vegetarian Chop Masala, a glorified but very dignified vegetable cutlet in a delicious gravy.

Fully carpeted with modern grey and black decor, Samudra has comfortable seating and the atmosphere of an Italian Trattoria, always busy and bustling. Bunto Singh personally goes from table to table looking after the customers' needs. Perhaps the best restaurant in Juhu Vile Parle Scheme, Sheetal Samudra deserves every bit of its success.

Sher-e-Punjab

Sher-e-Punjab
261/264 Shahid Bhagat Singh
Road
Near GPO
Bombay
Tel : 2621188, 2610431
Price : Moderate
Speciality : North Indian
Timings : Noon to 11.30 p.m.

The old Sher-e-Punjab is now refurbished, with all the trappings of a fancy air-conditioned restaurant— starched tablecloths, napkins, marble flooring, etc. Though it has lost some of the old dhaba charm, Ajit Singh Bedi, the son of Awtar Singh, the founder, is trying his best to retain some of the old recipes at prices affordable to his faithful old Mint Road customers. You can still find reasonably priced traditional Rogan Josh, Kheema Muttar, Sarson Ka Saag and Makki Ki Roti, (winter months only) and the famous Tandoori Chicken (Awtar Singh was the first to introduce the tandoori chicken to Bombay). But, do not order Sarson ka Saag in any other season, as it will be out of a can.

Other specialities are Bhuna Mutton, which was excellent with naan and the Chicken Adraki. Both have thick, spicy gravies. The Brain Masala Fry, is yet another house speciality. The rotis were excellent too. The vegetarians have a good choice here. We recommend Vegetable Navratan Korma, with baby corn, peas, carrots, mushrooms and paneer, Muttar Palak and the superb Maa Ki Dal, cooked with cream.

The place is clean and well-maintained. The water is filtered. The service is impeccable. As typical with most Punjabi food, we found the food rich and heavy on the oil.

Sriram Boarding House

Sriram Boarding House is the most unlikely place anyone would walk in for a casual meal. It has dark brown walls and blue Rexine seats. The area is divided with into two cubicles, a bar section and eatery, which is dark and dank. But the coastal food here is some of the finest in the area, and the prices rock bottom. Owner N. K. Samant, alias Shyambhai, says the recipes are all from his mother's kitchen.

Sriram Boarding House
Dandekar Building
220, Raja Ram Mohan Roy
   Marg
Girgaon
Bombay
Tel : 3881919
Price : Inexpensive
Speciality : Konkani
Timings : Noon to 3.30 p.m.;
   6.30 to 11.30 p.m.
Air-conditioned

Start with Shyambhai's superb version of Kokam Saar, a fiery aperitif, made from thin coconut milk, green chillies and kokum, the souring agent. The specialities here are Crab Masala, Shell Fish Masala, Prawn Masala, Fish Curry and Shark Masala Fry, all cooked in distinctly different, coconut-based curries with home-ground masalas. Our all-time favourite is the delectable Oyster Masala. The oysters, although small in size, retain all their juiciness and vitality even though they have been cooked. Even the Chicken Kheema and Chicken Masala were superbly cooked.

Instead of the usual rice, try Sriram's unique rotis instead. They are a cross between a paratha and a chapatti. Ask for one at a time, so that they arrive nice and hot. For snacks try the pan fried Bangda Chutney, mackerel coated with coarse black pepper, onion and chilli powder and fried dry, with the in house Usal Masala, spiced up sprouts, an unbeatable combination with chilled beer.

Definitely not a place for vegetarians. The kitchen is as clean as a pin and the water filtered.

Star of Asia Restaurant

Star of Asia Restaurant
5, Sheri House
Rustom Sidhwa
Fort
Bombay 400 001
Price : Inexpensive
Speciality : Muslim
Timings : 7 a.m. to 11:30 p.m.

The restaurant, which has its normal flow of Chai Brun (tea and a crisp roll, a breakfast special) regulars, suddenly gets packed around noon, when the cook ceremoniously breaks the atta (pastry) seal around a huge degchi of freshly cooked Kachche Gosht Ki Biryani (biryani made with raw mutton which is cooked along with the rice). Hot steaming plates of biryani are quickly served to expectant customers, who assemble with the sole purpose of enjoying this dish, which has made Star of Asia famous. A crisp Rice Papad, yet another speciality, along with fresh thick cut Kachoomar (salad) goes well with it. We also greedily tried out the Mutton Masala (mutton cooked in a thick, spicy gravy) which was mouth-watering, eaten with fresh slices of pav (fresh, soft, white bread).

By the time this book is out, Star of Asia will have opened its pizza parlour in one part of the restaurant. Yes, a genuine Italian pizza with freshly-made dough, Mozzarella, olives, sun dried tomatoes, etc. Said Mohammad Hassan, 'my partner has trained in the Mama Mia chain in America so it will be the best pizza in town.' Inshallah !

The restaurant, happily, has retained all the old decor, the fans, clock, chairs, marble tables, mirrors with hand painted landscapes of rivers and boatmen and Persian carpets on the walls. Worth a visit.

Swati Snacks

Swati Snacks is a popular eatery which specializes in a few traditional dishes. During peak hours there are more people waiting outside than inside this tiny restaurant which started twenty-six years ago.

Swati Snacks
Karai Estate
Near Bhatia Hospital
Tardeo Road
Bombay
Tel : 4920994
Price : Moderate
Speciality : Gujarati
  Vegetarian
Timings : Noon to 11 p.m.
Air-conditioned

The dishes are traditional Jain, Gujarati, Maharashtrian and South Indian recipes. We chose the Panki Chutney, delicate rice pancakes with a hint of garlic, steamed in a banana leaf, followed by Fada Ni Khichdi, whole wheat khichdi with curd. The other remarkable dishes are Ek Top Na Dal Bhat, vegetables, rice and dal, cooked together with coconut, and Thalipith Pithla, Maharashtrian mixed dal masala roti served with a thick besan relish. Asha Jhaveri, the owner, has recently added Kerala Appam with coconut stew and Dal Dhokli, a sweet-and-sour version of lasagne, to the menu.

End the meal with Malai Malpuda, little pancakes packed with rabdi and a slosh of flavoured syrup. Swati is also famous for breakfast (7 a.m. to 10 a.m.) when hot jalebis are served, chaat served right through until 11 p.m. and their fabulous home-made ice creams. Sitaphal and Cinnamon flavours are always available, but Fresh Peach and Yoghurt on Sundays only.

Decorated with taste, Swati Snacks has simple but elegant white walls, jute carpet, tables and benches. The open kitchen, though tiny, always looks tidy and clean.

Tanjore

Tanjore
Taj Mahal Hotel
Appolo Bunder
Colaba 400 039
Tel : 2023366
Price : Expensive
Speciality : North Indian
Timings : Noon to 3 p.m.;
    7 to 11 p.m.

One of the flagship restaurants of the Taj, Tanjore, serving Indian food, has held steadfast to its reputation for all these years.

We remember some foreign guests of ours being so taken with the Nawabi Sheekh at Tanjore, that they insisted on eating just that with endless rounds of draught beer. We lost count of how many kababs were demolished. The Raan is the main speciality. It was cooked to perfection, the body, the aroma and the taste. For chicken lovers, we recommend Murg Makhani, in tomato with a hint of methi (fenugreek). For the vegetarians, the best bet would be the Thali. If you are not that hungry, then try the Panchmela Bhindi, Faldaari Kofta Curry (dumplings of raw bananas in tomato cashew gravy), unusual but tasty along with Tadka Daal and Khasta roti.

For those with a sweet tooth, we recommend Lacchedar Rabdi. At Tanjore seating arrangements are separate balcony style, with gaddas and bolsters, overlooking the stage where traditional Indian dances are held every evening.

Tewari Brothers Mithaiwala

Situated at the Opera house junction, this mithai shop also serves some of the most delicious heavy snacks in the area. Their speciality is Raj Kachori, which is a huge puri, stuffed with boondi, boiled potatoes, sev, three kinds of chutneys and garnished with fresh coriander. It is nutritious, delicious and quite a deal at Rs 14 (all inclusive). Other equally good snacks are the Mixed Chaat, Papri Chaat and Dahi Kachori. One or two of these, drowned with a glass of chilled Lassi (buttermilk) makes an ideal brunch or lunch in the hot weather. Also try the famous Kulfi Falooda or one of Tewari's famous Boondi Laddoos.

Tewari Brothers Mithaiwala
3, Purshottam Building
M. P. Marg
Opera House
Bombay
Tel : 3614238, 3617465, 3627290
Price : Inexpensive
Speciality : North Indian Vegetarian Snacks and Mithai
Timings : 10 a.m. to 9 p.m.

The place has white marble flooring, no tables but a few seats against the wall, where you can sit and eat. There is no table service. You have to buy a token and collect your order from the counter. But at prices which are marginally higher than the roadside chaatwala, Tewari serves an extraordinary quality of snacks in air-conditioned comfort.

Definitely worth a visit.

Thai Pavillion

Thai Pavillion
Hotel President
Cuffe Parade
Bombay
Tel : 2150808
Price : Expensive
Speciality : Thai
Timings : 12.30 to 2.30 p.m.;
   7.30 to 11.30 p.m.
Credit cards accepted
Bar licence
Air-conditioned

As we entered, a beautiful Thai girl greeted us from the platform where she was busy carving sculptures out of fruits and vegetables. Thai hostesses in gold and silver lamé dresses led us into a spacious hall, in the middle of which stood a Thai temple with a huge bouquet of flowers in the centre. Tables and chairs were arranged at discreet distances and we were seated in one corner. On each table was a Thai orchid. It was like being transported to Bangkok, without the bother of catching a plane!

The Thai kitchen is a heady mix of intoxicating scents: sweet jasmine, sharply perfumed lemon grass, coriander, different types of ginger and refreshing lime, are all perfect foils for the coconut, shellfish, meats, poultry, and pungent shrimp paste.

There are so many delightful options that we suggest you skip the appetizers, and go straight into the herb and spiced salads which are absolutely superb. The simplest ingredients, like raw papaya and banana flower can take on many nuances. We recommend Som Tam, the tasty, tangy young raw papaya salad with crushed, roasted peanuts, and Yum Huapee, a spicy banana flower salad, flavoured with Namprik, a special chilli sauce imported from Thailand. The sauce is an exotic combination of red chilli, fried garlic, fried shallots, jaggery, tamarind, nampla (fish) sauce and shrimp paste. Enjoy the papaya salad first, before you take on the Banana flower salad, which is really spicy, but, nevertheless, an utterly delightful experience.

For the next course we recommend Pla Rad Prik, Red Snapper fish (specially flown in daily from Dhaka by the chef), crisp fried and treated with a tangy sweet-and-sour pepper sauce. Even though two supplementary sauces, a chilli nampla sauce and a chilli vinegar sauce, are provided, adding them to your dishes would be tantamount to 'tampering' with the original flavours.

After the delightful fish, there is an option of three curries. Gaeng Kiew Warn (green coconut curry with fresh coriander, Thai ginger, galangal, and lemon grass) Gaeng Phed, (red curry, a blend of red chillies, lemon grass and coconut milk) and Gaeng Massaman, a superb Lamb curry from Southern Thailand, rich with whole ground garam masalas. It is really a matter of personal preference, but we preferred the green curry. You can order your choice of chicken, prawns, meat or vegetables in any of the curries. The non-vegetarians, however, should try the lamb preparation. The meat was succulent and the curry unique.

Who can leave a Thai table without tasting the Tom Yum Koong, spicy Prawn Soup, and for the vegetarian, the same soup with vegetables, Tom Yum Phak, which are both superbly crafted.

Thai desserts, though presented beautifully, are never as impressive as their food. We do wish, however, that since Thai Pavillion is importing almost all their herbs and spices like makrut, pandanus leaves, shrimp paste, bird chilli, and Thai ginger from Thailand, they could also import their exotic fruit, like mangosteen, rambutan, etc., which would make a delightful ending to a meal.

Thai chefs Ms Vilaiwan, Ms Srirat are in charge of the kitchen, and Ms Sangde does the beautiful carving of fruits and vegetables.

The restaurant seats about 100, and is elegantly decorated and designed like a Thai pavillion.

Service is superb. An experience not to be missed.

Thaker Bhojanalay

Thaker Bhojanalay
31, Dadiseth Agyari Lane
Opp G. T. High School
Kalbadevi
Bombay 400 002
Tel : 2011232, 2061490
Price : Inexpensive
Speciality:Gujarati
   Vegetarian Thali
Timings : 11 a.m. to 3 p.m.;
   7 to 10 p.m.
Saturday evenings closed

The real test of any good restaurant is whether you frequent it or not. We go to Thaker Club at least once every two months for a wholesome tasty vegetarian thali. No doubt it is quite a pain to reach the place as it is located in a crowded lane in perhaps what is one of the most thickly populated areas of Bombay. You may have trouble finding it and parking is impossible. So the best bet would be to take a taxi. You may also be put off by the exterior and the fact that you have to hop over a gutter to enter the dimly-lit corridor which leads to the first floor where the restaurant is situated. But once you are in the restaurant and the food is laid out in front of you, all your efforts are well compensated.

Established in 1945, when the price of the Thali was just about a rupee, by Maghanbhai Purohit, Thaker Club has been consistently serving superb home-cooked hot food comprising of four vegetables (two green, one potato, one bean), two dals, yoghurt, lassi, rotis, bhakris (whole millet rotis), farsan (snacks), pickles, papad, salad and dessert—unlimited helpings, at a fixed price. We were told that one particular regular demolishes thirty rotis, mountains of rice, gallons of dal and śabzis and is still as thin as a toothpick! Maganbhai takes it all in his stride. Along with his son, he personally supervises the cooking and the serving—that perhaps explains the consistency and the quality which, according to us, has in fact gone up in the course of years. Of course, so has the price, which is now Rs 50 per person (all inclusive).

Our favourites at Thaker Club are Pooran Poli (sweet little breads stuffed with tuvar dal and jaggery), saturated with pure ghee, served every Wednesday and Pulav and Kadi served every Thursday night. The vegetables are changed according to the season and the tastiest are their bhindi, tendli and the potato preparations. The dal (Gujarati style with a touch of sugar) is something we can't stop sipping between the bites. The rotis are tossed onto your thali piping hot. It requires tremendous will power to be able to resist overeating at this place as everything is so delicious.

Thaker Club is packed during peak hours, and you may have to wait in the corridor with your token number, which is announced through a white fog horn. Then you proceed to the first floor. The inside of the restaurant has a clean marble floor with wooden tables and chairs neatly laid out. Service is super fast.

Gujarati Thali at Thaker

Thali Restaurant

Thali Restaurant
B, 1-5 Tara Baug Estate
297, Charni Road
Bombay 400 004
Tel : 3855934
Price : Inexpensive
Speciality : Gujarati
   Vegetarian Thali
Timings : 11.30 a.m. to
   3 p.m.; 7 to 10 p.m.
Tuesdays closed

There are still quite a few good thali places in Bombay. Thali Restaurant, near Charni road, has its own identity. Started in 1978 by Ajay Shah, Thali has been serving delicious food to its appreciative customers ever since.

We zero in on what we feel is the best item on the menu, Peas Palak. This does not mean that the other vegetables like Tendli, Black-eyed Beans and Vatana, are not delicious. It is just that we like to focus on one flavour at a time. The Potato Bhaji is superb and so are the Dal and Kadi Dal. The Jawar roti (without ghee) was extraordinary with the green bhaji.

Also try eating rotla with green chutney. For those on a diet, avoid the ghee and ask the waiter to give you plain rotis. There is no decor to speak of, and the walls are decorated with pictures of gods and goddesses. Service is extremely good.

La Brasserie

Despite the fact that the Brasserie, situated in the lobby of the Oberoi, is about to be dwarfed by Palms, the new buffet-style, international coffee shop of the Oberoi Towers, this is still one of our favourite places to 'hang out' in the city. Although a little too brightly lit, it is the perfect place to enjoy a late dinner, or a light lunch from the Salad Bar.

La Brasserie
The Oberoi
Nariman Point
Bombay 400 021
Tel: 2025757
Price : Expensive
Speciality : Continental
Timings: 7 a.m. to midnight
Bar licence
Credit cards accepted

From the 'light meals', the Pepper Steak and Fillet Mignon, a simple roundel of steak, grilled on lava stones are consistently good. The Pomfret Caviare, lightly poached fish with a black caviare sauce is delicate and delicious. Try the composed salads, Nicoise (green beans, capers, tuna and anchovies) and Murattier Salad (artichokes and asparagus on a bed of salad finished off with a walnut cream). For something more substantial, Harlequin Pasta, tri-coloured pasta with a mushroom and cheese sauce was good, but we found the green pepper (capsicum) unnecessary. Finally, the Pork Roll stuffed with prunes and served with an apple sauce was rather nice. Finish off with a walnut cream pie (soon to be replaced by a pecan nut pie), and an expresso, and you will have had a very satisfying dining experience. Wine by the glass is available as are Herb Teas.

The atmosphere at La Brasserie is relaxed enough for breakfast, yet special enough for a dinner out. The rich burgundy leather furnishings, rosewood trimmings, impressive looking bar and well spaced out perfectly set tables, are more conducive to fine dining than a casual snack. Excellent service.

The Great Wall

The Great Wall
Leela Kempinski
Sahar
Bombay 400 059
Tel : 8363636
Price : Expensive
Speciality : Chinese
Timings : Noon to 3 p.m.;
  7 to 11:30 p.m.
Credit cards accepted
Bar licence

Overlooking a gorgeous waterfall, the Great Wall has a clean, white decor which is only vaguely Chinese and an elegant ambience. Priceless Chinese jars and an antique robe at the entrance complete the scenario.

The cuisine is equally impressive. To start with, try the batter fried, translucent Phoenix Tailed Prawns and the Prawn Sesame Toast. For the vegetarian, the Sesame Beancurd Toast was unusual and the Onion Cakes were superbly flaky. All these starters should be eaten with the soup. For the non-vegetarians, we recommend the Hot and Sour with Crab meat instead of the usual chicken. It was quite unusual and delicious. The vegetarians should try Sam Piew Thona, a blend of mushrooms, carrots and preserved vegetables. Quite spicy but tasty.

At the Great Wall, we decided to go slightly spicy for a change and ordered accordingly. Pepper Blasted Prawns (with burnt red chillies and black pepper) were not as hot as the description and were memorable. Follow it up with Lobster in chilli and garlic sauce. All the seafood is superbly prepared without overcooking. Chicken lovers will be very happy with Yu Shiang Chicken, cooked in celery and chilli sauce. The Lamb in hot pepper sauce, too, matched the rest in quality and taste.

The vegetarians will be delighted with Fresh Tofu, done in chilli sauce, and the Spinach in Garlic Sauce. We recommend plain white rice to counter the spiciness of the main dishes.

After such a massive assault on the taste buds, dessert is a must to cool off. The Fresh Date Pancakes with ice cream is just the thing to finish off a grand gourmet experience.

The Outrigger

Despite this being one of the oldest restaurants in the Oberoi Towers, if we are in the mood for a lunch buffet, it is always the Outrigger that we opt for. Still very reasonably priced at Rs 225 (plus taxes), it is the ideal place to take guests whose tastes may be varied.

The Outrigger
The Oberoi Towers
Nariman Point
Bombay 400 021
Tel : 2025757 Ext: 6312
Price : Expensive
Speciality : Polynesian
Timings : 12.30 p.m. to
3 p.m.; 7 p.m. to 11 p.m.
Credit cards accepted
Bar licence
Air-conditioned

With an Outrigger boat to greet you at the entrance, a Mai Tai is the first step before embarking on a buffet to remember. Cold cuts and starters may include fresh Oysters on the half shell (in season), Gallantines (cold cuts in aspic), pâtés and a selection of salads, presented in shells. The main courses include a traditional roast, carved in front of you, with accompaniments, Polynesian and Chinese dishes which usually include fish, prawn, chicken and an equal number of vegetarian options, and consistently good Indian food. The assortment of desserts is impressive, but the Rasmalai is always superb.

The evening menu at the Outrigger is Polynesian. We haven't quite figured out what that means, but it smacks of Chinese with lots of sweet peppers. Favourites include Galbi Jim, smoked spare ribs glazed with honey, the Kona Kai Steamboat, a kind of do-it-yourself soup and the Chilli Chicken Maui. The Egg Drop Tomato soup is excellent. For the vegetarian, Beancurd Temura, deep fried with chilli oil and mustard sauce and the Vegetable Tahiti, stir fried with chilli oil and cashew nuts are popular choices.

The Outrigger is still a very decent place to lunch or dine, although the Oberoi does plan on changing the concept in the near future.

The Waterfall Café

The Waterfall Café
Leela Kempinski Hotel
Sahar
Bombay 400 059
Tel : 8363636
Price : Expensive
Speciality : Continental
Timings : 24 hours
Credit cards accepted
Bar licence
Air-conditioned

Of all the restaurants in this opulent, sprawling hotel, we prefer the Waterfall Café. The view, especially if you manage a window table, is splendid. From whichever angle you look, massive rocks, gushing waterfalls, lush fauna and flora, and, if you are lucky, a family of white ducks, are visible. The scenery and the palm lined drive up to the hotel, has calmed our much worn nerves on several occasions, (an added bonus is that the International Airport is two minutes away by road, and there is a free shuttle service). The subtle pastel tones are a refreshing change from the overbearing five-star Coffee Shops. In addition to the à la carte menu, which is extensive for a coffee shop, there are also lunch and dinner buffets, which we highly recommend.

From the menu, start with the Fresh Fruit Platter, which is served with honey and yoghurt. Move onto the Hungarian Goulash, a thick lamb and potato soup flavoured with paprika, garlic and jeera. The Delicatessen Platter also makes a substantial snack. You'll always find excellent Dosai, with chicken or prawn masala, which we hear is one of the owner favourite dishes. For a proper meal, go for Pepper Steak (imported T-bone and Sirloin are also available, in addition to local steaks). For the vegetarians, the Vegetable Cordon Noir, a cake stuffed with cream cheese and vegetables, is an adequate alternative. End on 'Never on a Sundae', a wicked combination of mousse, dry fruit and nougat ice cream.

There is sometimes a band in the evenings, which does transform this coffee shop into something more serious.

If you are catching a flight, inform the waiter, as a la carte service can be slow, and the bill formalities even slower. Although there are plenty of taxis outside, don't forget to ask about the shuttle service to the airport. Alternatively you can also hitch a ride with any of the airlines' coaches heading that way.

Trattoria

It is no quirk of fate that Trattoria was voted the best Continental Restaurant last year. The ambience is elegant and yet cosy, it is open when other restaurants close, and the food is consistently good.

Specialities include Carpaccio (wafer-thin slices of raw tenderloin garnished with parmesan cheese, mushrooms and olive oil). We relish it slowly while sipping on a glass of dry red wine. All the beef dishes here are excellent. For the vegetarians, we recommend Lasagne di Verdure Re Misticanza Di Formaggio (mixed vegetable lasagne). Rich, but nevertheless, delicious. The Spaghetti Alla Checca, simply done, with tomato, basil, garlic, mozzarella and olive oil, is a light, yet substantial alternative. For the more adventurous, Pasta with Pesto, a sauce made with fresh basil, cheese, garlic, nuts and olive oil, is a must. Then go for Picollo Melanzane Ripiene, Fonduta Di Pomodori (small brinjals on a bed of tomatoes, baked with cheese). Trattoria uses genuine Parmesan, the famous cheese made in the Parma region of Italy.

After all this surfeit of indulgence, you must try a deadly combination for which the Trattoria is famous. The rich, Bitter Chocolate Ice Cream, accompanied by a William of Orange (coffee with Cointreau and whipped cream).

In Italy, a Trattoria is generally a simple family run restaurant, often with decorative local pottery, plates and pans on the walls. The real atmosphere is created by the informality and enthusiasm of the customers. Trattoria at Hotel President is a slightly luxurious version, complete with serenading musicians. It doubles as the Hotel's twenty-four-hour Coffee Shop as well as a speciality restaurant and therefore lacks the down-to-earth atmosphere of its namesake.

Trattoria
Hotel President
Cuffe Parade
Colaba
Bombay 400 005
Tel : 2150808
Price : Expensive
Speciality : Italian
Timings : 24 hours
Credit Cards accepted
Bar licence
Air-conditioned

Trishna Restaurant & Bar

Trishna Restaurant & Bar
7, Rope Walk Lane
Next to Commerce House
Kala Ghoda
Fort
Bombay 400 023
Tel : 272176
Price : Moderate
Speciality :Mangalorean
  Seafood
Timings: Noon to 4 p.m.;
  6 p.m. to 12.30 a.m.
Sundays : Noon to 4 p.m.;
  7 p.m. to 12.30 a.m.
Credit cards accepted
Bar licence
Air-conditioned

A statue of Sai Baba on a high pedestal serenely overlooks this small, seafood restaurant, which has, in the last few years, become the rage of the city. Trishna was originally founded by B. V. Anchan forty-five years ago, when it was called Matraboomi Lunch Home, specializing only in South Indian foods. In 1989, his sons Vishwanath and Ravi transformed it into a modern, air-conditioned seafood place. Both the sons give their full time and attention to the restaurant, from the purchase of fresh fish and vegetables to the selection and grinding of masalas and supervising the cooking. The food therefore is consistently good. Trishna, unlike other Coastal restaurants which rely heavily on red chilli and kokum, depend on milder spices and lean more towards the Mangalorean use of tamarind and coconut paste. The flavours are therefore more subtle and easy on the stomach.

We tried out just about all the specialities on the menu and strongly recommend, to start with, Pomfret or Bangda (mackerel), steamed with mushrooms in a cabbage leaf, with just a touch of salt, pepper and butter. It is ideal for those who are not used to heavy spice. The fish was served deboned, which made it easy to handle and appreciate. The Crab Tandoori is the *pièce de résistance* of Trishna. The crab claws are heavy with meat, and the cooking time was just right, leaving the flesh still moist. If spice is not up your street, then try the crab boiled in salt, pepper and butter or the jumbo prawn done in the same manner. The other speciality worth trying out is Squid Chilli Garlic, done in a dry sweet-and-sour sauce, spiked with green chillies and heavy on the garlic. The crisp Lady Fish Fry and the Koliwada

Prawns are new additions to the menu which we recommend.

For the vegetarians, the Kadai Bhaji of fresh baby corn and mushroom, is worth trying, while the Hyderabadi Dal was superb, with a seasoning of fried mint, deep fried red chillies and garam masala.

The decor is conventional, with rough white coated walls, and comfortable, but slightly cramped seating. The service is superb. Go early to be sure of a table or prepare to wait for up to fifteen minutes.

Under the Over

Under the Over
Crystal
36, Altamount Road
Kemps Corner
Bombay 400 026
Tel: 3861393, 3882979
Price : Moderate
Specialities : American,
    Continental
Timings : 12.30 to 3.30 p.m.;
    7.30 to 11.30 p.m.
Credit cards accepted
Air-conditioned

With its stark black, grey and white decor, the work of local artists displayed (for sale) on the wall, and the spotlessly clean look, Under the Over provides the Bombayite with great Tex-Mex and European food at very affordable prices. Although this American-style bistro is famous for its Mexican-American specialities like Nachos (crispy tortilla chips with melted cheese), Tacos (crispy corn pancakes filled with chilli lamb, or vegetables, cheese and salsa), Steak Ranchero (with melted cheese, corn hash), Tostadas Pollo (chicken with re-fried beans and cheese sauce), Chimi Chongas (corn burritos with three salsas and re-fried beans), we feel that chef-proprietor, Rahul Akerkar turns out some great Italian dishes too. The Maccheroni al Arrabbiata, coated with a fresh tomato, mushroom and basil sauce and red pepper flakes, Pasta Siciliana, spaghetti with sun dried tomatoes, olives, capers, basil and parmesan, Vegetables Antipasta, vegetables grilled with olive oil and herbs and the Pizzas are our all-time favourites. Of all the pizzas, the Catanese with slices of grilled aubergine and capers is worth driving miles for. Thankfully, all the Italian pizzas (there are a couple of corn meal Tex-Mex ones too) are topped with mozzarella cheese and always arrive piping hot.

There is something for everyone on this menu. The Summer Spa is a selection of delightful calorie conscious salad meals. The Grilled Lemon Chicken (256 calories) and Shrimp with Bacon Bits (249 calories) are superb. Vegetarians are well looked after, as half the menu contains vegetarian options.

Desserts are less adventurous, but consistently good. The Jamaican Chocolate Mousse and Fruit Sorbet are worth trying out. It is a pity that there is no liquor or beer licence yet. A glass of wine or beer would make all the difference to this highly creative, quality conscious menu. A great place to take children of all ages.

Vintage

As you walk into Vintage, you are struck by an odd mix of old British and modern Indian decor. Pictures of Fox Hunting decorate the walls and the ornate furniture looks like an up-market dining-room in a fashionable enclave in Delhi. This is hardly a place you expect to be served traditional Hyderabadi food. We also expected to see a Muslim Bawarchi from Hyderabad do his salaams and the food to be served by hoors, but instead chef Harpal Singh, immaculately dressed in his whites and chef's hat, made his appearance. On the food front, however, we were not disappointed. Chef Harpal Singh

Vintage
4, Mandlik Road
Colaba Causeway
Bombay 400 039
Tel : 2856316, 2020292
Price : Expensive
Speciality : Hyderabadi
Timings : Noon to 3 p.m.;
   7 to 11.30 p.m.

has taken it as his life's mission to delve into classic Indian recipes. His rendering of Hyderabadi cuisine was almost as authentic as the best family homes in Hyderabad. The restaurant also serves North Indian and Continental, but it is the Hyderabadi cuisine which you should try.

The starters Shikampuri Kabab (a fist-sized, finely ground mince kabab, stuffed with rough cut onion and coriander in dahi chutney) and Dum Ka Kabab (finger shaped mince kabab), were unassuming and avoidable. Instead we recommend Chatpatta Chicken, a dry dish of batter fried cubes of marinated chicken, sautéed in curry leaves and green pepper. For the vegetarians there's Chatpatta Gobi, which is equally tasty.

We give full marks to Harpal for Pathar Ka Gosht. The mutton, with the bone, marinated with poppy seeds among other things, is then placed between two slabs of granite stone brought from the base of the Daulatabad Fort and fired from the bottom with charcoal. It is cooked for seven to eight hours until the meat is tender. It was invented by the Nizam's cooks for hunting picnics.

Harpal passed the next test as well, with flying colours. The ubiquitous Mirchi Ka Salan, large chillies which are a cross between capsicum and green chilli are cooked in a sesame and coconut sauce. It had the right taste and packed a kick, without causing any discomfort. Mop up the delicious sauce with Lachchedar Paratha. The Khatti (sour) Dal, cooked with tamarind, curry leaves, garlic, mustard seeds and whole red chillies, was also superb. If you still have some space left, try the Kachche Gosht Ki Biryani (meat and rice cooked together in a sealed vessel). The basmati rice was perfectly cooked, each grain separate and moist, but the meat was a bit over done. No Hyderabadi meal is complete without Khubani ka Meetha, stewed apricots with cream, very sweet but yummy or Azam Shahi, bread pudding soaked in cream and sprinkled with lots of nuts. Both were good, but the presentation could have been better.

We missed the regal service and ambience usually associated with Hyderabadi cuisine of this calibre. Nevertheless, this is a fine attempt at a complicated, time-consuming cuisine which is today rarely available outside a traditional home, even in Hyderabad.

Old world charm – Wayside Inn

Vithal Bhelwala

What was previously a tiny chaat shop, has now expanded into a 100-seater, deluxe restaurant, with a modern open kitchen and uniformed waiters. It was, in fact, great-grandfather Vithal who came from Surat and started hawking this mixture of puffed rice, sev, crisp puris, potatoes, onions, tomatoes, raw mango and the real zing, the sweet chutney made of dates and the spicy one made of chillies and garlic, a hundred years ago.

Vithal Bhelwala
5, A. K. Naik Marg
Near Excelsior Cinema
Fort
Bombay 400 001
Tel : 2044673, 2046205
Price: Inexpensive
Speciality : Maharashtrian
  Vegetarian Chaat
Timings : 9.30 a.m. to 10 p.m.
Partly air-conditioned

You still get great bhel on the streets of Bombay, but hygiene is not a strong point. Vithal provides a good alternative with amenities like filtered water, clean tables, decent crockery and cutlery, comfortable seating and good service. Once you specify how you like your bhel (spicy, sweet, with more lemon juice) it will be brought to you, ready mixed. If you're still not satisfied, there are more chutneys, lemon, onions and chilli powder on the table. The specialities here are Sev Dahi Potato Puri, Panipuri, served with chilled water seasoned with mint, cothmir, jeera, black salt, green chillies, ginger and lemon, and the special Bhel. Those looking for something more substantial should go for the special Pau Bhaji, soaked in Amul butter. Vithal, in keeping with their new, modern image, also serves sandwiches, idli, pizza, milk shakes, ice creams (try their delicious home-made sitafal ice cream) and fresh juices, but it is their Bhel and the other puri-based Gujarati snacks that reign supreme. Dry packed boxes of Bhel and Panipuri (you add the water to the masala) are available for those wanting to send Relief parcels overseas.

Wayside Inn

Wayside Inn
38 K D Marg
Kala Ghoda
Near Jehangir Art Gallery
Fort
Bombay 400 023
Tel : 244324
Price : Inexpensive
Speciality : Continental
Timings : 9a.m. to 7 p.m.;
Sundays 9 a.m. to 3 p.m.

The all-time favourite dishes with staunchly loyal customers here, are the ubiquitous Fish and Chips with Tartare sauce, or the Grilled Steak, garnished with brown onions and vinegar sauce. The fish was fresh, but a bit overdone. The Steak (medium rare) came exactly as ordered, with great French fries. For once simple Continental food without any of those white sauce bakes, often mistaken as the hallmark of French cuisine.

For those looking for a spicier dish, we recommend Chicken Vindaloo. Sunday is reserved for Parsi dishes when Dhansak, Patra Ni Machhi and Sali Boti are served. Looking at the kind of attention the owners, Mr and Mrs Patel, pay to the kitchen and upkeep of this simple restaurant, we feel confident talking about the Sunday specials, without even tasting them.

There are also daily specials, according to what is fresh in the market. The home-made desserts we recommend are the Mango Soufflé, Sitafal Kulfi (in season) and the Apple Pie. Beer is served.

Even though refurbished recently, Wayside Inn has fortunately kept the high ceiling supported by wooden beams, the Irani chairs, sideboard with old pottery and the old clock. The restaurant is cooled by old-fashioned fans. Service is attentive. Drinking water is filtered and safe. Definitely worth a visit for those looking for unpretentious Continental and Parsi food.

Yoko Sizzlers

Probably the best place for steaks and hamburgers in the suburbs, Yoko is perpetually crowded due primarily to its value for money concept. Huge amounts of food is piled on to sizzler trays, all for Rs 70. The choice of sizzlers is astounding, around forty-five, including nine for vegetarians. The Pepper Steak which came along with vegetables and Barbecue Sauce, was excellent, and so was their all-time hit, Chicken Shashlik, cubes of grilled chicken on a bed of rice with boiled vegetables (carrots, beans, potatoes) doused with their inimitable Barbecue Sauce. Our only complaint is that the food was sloppily piled onto the platter, and we had to try and figure out what exactly we were eating.

Yoko Sizzlers
10-11 West View
S. V. Road
Near Akbaraly's
Santacruz (West)
Bombay 400 054
Tel : 6492313, 6491528
Price : Moderate
Speciality : Continental Sizzlers
Timings : 10.30 a.m. to 11:30 p.m.
Air-conditioned

The restaurant also serves specialities on different days of the week, the most popular being Chicken Dhansak (Sundays) and Mutton Biryani (Fridays). Dhansak is usually a Sunday special, because you obviously need a snooze afterwards.

The restaurant is long and narrow, with tables jammed together. There are always people waiting. Reservation is essential and accepted, except at the weekend, when you should go very early or very late.

Zodiac Grill

Zodiac Grill
Taj Mahal Hotel
Apollo Bunder
Colaba
Bombay 400 039
Tel : 2023366
Price : Expensive
Speciality : Continental
Timings : Noon to 3 p.m.; 7 to
  11 p.m.
Credit cards accepted
Air-conditioned

Carrying the logo of the sun, Zodiac Grill at the Taj serves some of the most delicious, French inspired gourmet food under the sun. The setting is heavily comfortable, rather like a Gentlemen's Club. No unnecessary themes, no frills, nothing to detract from the sumptuous offerings.

Drinks over, do not hesitate about the first course, just plum for chef Hemant Oberoi's superb creation, Camembert Dariole, described as a hot lush cheese soufflé, delicately glazed with cream sauce. There are no words to describe this miracle of a dish, which has to be tasted to be experienced. Those who are not into cheese can opt for Scallop Delphinus, a combination of imported scallops and curried prawns grilled to perfection and dressed with a saffron ginger vinaigrette.

We suggest that you skip the soups and save your appetite for yet another brilliant creation from chef Oberoi, Chicken Zodiac—a delicate puff pastry, enclosing a succulent breast of chicken, stuffed with creamed carrots, leeks and mushrooms enfolded in spinach. Surrounding Chicken Zodiac is a brilliant brown sauce made from reduced meat stock, supported with a dainty dish with steamed Broccoli, creamed baby carrots and baked potato, all very beautifully presented. Yet one more heart-stopping dish added to the new menu, is Tiger Prawn Nebule. Tiger Prawns are pan fried with ginger, Hoisin sauce and garnished with Sushi! It was heady, intriguing and certainly innovative.

For the vegetarians, keeping with the times, we recommend Pasta Sculptoris, Italian pasta with exotic pesto sauce garnished with sun dried tomatoes. Also Pan Aerostatique, a *mélange* of vegetables encased in puff pastry. Very light but satisfying dishes.

In between courses, a salad trolly is wheeled around for you to make your own, as it were. The bread basket is a speciality of the Zodiac. From the assortment, we recommend Cinnamon Bread. The French house wine, a Bichot, was dry, smooth, full bodied and worthy of the high standard of cuisine served.

To end such a fabulous meal, order the equally fabulous, Kahlua Mousse, made with Mexican coffee liqueur, which, like the Camembert soufflé, you must have if you come to the Zodiac.

The decor of Zodiac takes you back to the early Forties when comfort was the king. Huge chandeliers, heavy drapes and mirrors. Well-laid-out tables with exclusive Doulton crockery and silver cutlery on a starched tablecloth. Service is superbly discreet. An ideal place for a romantic rendezvous and for those interested in the serious art of elegant dining.

The prices here are as haute as the cuisine, but worth it.

Silver service at the Zodiac Grill

Calcutta

The Bengalis have a veneration for food similar to that of the French. It is a mystique that borders on mysticism. The appreciation of good food is a snobbish cult, as essential for a 'cultured' person as a passion for literature, nostalgia and politics.

The pot pourri of cultures which have influenced the history of the city—Turkish, Armenian, Greek, Portuguese, British. Recently, Chinese and Muslims (from Bangladesh) have had a similar effect on eating habits. Calcutta lived longest under British rule. It was, in fact, the capital of British India until 1911. During this time, an Anglo-Indian or Colonial cuisine was established and adopted by both the British and the upper class Bengalis. Dishes like Devilled Eggs, Potato Chops (filled with kheema) and Worcestershire sauce were inventions of the cooks of the time which unfortunately are not available in any restaurant in the city.

The Bengali may have become a product of both cultures, but he never gave up his language, literature or food. Unlike Mughal cuisine which filtered down from the royal kitchens, the root of Bengali cuisine is rural. Seasonings may be nothing more than mustard (either in the mild form of a tadka, or a vigorous mustard paste), green chilli, ginger and the famous Bengali oomph, panch phoron, a five-spice powder containing kalonji, methi, jeera, saunf and radhuni. The excellence of the dishes derives from the subtlety and simplicity of the ingredients. Like Chinese food, nothing is wasted or considered too lowly to be concocted into or incorporated into a dish. Take Kachur Sag, the stem of the taro plant, which is cooked with prawns or fish head. Any true son of the soil would kill for it. Similar reactions are aroused when you talk about banana stems and flowers, and each dish is eaten individually, with a little rice, almost in courses, so that flavours do not overlap. As it is not a lavish cuisine, it isn't an expensive one either.

A typical Bengali meal would begin with a bitter vegetable dish like shukto, a subtle concoction of vegetables and fish to which karela (bitter gourd) is added. This would be followed by dal (usually cooked with a fish head) accompanied by a dish of fried potatoes or brinjals. Then comes the core of the dinner, the fish and if you're lucky, prawns too. In fact, Bengalis love fish, especially the sweet water variety Elish or Hilsa so much that, if they can afford it, they even have it for breakfast! Other fish you are likely to find in restaurants include rui, bekti, topsey and pabda, and, of course, anything from lakes, rivers or ponds. The head and tail are considered the best parts of the fish. Salt water fish, like pomfret, which has become so exorbitant in Bombay, goes for peanuts in this city. As in Kashmir, fish, considered a 'vegetable of the sea', is eaten by Hindu Brahmins in this part of the world. Chutneys are an integral part of the meal. Whether they are made from mango, papaya, tomato or radish, they are almost eaten as a separate course, not just as an accompaniment to liven up other things.

No Bengali meal is complete without dessert, whether it is their delectable mishti doi, yoghurt sweetened with date palm jaggery, rossogolla or sondesh.

When you first hit Calcutta everybody tells you that authentic Bengali cuisine, like other regional cuisines in India, is only possible at home. This may be true of certain delicacies. Nevertheless, we found Aheli could lay on a splendid Bengali feast, and both Suruchi and Siddheshwari Ashram have a more home-style approach. For Muslim food, the area around Zakaria Street is the place. Although Nizam's, in the New Market area discovered Calcutta's original fast food, the Kathi Kabab, their Mutton Chap is excellent too. Watch out for inexpensive restaurants in this city. They tend to be grotty and unhygienic.

Despite all the hype, we found both the old Chinatown and the new one in Tangra unreliable for good food, but the former is still high on atmosphere. Tangra, an area of tanneries on the way to the airport, is the most unlikely place to house the new Chinatown. Dimly lit, almost like the movie set of a suspense film, with ramshackle old houses, homes which allow you to share a little of what it means to be Chinese in India today. These places are not for the discerning diner at all, but provide home spun stuff in very basic surroundings.

If budget is no constraint, then a visit to the Rotisserie at the Oberoi, to savour the Anglo-Indian and Continental delights of Chef Alphonso Gomes, is a must. Last but not least are some tips for those with a sweet tooth. Bengali sweets have the edge on other Indian sweets as they are made with a cottage cheese called chhena, and not mawa. For rossogollas, although K. C. Das has made a name for himself with the tinned version, we would recommend the original, Naveen Chandra and Mithai. For sondesh, made with both sugar and palm jaggery,

Bheem Nagin Bow Bazaar, Nakur and Shyambazaar are the places. And mishti doi is available again at Shyambazaar and Sen Mahasay.

One of the most versatile restaurants in the city is Sonargaon, at the Taj Bengal. Popular for his North Indian specialities, chef Zakaria is also a wizard with traditional Bengali food and mouth-watering, delicate, totally vegetarian Rajasthani specialities which, although not on the menu, can be specially ordered.

Vegetarians should watch out in this city, as we suspect that many vegetable preparations in smaller Bengali restaurants contain a discreet bit of fish here or there.

In short, we found Calcutta, of all the cities in India, could be a real Epicurean delight, and Bengali cuisine, along with French and Chinese, has surely done a great service to mankind.

A meal for one person

Inexpensive: under 100 rupees
Moderate: 100 to 250 rupees
Expensive: over 250 rupees

Aheli

Aheli
Quality Inn
12, Jawaharlal Nehru Road
Calcutta 700 013
Tel : 2430220
Price : Moderate
Speciality : Bengali
Timings : 12.30 to 3.30 p.m.;
   7.30 to 11 p.m.
Credit cards accepted
Air-conditioned

As soon as you enter Aheli, the traditional Bengali welcome is overwhelming. The captain, Mukhsha Puriveshar, then hands you a pretty menu, on the cover of which is a mother feeding her little son. Despite the cliché, it does make you sigh.

The decor is chic—a huge skylight in the middle of the ceiling, well-laid-out tables with elegant cane mats, and yet a very homely atmosphere. Our experience at Aheli was exactly as it is described in its menu, which is worth quoting. 'Bengali cuisine is quite like Bengali music or poetry. Warm, sensitive, romantic and crowded with memories. One has to approach this food the way one would make an effort to understand music or poetry.

In a rather leisurely pace, item by item, travelling from warm rice and lentil to a warmer phase of meat and fish, eventually ending up with the cool luxuries of curd and Sondesh.

We recommend you start off with Aam Poraa Sharbot (a tangy drink made from raw mangoes) to whet your appetite. Move on to Chingri Jogey Chamotkar. A real chamotkar (miracle) will happen when you eat this dish, made with fresh, medium-sized prawns and coconut milk, served with fluffy basmati rice. You are immediately transported to heaven, where you lie in total bliss, savouring the morsels, till you reluctantly come down for the next dish. No Bengali feast is complete without the Bhaapaa Ilish Shannaakaar (steamed hilsa with mustard paste and green chillies). This can be followed by Taatkaa Mochaar Ghonto (banana flowers and potatoes cooked in grated coconut) and Shukto Rey, mixed vegetables with Radhuni, cooked with typical Bengali spices. Finally, of course, no Bengali meal is complete without the chapatey chutney—made of raw papaya, dates, raisins and ginger.

From the range of deserts (mishti), we recommend the Monolobha Maalpoa or Sheetal Doi Mishti.

Aheli also serves a typical Bengali thali, incorporating all the above dishes and many more, but we feel it is much more exciting to order from the menu, to suit your taste, budget and appetite.

A Bengali lunch

Amber Bar & Restaurant

Amber Bar & Restaurant
Sagar Hotel
11, Waterloo Street
Calcutta 700 069
Tel: 6486746/3477/6520
Price : Moderate
Specialities : Moghlai
Timings : 11 a.m. to 11 p.m.
Credit cards accepted
Air-conditioned

By now an institution in Calcutta, Amber has its regular clients who swear by the Mutton Peshawari Barra (roast leg of mutton). Although it is one of the biggest restaurants of its kind with three floors of dimly lit interiors, it is still difficult to find a place to sit during peak hours.

Stick to the Moghlai food at which the restaurant excels. Besides the Mutton Barra, (pieces of mutton in a dry roasted masala) and the Tandoori chicken, the daily specials worth trying out are—Chicken Masala Kabab on Mondays, pieces of boneless chicken in a brown gravy; Chicken Chilli Kabab (Tuesdays); Chicken Tangdi Kabab, basically a tandoori leg of chicken in the usual tandoori masala (Wednesdays); Fish (Betki) Masala Kabab, in a dry garam masala (Thursdays); Mutton Reshmi Kabab (Fridays); Chicken Boti Kabab (Saturdays) and Mutton Bara Kabab (Sundays). The tandoori roti was superb.

The service is good and tableware elegant. If you are interested in good Tandoori food and heavy, rich Moghlai fare, in air-conditioned comfort and without worrying about your bank balance, then Amber is the place for you. Amber was the first taste of Punjab for Calcutta.

Aminia

The strong whif of Kashmiri zafran (saffron) and kewra hits you square in the nostrils as you enter the huge crowded hall of Aminia. Jam packed with no-nonsense foodies (about 200 of them at any one time), they are all tucking into what is perhaps the best Muslim Biryani in Calcutta. We found the kewra and rose flavouring a little too strong, but otherwise the rice was cooked to perfection, as was the chicken. Priced at Rs 19 (plus taxes), it is a complete meal. Also worth trying is Aminia's Special (mutton, egg, potato and tomato) curry; a bit greasy, but tasty all the same, to be eaten with thick hot tandoori or roomali roti. Other items on the limited menu include Chicken Do Piaza, Mutton Afghani curry, Chicken and Mutton Chop and some vegetables like Palak Paneer and Mixed Vegetables.

Aminia
6A, S.N.Banerjee Road
Opp Elite Cinema
Behind Oberoi Grand
Calcutta 700 013
Tel : 2441318
Price : Inexpensive
Speciality : Moghlai
Timings : 11 a.m. to
   11.30 p.m.

The furniture is old-fashioned, with long wooden tables, dormitory style, which are shared. They are cramped together to accommodate as many customers as possible. The place is always full, bustling with hungry regulars, tucking into tasty, good value food. There are mirrors on the walls and a huge service counter near the kitchen.

Chinoiserie

Chinoiserie
Taj Bengal
34-B, Belvedere Road
Alipore
Calcutta 700 027
Tel: 2483939
Price : Expensive
Speciality : Chinese
Timings : 12.30 to 3 p.m.;
    7.30 to midnight
Credit cards accepted
Air-conditioned

Chef Brando, who was previously with the Golden Dragon at the Taj Mahal Hotel in Bombay, is the force behind the Chinoiserie, which is positively the best Chinese restaurant in Calcutta.

We strongly recommend the following: Chicken Curd Soup, Fish Bonfire (steamed Betki in a light clear sauce with a hint of ginger), followed by the Konjee Krispy lamb which has an exotic sweet-and-sour taste, and Mixed Vegetables in satay sauce. If you are still hungry, then ask the chef for his Chilli Potato (no jokes), it is simply mouth-watering.

For dessert, try their toffee apple with deep fried (yes fried) ice cream. The Chinese really know how to balance sweet and sour, and in this case hot and cold!

The Chinoiserie is decorated with original mother-of-pearl pictures. The crockery and cutlery is exclusively designed for the restaurant. With all this and the excellent cuisine, a trip here is a culinary pleasure.

Chinese condiments

Kafulok Restaurant

We were told to go to Tangra for 'authentic Chinese'. Well it was authentic in so far as the Chinese who live there served what they ate themselves. We sometimes forget, though, that many Chinese living in India are born and bred here, without having set foot in their homeland. Their tastes are therefore influenced by rice, dal and spices, as much as noodles and stir fry. So forget about steamed lobsters, jumbo prawns and Peking Duck. The 'Indian Chinese' food here is far from Beijing, but delicious.

Kafulok Restaurant
47 South Tangra Road
Calcutta 700 046
Tel : 2451953
Price : Moderate
Speciality : Chinese
Timings : 7 p.m. to 10 p.m.
Air-conditioned

At Kafulok, the toss fried Chilli Prawns were fresh and the Lemon Chicken, tasty in a thick, but not glutinous, lemony sauce. Avoid the fried rice, and take on fresh home-made rice noodles instead. Chilled beer is served. Bisleri water is also available. The owner, H. P. Chen, takes the orders, the cooking is supervised by his pretty wife. The rest of the family serves. There is a separate 'family' room where you are allowed to drink your own booze, with no cover charge! This is one of the more organized restaurants in Tangra. It even has a printed menu.

The decor is typical of a Chinese soup kitchen. Wooden tables and chairs covered with a red tablecloth, cheap Chinese bowls and plates, and a few Chinese wall hangings and calendars.

Lakhanlal Hotel

Lakhanlal Hotel
88, S. L. Banerji Road
Near Elite Cinema
Calcutta
Price : Inexpensive
Specialities : North Indian
  Vegetarian
Timings : 9 a.m. to 3 p.m.;
  7 p.m. to midnight

Lakhanlal is one of the few pure vegetarian restaurants in Calcutta where you can be sure there is no fish in sight, or even lurking about inconspicuously in their delicious dal. The vegetable dishes vary from day to day according to the season. There is no menu card and the daily specials are rattled off verbally by the over efficient waiters who serve you within minutes of your placing the order. We tasted and recommend Karela Potato, a dry concoction of these two Bengali favourites, Potato Pumpkin in a light soupy gravy and the dal. Rotis are served hot and the whole thali costs as little as Rs 10 (all inclusive). The food is tasty, wholesome and truly satvik. Home-made curd is available and an extra portion of rice costs a mere Rs 2.40.

The exterior is like a shop, with matkas of freshly-made dahi displayed in the window. Inside, there are wooden tables and chairs laid out without any noticeable decor. The owner, Lakhanlal Chaurasiya, has maintained the same quality ever since he opened the shop fifty years ago. This is a great place to eat if you are looking for simple, home-made vegetarian food, at ridiculously low prices. Avoid peak hours, or prepare yourself for a long wait.

Nizam's Restaurant

Nizam's Restaurant at Hogg Street is just for that—hogging! It has a limited menu, but almost everything is good quality and value. On top of the popularity chart is the Mutton Kathi Kabab (pieces of boneless, cooked meat wrapped in a roti along with onions), which, the Management claims, is carried by travellers to eat on the plane and to share with their friends and families in other cities and countries.

Close on the heels of Kathi Kabab is the ubiquitous Chicken Chap. Even though there could be many contestants for the best Chap in Calcutta, we thought the one at Nizam's was the best. The flavour was subtle and yet tasty. Chap is actually the half-breast portion of the chicken, or a goat chop, which is marinated in a special masala and then left to stew in a huge kadai, simmering on coals. In most cases, the kadai is kept at the entrance of the restaurant, so that the aromas can lure prospective customers. The other recommended dishes are Khiri (udders) Kabab Roll, Chicken Rozella (chicken curry with a full egg, tomato and potato) and Murg Mussallam. Tandoori roti and Roomali roti are both priced at Rs 1.50 only.

The decor is basic, a bit like Bombay's Irani restaurants, with wooden tables and mirrors. The preparation and cooking is done in an open kitchen, in full view of the customers.

Definitely worth a visit. A new branch in Bangalore has recently opened.

Nizam's Restaurant
1, Hogg Street
New Market
Calcutta 700 087
Tel:299397
Price:Inexpensive
Specialities : Tandoori, Moghlai
Timings : 10 a.m. to 11.30 p.m.
Only take away up to 1 a.m.
Credit cards accepted

Rotisserie

Rotisserie
The Oberoi Grand
15, Jawaharlal Nehru Road
Calcutta 700 013
Tel: 292323
Price: Expensive
Speciality: French
Timings: 12.30 to 3 p.m.;
    7.30 to 11 p.m.

Hilsa of the Hooghly

In terms of impeccable service and five-star luxury both the Taj and Oberoi group of hotels ride neck and neck for the top ranking. In terms of fine cuisine, it is really a matter of who has the best chef, in any particular city. There are times when a chef produces such dazzling dishes, that you even forget about five-star prices, or rather five-star taxes.

One simple man (or woman) can make the difference between an extraordinary and mediocre restaurant. Chef Alphonso Gomes at the Rotisserie, Oberoi Grand is one such man. He is the type of chef, quiet and unassuming, who will go down in the history of Indian cuisine for having perfected just one single dish, which truly is a masterpiece of culinary wizardry. We would even go to the extent of saying that if you have to try only one thing in Calcutta, budget permitting, it has to be chef Gomes smoked deboned (entirely!) hilsa, the prized fish of the Hooghly. It was our good fortune that we happened to be in Calcutta during the rains, the peak season for this city's favourite fish. Chef Gomes had bought it fresh that morning from the local Manektala Market, looking as if it had been chiselled in sterling silver with shocking pink gills and bright, sparkling eyes.

We had tried Hilsa or Elish, as it is known as here, steamed in a banana leaf with a moat of fiery mustard sauce; we had tasted it reconstituted deboned, mixed with masalas and made into its original shape; we had even tasted it stuffed; but never with a fresh water fish. Hilsa, we have decided, prepared this way, is surely one of the most rewarding experiences of the gourmet world.

At the Rotisserie, the fillets (served with dainty vegetables in the European mode) released thousands of pleasant sensations, awakening our taste buds to the optimum capacity. Hilsa is the king of the sweet water tribe, doesn't need much pampering or camouflaging with masala.

As much as we love the ritualistic play with the deboning of a hunch of Hilsa, we have to admit that there are times when you long for the service to be smart, the crockery and cutlery outstanding and the fish filleted. Despite being into rich gourmet food our daily diet is actually quite puritan compared to most. But once in a while comes an irresistible urge for a piece of steak. We have 'given up' beef many times but when the urge is aroused we generally fine into it. After having spent several days 'tasting' in Calcutta, a simple grilled steak at the Rotisserie gave us more pleasure than any of the fancy French dishes of the week. Accompanied by lightly buttered string beans, glazed baby carrots and baked potato with sour cream—a glass of Beaujolais red wine, we were at peace with ourselves and the world. 'Local Beef,' said chef Alphonso, 'is good in Calcutta,' and we nodded in agreement, our mouths full of the succulent meat. The accompanying sauces (Béarnaise, peppercorn and mushroom) were all delicious—Alphonso also does an extraordinary grilled Bekti (another marvellous estuary fish) in cream, wine and saffron sauce with a hot mini naan rather than bread to mop up the delightful gravy—a true miracle of East meets West.

One could make a full meal out of any of the above three extraordinary dishes—but we would recommend taking Hilsa or Bekti as a starter and finishing off with grilled steak for a total experience.

Chef Alphonso started his career in 1969 and did stints at the Oberoi Hotels at Delhi and Kathmandu before coming to his home city of Calcutta, as Executive Chef at the Oberoi Grand, which he loves, more so since, he says, 'the market to buy the fresh stuff is just next door.' Working under European chefs, Bob Cardinan from Italy, Wiltbodt from Germany, gave him the insight into the world of European cuisine and he obviously turned out to be an A-grade student—he now applies the craft to creating European dishes out of local ingredients. Smoked Hilsa is his creation and masterpiece—a culinary adventure you should not miss.

Royal Indian Hotel

Royal Indian Hotel
147 Rabindra Sarani
Calcutta 700 073
Tel : 2381073
Price : Inexpensive
Speciality : Moghlai
Timings : 11 a.m. to 11 p.m.
Partly air-conditioned

This ancient eatery, established nearly ninety years ago, is popular like Nizam's, for its Mutton Chap. In fact, the owner, Mehmood Afzal, claims that the dish was created by his forefather, Ahmed Hussain. Even though Muslim restaurants all over Calcutta serve chicken, fish as well as mutton chaps, the real Chap, Afzal claims, is made of mutton that comes from the back portion of the goat, called 'pudh ka piece', which is then pounded and marinated in a secret blend of masalas, and finally slow cooked in a kadai on gentle glowing coals. It was also quite comforting to hear that the owners eat their own Chaps, in the restaurant itself.

For those who like their food rich and spicy, the Royal Chap is brilliant. Worth going all the way to the Harrison Chitput crossing. The good old electric tram will take you there, if you have enough time. Also recommended is the Biryani.

The modern decor is basic and nothing much to talk about. One wonders what happened to all the wonderful old furniture and fixtures that must have existed when the restaurant started ninety years ago. The air-conditioned section on the first floor is well maintained and is recommended for comfortable dining.

Shiraz Golden Restaurant

Few dishes around the world have the mystique or appeal of a biryani. Emperor Shahjahan ate it, so did the Nawabs of Lucknow and Hyderabad. Each had his own jealously guarded recipe, handed down from generation to generation.

Shiraz Golden Restaurant
56 Park Street
Calcutta 700 017
Tel : 2477702
Price : Inexpensive
Speciality : Moghlai
Timings : 5 a.m. to 11 p.m.
Partly air-conditioned

Shiraz serves more plates of biryani (about 2500 a day) than any other restaurant in Calcutta, claimed the owner Mohammed Shaukat Ali. 'We use only desi (farm reared) chickens and are generous with Zafran.' The recipe he follows was created by his late father, Arshad Ali. A plate of fragrant biryani is as little as Rs 17 for mutton and Rs 18 for chicken. While the biryani is served daily, other specials like Kachi Qualia (mutton with a boiled potato, in curry) appears every Tuesday and Saturday. Nargisi Kofta (minced mutton balls in a thick tomato and onion gravy), on Mondays and Fridays, and Reshmi Kababs, on Wednesdays and Sundays. Tandoori roti is only Rs 1 each. Wonderful food and great value. The owner promised to instal an Aquaguard by the time this book is out; if not, it is advisable to carry your own bottle of water.

Decor is non-existent. The paint is peeling off the walls, and the air-conditioned section upstairs is best avoided. It is much more interesting to eat downstairs to get the whif of the chops cooking in the open kadai, and observe the raunak (hustle and bustle) of one of busiest streets of Calcutta, while you wait.

Siddheshwari Ashram

Siddheshwari Ashram
19 Rani Rashmoni Road
Near Society Cinema
Calcutta 700 087
Tel : 244 2103
Price : Inexpensive
Speciality : Bengali
Timings : 8 a.m. to 2 p.m.;
    7.30 to 11 p.m.

Established in 1920, Siddheshwari Ashram (nothing whatsoever to do with your spiritual needs) has been drawing crowds eager for 'home cooked' quality food, with an emphasis on fish, Bengali style.

The fish repertoire includes: fried Rui roe (a bit of a tongue twister in more ways than one) is only Rs 3; fried Rui (superb); Rui curry (in an onion, tomato and potato gravy); and a small river fish called pabda (which comes whole with the head) in a similar gravy to the Rui. It is a wonderfully delicate fish. The cherry on the cake is Elish (Hilsa), which we recommend you eat last, as it comes steamed in a light mustard gravy, which does not rise up your nostrils with the same fierce intensity as many of its cousins. And finally dal. Do not avoid it just because it is cheap and sounds familiar. It is, in fact, the most delicious moong dal we had ever eaten, which we suspect is cooked with Rui fish head, for flavour. Rice is an incredible Rs 1, for a mountain of a portion.

The only thing missing on the menu was the special Chingri Malai Mach (prawn cream curry). 'Prawns are expensive and not always available. Besides tables are shared and we don't want those who cannot afford prawns to be envious of those who can. That does not go with the socialistic theme of Calcutta,' said the owner. 'Rui, on the other hand is always available and is within everyone's budget.' There is no printed menu here, as most clients are regulars.

The restaurant is on the first floor of a house, and no effort has been made to make it look like anything else. The service was on clean banana leaves, no cutlery. The appreciative licking of the fingers, sucking at the fish head, vacuuming the tiniest bit of fish meat in the crevices, is part of the fun. Eating at Siddheshwari is serious business—a place to sharpen your gastronomic skills, not your conversational ones.

No mishti (desserts) here. Amble over to Mithaai a sweet shop located at 48 B, Syed Amir Ali Avenue nearby, for the softest, spongiest rossogollas in town.

A wedding feast

Suruchi

Suruchi
89 Elliot Road
Calcutta 700 016
Tel : 29-1763/ 20-9152
Price : Moderate
Speciality : Bengali
Timings : 11 a.m. to 10 p.m.

What strikes you as you enter this scrupulously clean hall, is that the food is cooked and served only by women, who belong to this women's institution. Suruchi is mostly patronized by students and housewives, and lot of white collar executives looking for home style food, in clean surroundings.

There are fixed lunches (thali), as well as à la carte. The price depends on the type of fish you choose. For example, a vegetarian lunch is Rs 14, Rui fish lunch is Rs 20, Elish (hilsa) is Rs 26, Bekti is Rs 28. There are two vegetables included, Alu Bhindi and Mochar Ghanto (a dry vegetable dish made from the banana tree flower)—both excellent. The small Chitol Rossa (sweet water fish in a tomato and onion gravy) was tremendous. Bekti jhol, a thick fillet of this buttery fish, and Elish (hilsa) Vapa in a fiery mustard sauce, was a fitting climax to the meal. In between, we picked at the gorgeous raw papaya, mango and ginger chutney. This is a must with every good Bengali meal. Soft drinks are available, and for those with a sweet tooth, mishti doi (sweet yogurt) was a perfect end to a perfect Bengali meal.

The Dhaba

For a taste of the Punjab in Calcutta, make tracks for the Dhaba. Managed by the young Prit Pal Singh, who is the third generation of owners and started off with a small shop serving lassi and samosas to lorry drivers, on the highway. Today the same Dhaba has developed into a three-level restaurant, with an air-conditioned section, as well as a terrace garden. It is surprisingly clean and well kept, with an Aquaguard filter for safe drinking water and clean bathrooms.

The Dhaba
P-23 Ashutosh Chowdhury
  Avenue
Calcutta 700 019
Tel : 746227
Price : Inexpensive
Speciality : North Indian
Timings : 11 a.m. to 11 p.m.
Credit cards accepted
Partly air-conditioned

Almost all the items on the menu are tasty, plentiful and definitely good value. Full Tandoori chicken is only Rs 40 and Sarson ka Sag and Makki Ki Roti are available during season. Maasi, an old lady from Prit Pal's village in Punjab cooks the sag and roti. For the non-vegetarians we recommend Chicken Bharta, made with boneless chicken and cream. The chicken roll, a sort of a kathi kabab, with diced pieces of desi chicken cooked in a dry ground masala and wrapped in a baida roti with green chutney and onions, makes a great snack. Yet another masterpiece here is the Maa Ki Daal, served with a dash of white butter. The yoghurt is made on the premises. The special tea, made with milk and Red Label tea leaves and no water, is a must.

It's a taste of Punjab all the way through.

The Sonargaon

The Sonargaon,
Taj Bengal
34-B, Belvedere Road,
Alipore
Calcutta 700 027
Tel : 2483939
Price : Expensive
Speciality : North Indian,
   Bengali
Timings : Noon to 3 p.m.;
   7.30 to 11.30 p.m.
Credit cards accepted
Bar licence
Air-conditioned

Chef 'Zaks' as he is affectionately called by his co-workers has, besides perfecting Moghlai cuisine, put his own creative touches to the mainly North Indian menu at the Sonargaon. The Palak Roomali roti is so deliciously moist that it could be eaten on its own. Dhania Chicken in a light gravy, with a hint of cashews, and the subtle papaya pickle, are amazing. Goolar Kabab, shaped like an oversized mushroom, was excellent. The huge Khandani Naan is a flamboyant version of the ordinary naan, but cooked with milk and cream. It makes quite an impression. The fine ground Kakori Kabab, though originally created for the toothless Luckhnavi Nawabs, simply disappeared as soon as it entered the mouth.

For the vegetarians, we highly recommend the Hara Tawa Kababs (made from finely ground spinach and channa dal), Paneer chutney tikka, Palak Paneer Bhurjee and Dal Sonargaon, cooked to perfection and garnished with fresh cream. Kulfi is home-made, light and delicious.

Sonargaon was packed, even on a weekday. Obvious testament to the consistently good quality of the food. Chef Zakaria is also prepared to create dishes outside the menu.

Though the 'village square' decor is rustic, the seating is modern and comfortable.

Zaraanj

Though the name means a small Indian village, Zaraanj looks more like a Japanese one, with little waterfalls, bridges and tables laid out to face the glass enclosed tandoor. The bar, excellently placed under a skylight, makes waiting pleasant in case the restaurant is full, which it is most of the time. The speciality here is Zaraanj's Raan (roast leg of lamb). Although the most popular item on the menu is the more common, Murgh Nawabi (boneless chicken). For fish lovers, there are Macchi Masal Kabab (Bekti fish), and Tandoori Jeenga. Best of all was the non-spicy Peshawari Barrah (succulent pieces of lamb marinated in yogurt and grilled in a tandoor).

Zaraanj
26, Jawaharlal Nehru Road
Calcutta
Tel : 2495572/9744/0369/0370/ 9322
Price: Expensive
Speciality : North Indian
Timings : 12.30 to 3 p.m.; 7.30 to 11 p.m.
Credit cards accepted
Bar licence
Air-conditioned
Reservation essential

For vegetarians, there are Dal Ke Kabab, made of channa dal mixed with yoghurt into balls and then cooked lightly in the tandoor. Maa Ka Dal, the all-time favourite, is here too, to be eaten with Lachchedar Tawa Paratha. The cuisine is of a high standard, as is the service, by Catering College boys dressed in dark Nehru suits.

Zaraanj is the kind of place you could entertain in style.

Delhi

Delhi, being the capital of the country and the seat of Parliament, attracts, on the whole, more conservative, traditional kind of people, whose tastes in food follow much the same pattern as their lifestyles; at best ethnic sophistication, at worst, downright gaudy. Whether it is up-market dining or snacking on the street, the choice of dishes varies little. It is simply the quality of ingredients used and the presentation, as well as the location, of course, that establishes the boundaries.

Although the city has had a number of varied rulers, who in turn left a myriad of cuisines behind, not much trace of these legacies can now be found outside private homes. As recently as ten years ago, you could still find a slow cooked, authentic Kashmiri Rogan Josh and many a superlative Muslim biryani, without having to tunnel your way through the grottiest parts of town. The restaurant scene today is moving wholeheartedly towards a synthesis of Moghlai and Punjabi food. Kormas, koftas and kababs are increasingly popular, with the 'melt in the mouth' kakori kabab, a native of Lucknow, on almost every restaurant menu and roadside kabab stall.

The Punjabis came to Delhi in 1947. Armed with their tandoors, healthy appetites and their skill for making great parathas and rotis, they set up small, home-spun places of culinary feasting, the dhabas, and have never looked back since. Many dhabas in the city have been replaced or 'upgraded' into multi-cuisine, air-conditioned restaurants, serving standard masala fare, of no particular identity or origin. However in deepest Azad Market, in the wholesale area of the city, you can still find a tender mutton 'chap' at Sardar Inderjit Singh ka Dhaba. A great Delhi favourite is Kali Dal, a rich, creamy, slow-cooked sensation, which has become the perfect accompaniment to kababs. Without doubt, Bukhara, in the Maurya Sheraton, serves the best Kali Dal in the city. New Tera Hotel, in Karol Bagh, serves exceedingly good vegetarian Punjabi food, including an excellent Kali Dal, all cooked in pure ghee!

We feel that of all the dishes in this fusion of Moghlai and Punjabi, the Tandoori Chicken, with its sister, Butter Chicken, are what Delhiites crave for most. We endured a number of restaurants which serve the above two favourites as their 'specialities', each one boasting that theirs was the biggest and the best. By the time we reached the eleventh or so Butter Chicken, we proclaimed ourselves experts on the subject, and voted Minar, in Connaught Place, the creamiest, most tender chicken of them all.

North West Frontier cuisine, with its emphasis on kababs, rotis and the carefully marinated leg of lamb, Raan, couldn't fail in this city. However, this too seems to have lost its authenticity in favour of a more Punjabi influence.

With the constant pressure that chefs must be under to provide something different within the existing framework, it is a wonder they manage to come up with anything very unusual. But Chicken Malai Kabab, where cream replaces the dahi in marination, and cheese the masalas, is a winner, and due to the constant movement of chefs from one restaurant to another, can be found all over the place.

Old Delhi, rambling, busy, dusty and crowded, still has a certain charm, but it is difficult to recommend many establishments because of the unhygienic conditions and poor quality of food. If you don't mind taking a risk, then street food is your best bet here. Paratha Gully, the wholesale Pickle Market and the numerous Bhajia stands around Chandni Chowk are the places to look out for. Many of New Delhi's roadside Chaat vendors have smartened up their operations, or disappeared altogether. Most residential areas, however, still have their corner chaatwalla, and the familiar carts selling juicy carrots and white radish in winter and fresh fruit in summer. We find Nathu's in Bengali Market a good, centrally-located place to try out Chaat and Channa Bhatura alike.

In the moderate range of restaurants, things do sway a little from the Tandoori brigade. Coconut Grove serves some excellent Kerala and Chettinad dishes, and other specialities from the South. You can find a very decent range of consistently fresh salads at Potpourri. And you still get the best Muslim food in town at Karim's, in Nizamuddin.

From the top range in Delhi, you can have a field day as far as choice is concerned. For quality European cuisine, simply prepared, we would plum for the quiet intimacy of the Grill Room, at the Holiday Inn Crowne Plaza. But for an evening to remember, the Orient Express, at the Taj Palace, is undoubtedly the place. For a touch of exotica, there is simply nowhere quite like Baan Thai, at the Oberoi. Those with traditional tastes should try Dehli-ka-Aangan, at the Hyatt, with its refined, elegant cuisine and imaginative vegetarian dishes.

If you love kababs, tandoori and a great selection of rotis, then

Delhi is the place for you. The city, despite its vegetarian population, is still 'meat centric', chicken being the favourite. Mutton, fish and prawns are all accepted by the Delhi palate, but being nowhere near the sea, you have to be a little choosy where and when you eat seafood. This is clearly not a city for a culinary adventure.

A meal for one person
Inexpensive: under 100 rupees
Moderate: 100 to 250 rupees
Expensive: over 250 rupees

Al Kauser

Al Kauser
Corner of Sardar Patel Marg
  and Kautliya Marg
Diplomatic Enclave
New Delhi 110 021
Tel.: 3015183, 3010427
Price : Moderate
Speciality : North Indian
  Kababs
Timings: 6 p.m. to midnight

As the city of Delhi becomes more and more spread out, the chances are that if you feel like Muslim type kababs, it would entail a mean trek across town, through the traffic, dust and grime, to old Delhi or thereabouts. Refreshing then to find a clean halal kabab stand in the up-market area of Chanakyapuri in central Delhi. The owners apparently own the spacious house opposite and started the stand in response to the growing demand for a quick evening snack, outside five-stars, in this area. The speciality here is the kakori, melt in the mouth, mutton kabab. You can be fairly sure that the meat and chicken here is fresh by the incredibly fast turnover. As fast as orders pour in from passing cars, a couple of cooks mould their pre-prepared finely-ground meat, onto skewers. We also recommended the Tandoori Chicken. However, the green chutney lying in buckets in front of the counter, is avoidable. There is ample parking, so you could eat in your car, or take away.

Not cheap in comparison to stalls of this kind in other parts of Delhi, but worth it for the convenience and cleanliness alone.

Baan Thai

It is difficult to write about the Baan Thai without running the risk of using repetitive superlatives. That said, we found this the most exquisitely decorated, most authentic speciality restaurant in Delhi.

Step inside the impressive Burma teak doors of this elegant Thai Home and you feel you have been beamed to Bangkok. The scent of fresh orchids fills the air and tasteful *objets d'art* greet you discreetly at every corner. Thankfully, there are no gushing waterfalls or fish ponds.

The food at the Baan Thai is

Baan Thai
The Oberoi
Dr Zakir Hussain Marg
New Delhi 110 003
Tel : 4363030; Fax : 4360484
Price : Expensive
Speciality : Thai
Timings : Noon to 3 p.m.; 8 p.m. to midnight
Credit cards accepted
Bar licence
Air-conditioned

beyond reproach. Chef Prakob, from Bangkok, has a master hand. He manages to retain authenticity without any compromise. His Tom Yam Goong soup, the yardstick by which Thai food can be judged, was simply the best we have had in India. Fragrant with lemon grass roots, Thai ginger (galangal), kaffir leaves (magrut), and fish sauce (nam pla), it is served in a steamboat. There is enough to feed a hungry Thai army. All the cold starters were both delicious and yet extremely light. Som Tum (raw papaya salad) Pla Koong (spicy prawns salad) and Laab (minced chicken with mint) contain no oil at all.

You must try the Poo Phad Phong Karee, baby crabs cooked in a sinfully rich sauce of cream and whipped eggs. Pla Kra Phong Thod Krathieum Prik Thai, is a bit of a mouthful, but a perfectly finished crisp pomfret in garlic and black pepper. We also enjoyed the Khao Ob Sapparod, fried rice tossed with chicken and shrimps, topped with sweet, shredded pork and served in a scooped out pineapple shell. Of the curries, Kaeng Kieo Wan, a green coconut curry with chicken and baby aubergines, was a good example of the cross cultural origins of Thai cuisine.

The portions at the Baan Thai are reasonably hearty, so it may be difficult to try out a variety of dishes. If this is the case, we would suggest that you go for the Tom Yam Goong, the creamy crabs and the rice in the pineapple shell. They are almost worth driving across the country for!

Baan Thai also has a charming private bar, serving all the usual cocktails, in addition to some very refreshing coconut-based Thai ones, all garnished with orchids.

A Thai touch – chef Prakob

Basil & Thyme

Any restaurant in this hyper-fashionable shopping complex is off to a good start with its up-market captive clientele. Though stark (bare walls), the decor is tasteful and contemporary. At lunch-time, the place takes on the frenzy of the stock exchange. Flying kisses are exchanged, saris are studied, and everybody (mostly expat and trendy, Indian women) is too busy, 'catching up' to worry about the food, which was nice, simple European fare but certainly not worthy of all the hype.

Basil & Thyme
Santushti Shopping Complex
New Wellingdon Camp
New Delhi 110 003
Tel: 6887179, 6887180
    Ext:111
Price: Moderate/
    Expensive
Speciality : Continental
Timings: 10.30 a.m. to 6 p.m.
Air-conditioned

The cold Tomato Soup crunchy with fresh leeks was velvety smooth and reminded us of an Andalusian gazpacho. The Avocado and Tomato Salad was simple and straightforward as was the Greek Salad with slices of feta cheese, tomatoes and a few olives drizzled with olive oil. We found the terrines visually appealing but on the bland side. However, the bechamel sauce which accompanies them was good, perked up with a dash of wicked tobasco.

A comforting thought is that the menu at Basil & Thyme changes every day, although the style remains the same. You can be sure of a vegetable terrine, pâté, quiche, stuffed croissant and salads whenever you visit. If you are browsing around Santushti, then Basil & Thyme is a lovely place for a light lunch.

Bukhara

Bukhara
Maurya Sheraton Hotel
Diplomatic Enclave
New Delhi 110 021
Tel: 3010101; Fax: 3010908
Price : Expensive
Speciality : North West
Frontier (Indian)
Timings : 12.30 to 2.45 p.m.;
  7.30 to 11.45 p.m.
Credit cards accepted
Bar licence
Air-conditioned

The oldest and probably most popular five-star Indian restaurant in Delhi, Bukhara is the baby of chef Madan Lal Jaiswal,[*] a down to earth chap, who is not afraid of getting his hands dirty. His early experience at Moti Mahal, the 'in' restaurant in Delhi of the Sixties, and later a trip to Pakistan, paved the way for his interest in tandoori food and recipes from the North West Frontier.

This small (for its stature) restaurant is the flagship for four clones worldwide, the last of which was opened in 1991 in the Royal Orchid Sheraton, Bangkok. The theme of Bukhara is probably as much to do with its popularity as the food itself. Tree trunk tables and menus, an open style kitchen, checked bibs, and you have to eat with your hands. This may not seem so unusual today, but when the restaurant was opened in 1977, it was a pretty extraordinary concept.

Despite efforts to copy features of the restaurant, even its menu, there is nothing quite like Bukhara's Kadri Naan and Maa Ki Dal. The dal (urad) is put on coal in a large brass handi overnight. The next morning, spices, ginger, garlic, fresh tomato purée, butter (lots of it) and red chilli are mixed in, and finally, Madan Lal gives his own last minute 'tadka' just before serving. The longer the dal cooks, the better and richer it is.

Apart from Bukhara's standard favourites, like the Raan, Chicken Malai Kabab and Kadak Seekh Kabab, we found the vegetarian options surprisingly creative for a meat-based cuisine. The Tandoori Capsicum,

---

[*]   Chef Madan Lal died in a tragic road accident a few weeks after we interviewed him. The restaurant continues in his spirit, of course.

with a delightful stuffing of cabbage and kishmish, the Tandoori
Stuffed Potato and Tandoori Salad on a skewer, were all
mouth-watering. The Jinga Jalpori was also excellent.

A landmark in culinary achievement. Definitely worth a visit.

*The late chef Madan Lal –
the man behind Bukhara*

Captain's Cabin

Captain's Cabin
The Taj Mahal Hotel
1, Mansingh Road
New Delhi 110 011
Tel: 3016162; Fax: 3017299,
3012853
Price : Expensive
Speciality : Seafood,
Continental
Timings : 12.30 to 2.30 p.m.;
7 to 11.30 p.m.
Credit cards accepted
Bar licence
Air-conditioned

The catch of the day

Tucked away next to the large, sprawling coffee shop, Machaan, is this little known gourmet corner of the Taj and designed as a ship bar, we didn't expect much. Captain's Cabin is worth visiting for Prawn Fantasy. Expensive but worth it. Inform chef Sanjay Vij and he will personally supervise the operation.

The prawns in question are jumbo, four of them on a plate, each prepared in a different but harmonious manner. One is just plain grilled (in the shell). The second is pan fried with a topping of fresh tomato sauce, flavoured with basil and garlic. The third is fried in cornflakes—quite a novel idea, which keeps the prawn crisp. And last, the best Thermidor (light on the cheese) we have tasted in Delhi. Wash this down with a glass of Chablis if you are feeling extravagant, or Riviera white. If you doubt that four prawns are enough, start the meal with Prawn Chowder or the deliciously flavourful Hungarian Paloc soup.

From mid-October until June, you can feast on a seafood buffet lunch at the Captain's Cabin. We can't guarantee that jumbo prawns will be there, but you can be sure of a large selection of fresh seafood every day.

Casa Medici

Some good Northern Italian cuisine, served as it should be, is now under way at this grand old, rooftop restaurant, with its flowing drapes, lofty spaces and fabulous views of the city. Do not prepare yourself for pizza and pasta. This is neither fast food nor a Neapolitan trattoria. Chef Roberto Gueilemoto, who joined the Taj in July 1993, presents heavy Italian country fare. Blond hair and blue eyes he may have, but the Italian charm is present in every course.

Casa Medici
The Taj Mahal Hotel
1, Mansingh Road
New Delhi 110 011
Tel: 3016162; Fax: 3017299, 3012853
Price : Expensive
Speciality : Northern Italian
Timings : Dinner only (à la carte)
Credit cards accepted
Bar licence
Air-conditioned

We kicked off with Vitello Tonnato—boiled veal, sliced, and served with a deliciously thick purée of capers, tuna and mayonnaise. The farmer's-style Minestrone had been cooking for four hours and was served with a garnish of olive oil, black pepper and Parmesan. Then came the pasta—whoops, beware of the enormous portions. Although the Fusili al Quattro Formaggi (Bel Paese, Parmesan, Gorzongola, Fontina) was truly a feast, it was heavy. We preferred the relatively simple, more familiar tomato based, Siciliana sauce. The Prawns, jumbo, with a sharp Salsa Verde, a green sauce made with fresh parsley, garlic and white wine, ended our meal and any prospect of being able to make a quick dash before the bill arrived.

Roberto is soon to change the entire Casa Medici menu, making it more regional and therefore more specialized. It will feature several imported items, like Italian salami, Prosciutto ham, different types of pasta, Porcini mushrooms, and a range of Italian cheeses, as well as good, strong Italian coffee served out of traditonal Neapolitan coffee percolators.

Like any memorable eating experience in Europe, the food should be savoured, not rushed. Leave the chef time and space to create and pamper you. He is certainly capable of both. The service, needless to say, is excellent.

Chor Bizarre

Chor Bizarre
Hotel Broadway
Asaf Ali Road
New Delhi 110 002
Tel: 3273821–5
Price : Moderate
Specialities : North Indian,
  Kashmiri
Timings: Noon to 4 p.m.; 7.30
  to 11.30 p.m.
Credit cards accepted
Bar licence
Air-conditioned

Hype, hype and more hype has been the crowning glory of this relatively new (1990) Delhi eatery. Understandably, Rohit Khattar, the managing partner, had to put all those years of hotel management in the US, coupled with American marketing skills, to some use.

The theme is irregular: a motley collection of antiques and bric-à-brac (all for sale), to the sounds of old, familiar Hindi and American film songs. The food, though varied, offers, perhaps, too much of a choice. The salad and chaat bar, in the 1927 Fiat, is almost as gimmicky as the vehicle itself. The tandoori items are above average by Delhi standards, especially the Ghazab Ka Tikka (chicken malai kabab) and Murgi Se Pehle (egg stuffed with cheese and roasted). But it is the much underrated Kashmiri Wazwan cuisine which reigns supreme. Try the Kashmiri Tarami—the traditional 'thal', which one has to sit around at a Wazwan feast of thirty-six courses. This one gives you a sample of Kashmiri Muslim cuisine; the Tabak Maaz (deep fried ribs) were superbly crisp, Goshtaba, rather like a 'desi' cold cut, and Haaq, luscious and creamy.

A great deal of effort and planning has gone into this venture, including the menu design, food descriptions, and a whole bunch of Kashmiri cooks. It is refreshing to see so much entrepreneurial skill being put into a restaurant, and that too in Delhi. Hotel Broadway is well off the beaten track, but funky enough to merit a visit.

Before or after dinner, you must visit Thugs, the pub on the first floor. This bar has received much publicity and it is, in fact, quite a simple place to hang out, rather than the high tech den it is made out to be. Paintings of movie gangsters, both Indian and foreign, stare at you from the walls and many of the cocktails, with amusing names like 'Lilly don't be silly', 'Liquid Oxygen' and 'Loin's Punch', are dedicated to them. Foreign and Indian drinks are served.

Coconut Grove

Coconut Grove is one of the few South Indian restaurants in New Delhi not to serve the typical South Indian vegetarian fare. In fact, Coconut Grove specializes in South Indian non-vegetarian food, quite contrary to the general feeling that 'Southy' food is all idli, dosa or sambhar.

Coconut Grove
Ashok Yatri Nivas
19, Ashok Road
New Delhi
Tel : 3324511-230, 3713052
Price: Moderate
Speciality : South Indian
Timings : Noon to 3 p.m.; 7 to 11 p.m.
Credit cards accepted
Air-conditioned

We had the most delicious Chicken Stew, served with Appam, moderately spiced, and cooked in coconut milk. The Appam, made of stone ground rice, fermented overnight with toddy, is cooked on a griddle in the restaurant itself in front of the customer and is served hot. Appams are also served with a very good vegetable stew. Pepper Chicken Chettinad, Konju Thenga Curry, a Kerala prawn curry, are the other non-vegetarian specialities. For the vegetarians, Kootu Curry (assorted vegetables in coconut curry) and Vathal Kolambu (vegetables cooked in tamarind sauce), a Chettinad speciality to be eaten with appams or rice, were the best of the lot.

The traditional music can be a bit monotonous at first, but you soon get used to it. Once in a while, when you feel like a change of flavours and cuisine, try the Coconut Grove.

Colonel's Kabab

Colonel's Kabab
29/1, Defence Colony Market
New Delhi
Tel: 462438
Price : Moderate
Specialities : North Indian
Timings : Evenings only
Air-conditioned

The young enterprising Bobby Kochhar started this mainly kabab stall in 1990. Today it is not only the talk of Defence Colony and south Delhi, but all over the city. People drive miles, especially in the evening, to crowd around outside, take away or try their chance for a table upstairs in this crowded, contemporary-style, fast food restaurant. The young man is obviously giving the city what it wants, familiar food, clean surroundings and reasonable prices. Vegetarian dishes are limited to the standard dal, paneer, aloo and korma. The accent is really on the kababs—Afghani (chicken pieces marinated in cheese and cream), Malai, the same as Afghani, but with butter and khoya as well), and Haryali (green masala and butter).

We didn't try, but saw a great many people having a whale of a time with the sizzlers, the Chicken Haldighati in particular (onion, saffron and butter).

Hats off to a young chap with a keen nose for current trends and creativity within a standard culinary framework.

D's Biryani Corner

Though not the best biryani we have ever tasted, D's is certainly the better of what is available in this price range. Both the chicken and mutton biryani are sealed in individual earthen pots with atta (dough), and then steamed in the tandoor. The other speciality of D's is the Sikandari Raan which (prompted the maroon Pathan-suited waiter) is the cheapest in Delhi. The water is filtered and served in copper glasses.

D's Biryani Corner
91/93 Under the Defence
  Colony Flyover
New Delhi
Tel : 692067, 690067
Price : Moderate
Speciality : Muslim.
Timings : 11 a.m. to 11 p.m.
Air-conditioned

Seating is on the first floor, the ground floor level is only for take away. The decor is simple, with five or six tables all crowded into one tiny space. Waiters wear achkans and the service is excellent. The only inconvenience is the constant vibrating of the restaurant due to the vehicular traffic on the flyover above.

Most of D's business is take away.

Dehli-ka-Aangan

Dehli-ka-Aangan
Hyatt Regency
Bhikaiji Cama Place
Ring Road
New Delhi 110 066
Tel: 6881234; Fax: 6886833
Price : Expensive
Speciality : North Indian
Timings : Noon to 2.30 p.m.;
    7.30 to 11.30 p.m.
Credit cards accepted
Bar licence
Air-conditioned

Dehli-ka-Aangan, we were told, is the first speciality restaurant in the world to feature Delhi cuisine, i.e., it takes from Muslim, Kayastha, Baniya and Punjabi influences. We found the explanation more confusing than the wonderful food and decor. It is certainly the first Indian restaurant we have come across which emphasizes style, comfort and an aesthetic sense, without smothering you with Indian artefacts, or trying to recreate an Indian era. It is decorated in muted shades of terracotta, pink and grey, and has a very interesting wooden inlay pattern on the parquet floor, which is repeated on the ceiling and on the tables. One of the best things about this restaurant is that there are no 'leftover' Indian smells as you walk in, and happily, no carpets to absorb them.

Everything we were served, course wise, was gentle on flavours and spices. The highlight for us was the exciting vegetarian creations. For once, the pure vegetarian is not treated as an after-thought, having to leaf through the menu to somewhere before desserts. The Tohfa-e-Zameen, a yam and pomegranate shammi, and the Khumb Paneer Sheekh, with paneer and dried plums, were as succulent as their meaty cousins, but more interesting in texture and content. For the main course, Bharwaan Zafraani Guchchi, stuffed morels in a saffron sauce, and Khazaana-e-lazzat—raw banana koftas, were a unique experience. If, after all this, you must have meat, then plum for the Murg-e-Firdaus (paupiettes of chicken prepared the French way, using Indian spices.

Jigs Kalra, the food consultant who was the brains behind the concept of Dum Pukht at the Maurya Sheraton, has been brought in to add even more excitement to this restaurant.

At last a dignified, yet not overly formal place to enjoy the charm of the Orient, without harsh spices, odours and artefacts.

Dum Pukht

Top marks for conceptualization must go to Dum Pukht. Revival of the age-old concept of fine dining is nothing new, but highlighting a chef in a country where chefs are rarely remembered, is something of a first.

Six years on, the regal elegance still plays to packed houses. It offers the Delhi élite identifiable dishes, graciously served, and the foreigner, for an indigenous, mildly-spiced cuisine, served in courses, similar to the European mode.

The richness of Lucknow cuisine is not unknown, it is just difficult to get right, in an era where speed is the ultimate factor. The dishes here are taken from the court of Nawab Asaf-ud-Daulah of Avadh, who, by chance, stumbled upon food being slow-cooked in sealed vessels, and decided that this method, with more refined ingredients, was going to be mastered in his court.

Dum Pukht
Maurya Sheraton Hotel
Diplomatic Enclave
New Delhi 110 021
Tel: 3010101;Fax: 3010908
Price : Expensive
Speciality : Avadhi (Lucknow)
Timings : 12.30 to 3 p.m.;
  7.30 to 11.30 p.m.
Credit cards accepted
Bar licence
Air-conditioned

Certain dishes on the menu are superlative. The soft Kakori Kabab, originally created so that the ageing, toothless Nawab could still enjoy kababs without chewing, really does melt in your mouth. It is presented with a heavily saffron coated sheermal, which frankly is over the top. The Murg Khushk Pardah (chicken in a veil) is a light, almost Continental casserole, which arrives in a veil of pastry. We found the biryani good, but not extraordinary. Leave room, however, for the shahi tukra, which is superb.

The vegetarians get a bit of a raw deal (after all, the Nawabs were all meat eaters). That is not to say that the chefs do not give it a bash. But ultimately, it is the experience of dining in style, Indian style, to the very pleasant fusion sounds of Brian Silas on the grand piano, accompanied by Indian instruments, that counts. A flagship restaurant worth its metal.

Dum Pukht has two clones, one in the Searock Sheraton in Bombay, and the second at the Bangalore Sheraton.

El Arab

El Arab
13, Regal Building
Connaught Place
New Delhi
Tel : 311444, 344754
Price : Moderate
Speciality : Middle Eastern
Timings : 11 a.m. to 10 p.m.
Credit cards accepted
Air-conditioned

El Arab has created a niche for itself for dishes inspired by the Middle East. It has a daily buffet (Rs 90 plus taxes) consisting of three salads, one fresh cheese dip, Moussaka, Humous, Dolmas, Baba Ghanoush, Falafel, two types of beef and one chicken, all mildly spiced. One or two Indian vegetarian dishes are also thrown in to please the 'desi' palate. For those interested in quantities, the buffet is ideal.

We would recommend the vegetarian Moussaka, a rich casserole of deep fried slices of aubergine, tomatoes and dry fruit, topped with melted cheese. You could also try Baba Ghanoush. The vegetarian version is made with aubergine, smoked over charcoal, peeled and mixed with tahini (sesame sauce), lemon and garlic. The non-vegetarian version contains mince as well. This is to be eaten with pitta bread, which is almost authentic here.

Aish Al Saraya (Honey cake) is a Mediterranean dessert, which you can follow with a truly dramatic Turkish coffee. Yes, this is the real thing, made in individual copper pots, in which fresh ground coffee is brewed along with cardamom and sugar to a thick, almost syrupy consistency, so that you almost eat your coffee. It's fragrant, delicious and a real treat.

Except for the above mentioned, the rest of the dishes have, unfortunately, suffered a strange metamorphosis from the original Arabic flavours.

El Arab is situated on the first floor of the Regal Cinema building. The place has wooden flooring and comfortable upholstered seating. The owner, Magda, and head waiter, Jagdish, are anxious to please and could be contacted to prepare dishes of your choice.

El Arab is definitely not a gourmet restaurant, but definitely worth the trip for some of its exotic Arab food and the aromatic Turkish Coffee.

Frontier Samosa Shop

Yet another tiny eating institution, Frontier has been serving 'heavy snacks' for the last fifty-five years, the taste and flavours of which no one else has been able to duplicate.

Owner Munilal looks very striking, with his big blond (!) handle bar moustache, and a white towel wrapped around his head as a makeshift turban. He presides over the frying as well as the service. Samosas and kachoris are served with channa and vegetable on the side, a full meal in itself. You can follow this with hot jalebis, warm gulab jamuns soaked in rose syrup, and sweet as hell imartis. Everything is Rs 3 per plate. Saves complication at the cash til.

Frontier Samosa Shop
N-4/15 Panchkuian Road
New Delhi
Price : Inexpensive
Speciality : Indian snacks
Timings : 10 a.m. to 7 p.m.

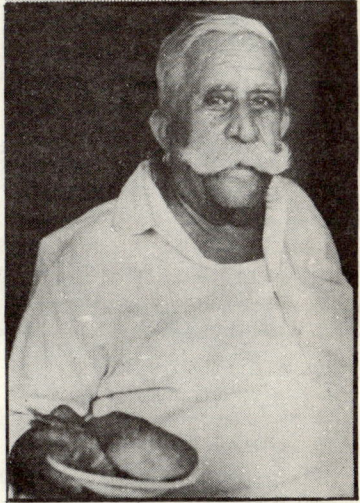

Munilal and his samosas

Ganesh Restaurant

Ganesh Restaurant
Chowk Gurdwara Road
Karol Bagh
New Delhi
Tel: 5720944
Price : Inexpensive
Speciality : North Indian
 (fish only)
Timings: Evenings only

For thirty years now, Hari Singh has been frying fresh singada fish for his Karol Bagh regulars, come rain, shine or 'off season'. The fish is marinated in a very light red masala and deep fried in a large cast iron kadai, bang in front of the little shop. It is always crisp, fresh and he shuts shop when the last piece is over, which is usually pretty early (9 p.m.) by restaurant standards. Most people take away, since standing around on the corner of this busy main road can be a little awesome.

Gulati Restaurant

What is striking about Gulati's, is the total dedication to pleasing the customer. The quality of the food, as well as the ambience, is equally matched. The decor is mostly huge, specially-commissioned paintings of the Himalayas that are up on the walls. They are actually very striking, and gives you something interesting to do while waiting for your order.

Gulati Restaurant
Pandara Road Market
New Delhi 110 003
Tel : 388836, 388839, 385559
Price : Moderate
Speciality :North Indian
Timings : 12.30 to 3 p.m.;
 7.30 to 11 p.m.
Credit cards accepted
Air-conditioned

The young Vinod Gulati, of the Gulati family, is perpetually improving the dishes, and coming up with something new. His Hara Shorba (green peas and spinach) soup is a delicious, as well as a healthy starter. He has also modified the ubiquitous appetizer, Jal Jeera, by adding a touch of ginger for an extra zing. On the non-vegetarian front, we recommend Gulati's Kalmi Kabab (grilled chicken legs) and Reshmi Kabab (grilled minced chicken kababs). For the vegetarian, Sarson Ka Saag (in winter only) and Malai Kofta, are excellent. Khasta Roti could be eaten on its own. A decent, middle of the road place, with good quality food and service.

Gulu Meatwala

Gulu Meatwala
Opp Delhi Transport
Licencing Authority
Rajpur Road
Civil Lines
New Delhi
Price : Inexpensive
Speciality : North Indian
Timings : 11 p.m. to 3 p.m.
Tuesdays closed

It was a case of love at first bite. We waited our turn patiently as Gulu, the chubby meatwalla, sat in his kiosk, like a king on his throne, surrounded by huge pateelas containing a magic potion called mutton masala curry, which he rationed out to those who had found the time to queue up at noon. Situated opposite the Delhi Licencing Authority, Gulu's 'eatery' remains open only from 11 a.m. to 3 p.m., or until the food is sold out, which is usually well before 3 p.m. The day we were there, the fluffy, long grained, onion scented rice, was sold out by 1 p.m.!

Mutton masala is all you'll get here, so don't expect to be spoilt for choice. With the mutton, you can have onion pullav or tandoori roti, for the set meal. You pay your money and receive two coupons, one for the meat and one for either the rice or the tandoori rotis, which are made in three tandoors, working non-stop to satisfy the demand. There is no proper seating, only tables scattered under the shady trees, but you'll be lucky to find a place. Onion rings and green chutney are available on the self-service counters, but not essential, as the mutton masala is cooked to perfection. However, being spicy, you definitely need the rice or rotis.

You have to see the flurry of activity that surrounds Gulu's stall to believe it. There is no pushing or shoving. It is a silent, almost stoic procedure, that takes you on a conveyor belt from the mutton, through to the rotis and onto tables under the trees. When we finally got our share of the dish (we jostled, but in vain) and tasted it, first with the fluffy onion pullav, we experienced a kind of rare gastronomic high.

The dish was full of tender meat (one chop and one marrow bone) and the gravy was thick with mince meat, fresh tomatoes cooked in home-ground spices, the true balance of which is a secret which only

Gulu the meatwala knows, and would not reveal!

Gulu also does paneer peas for the vegetarians at the same price (Rs 20). However, it is the mutton masala curry, which he has been serving for the last twenty-five years that is worth going across Delhi for.

Lunch-time rush at Gulu's

Karim's

Karim's
168/2, Jha House Hazrat
Nizamuddin West
New Delhi 110 013
Tel : 4635458, 4698300
Price : Moderate
Speciality : Muslim
Timings :12.30 to 3.30 p.m.;
  6.30 to 11.30 p.m.
Mondays closed
Credit cards accepted
Air-conditioned

You are greeted at the entrance of this busy Nizamuddin lane by two maroon, salwar kameez clad bearers who help you park your car, and lead you through the maze of over-crowded alleys, to the restaurant. This is an important and apprecia-ted gesture on behalf of the Management. The restaurant is not be an easy place to locate.

Karim's (actually called Daster Khwan-E-Karim) cuisine draws its inspiration from Mughal kitchens, serving traditional dishes without compromise. The meat is strictly halal, and no colour or artificial flavouring is used in the tandoori items. We found the cuisine consistently good, and the chef, Mohammad Akhil, very adept at turning out dish after dish of honest to goodness, full-flavoured, Moghlai food. We liked the Sheekh Kabab the best. Even though the soft kakori kababs have a lot of admirers, (we heard a foreigner describe them as Indian pâté), we, being in full possession of our teeth, still preferred the texture of the sheekh kababs, made with roughly-ground minced meat. When grilled perfectly, these too melt in the mouth, and at the same time have a bite to them. At Karim's, the kababs were worth dying for.

The Meat Burra was soft and tasty, but a bit fatty. The chicken Afghani, made with tender pieces of diced, boneless chicken, was excellent. Dil Bahar Do Piazza mutton chop, cooked in whole spices (full red and green chillies, full black pepper, elaichi, lavang, jeera, sabut dhaniya, etc.), without any onions, was unique in taste and full flavoured. The Rogan Josh was superb, but the Biryani was disappointing, compared to the other dishes. The butter naan was marvellous, and the dessert called Kheer Benajir (double cream with rice), was an appropriate ending to a superb Moghlai feast.

There is a blow up of the city of Samarkand on the wall, along with Kashmiri carpets. The seating is ordinary but comfortable. The emphasis here is obviously on food.

La Piazza

Without a word of exaggeration, this is one of the finest restaurants in India, serving some of the best and most authentic Italian food we have ever had. Everything is pure perfection. The people at the Hyatt have left no stone unturned and spared no expense to make this a very special place. 'If you're going to do something, you may as well do it properly or not at all,' said a confident Stephen Magor, Director of Food and Beverage.

The decor is elegant and yet casual, more up-market than a trattoria but not so 'haute' that you can't relax. The flooring for a start,

La Piazza
Hyatt Regency Hotel
Bhikaiji Cama Place
Ring Road
New Delhi 110 066
Tel:6881234; Fax:6886833, 6876437
Price:Expensive
Speciality: Italian
Timings:Noon to 3 p.m.; 7 to 11.30 p.m.
Bar licence
Credit cards accepted
Air-conditioned

is made up of stone tiles which have been laid in a terrazzo pattern worthy of any Italian palazzo. The walls are white and the simple, black wrought iron chairs marry perfectly with the warmth of wood and stone. Thankfully the tables are far enough from each other so you don't have to endure somebody else's conversation. Stark, white thirteen-inch diametre plates imported from Thailand are a perfect setting for the beautifully presented food. Pasta and soup is served in specially designed, rustic ceramic bowls.

It is impossible to appreciate this well-thought-out menu on one visit alone. We can highly recommend all the starters: the Warm Shellfish Salad (imported scallops, crayfish and prawns) with batons of fresh green and white asparagus, the Carpaccio, wafer-thin slices of tenderloin, with a traditional cracked pepper and mustard dressing, Artichoke Mousse, made with fresh artichokes, slightly smoked Marinated Salmon and the wonderful assortment of cold Italian specialities known as Antipasti (non-vegetarian and vegetarian). You are spoilt for choice with pastas. Almost all of them are brought in from Italy (spagettini, fettucine, penne, pappardelle), with sauces as exotic and diverse as seafood and parma tomatoes, gorgonzola cheese, tomatoes, chilli and garlic and the more familiar Bolognese. 'We could make our own pasta,' said executive chef Marcus Schneider, 'but the quality of wheat would not make it authentic.' Marcus is responsible for setting up the restaurant along with his sous chef, Hermann Grossbichler.

The Panfried Salmon with Sundried Tomatoes on a bed of spaghetti squash (specially grown pumpkin which after cooking separates into spaghetti-like strands) was the ultimate for us. Baked Duck Breast with black olives and Breaded Veal Escalopes with parma ham and parmesan are two of the very exciting main courses. If you are a pizza lover, fear not, all your favourites are here (baked in a wood fire oven with a regulated temperature control so that your pizzas are always perfectly cooked), including a truly delicious one with goat cheese, sundried tomatoes, roasted garlic and basil. If you prefer something more familiar, go for the Pizza Poorva Paschim, with chicken tikka and paneer!

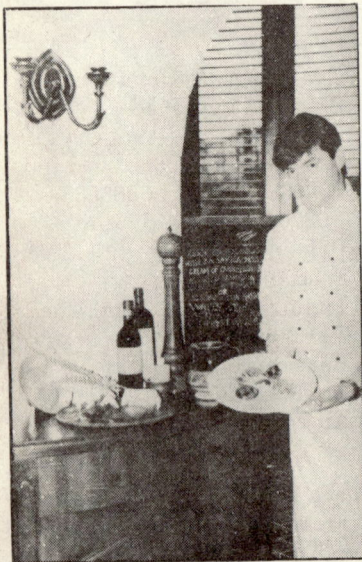

Desserts stretch to creamy Venetian tiramisu and Sicilian cheesecake with pistachio sauce. Wind up with a genuine Italian expresso or capuccino.

Chef Hermann Grossbichler

La Piazza offers a good selection of classic Italian wines, sparklers and champagnes.

On Sunday afternoon, the restaurant has a family fiesta with an antipasti buffet and free wheeling waiters taking around a variety of hot dishes straight from the kitchen. An amazing, eat as much as you like, gourmet extravaganza for Rs 350 (plus taxes).

If you feel like experiencing the grace, elegance and good food of Italy, let La Piazza transport you there for a magical couple of hours.

Minar Restaurant

Minar boasts of its own version of Butter Chicken and Shahi paneer, which are both sinfully luscious. We found they also do wonderful things with offal, like brain, liver, kidney, without the usual gravies. Service does take a bit of time (fifteen to twenty minutes), as everything is freshly made. Our brain curry arrived steaming, fragrant with cracked black pepper, and spices totally different from the butter chicken gravy. The wonderful thing about Indian food is that, if properly cooked with fresh ingredients and stone ground masalas, it beats all cuisines in intensity of taste and flavour. This was exactly the case with the Brain Masala, as well as with the Maa Ki Daal. The Tandoori roti was crisp and soft, and served one at a time, in perfect rythym with our eating pace.

Minar Restaurant
L-11 Connaught Place
New Delhi 110001
Tel : 3323259, 3328778
Price : Moderate
Speciality :North Indian
Timings : 11.30 a.m. to 11p.m.
Tuesdays closed
Air-conditioned

The other specialities at Minar are the freshly made delicious chicken soup (more like a broth), bara kabab, malai kofta to be eaten with Missi Roti or Khasta Roti.

Minar is scrupulously clean, with huge paintings of Krishna gamboling with his pretty gopies, on the walls. The ceiling has a huge circular, lit, floral fresco. The seating is cushioned and comfortable, and the formica tables are clean and functional.

No doubt, just about every medium priced restaurant in Delhi, serves similar food, at virtually the same prices, but we felt that the intensity of flavours, taste, and the dhaba-like simplicity of the dishes at Minar, was a cut above the rest.

Moti Dhaba

Moti Dhaba
Shop 2, Azad Market
Old Delhi
Price : Inexpensive
Speciality : Muslim
Non-vegetarian
Timings: Evenings only

Squashed in between wholesale cloth and canvas stores in this old and rather run down area of town, is a series of small restaurants serving typical Muslim favourites—brain, kheema and other offal. Although they all seem to be popular, Moti Dhaba is one of the oldest and most respected (so all the shopkeepers told us). A young man in a white Reebok sweatshirt prepared Bheja (brain), in fresh green masala to order (onions, ginger, garlic, chilli, tomatoes and cothmir) on a large tava which takes up most of the shop. The Kheema (obviously beef, at these low prices) and Gurda Kapura (goat kidney and udder) were all well up to our expectation. None of the dishes were either over spicy or oily.

Not the kind of place to take your mother, but perfect when you get that desperate need for a quick, fresh, meaty nibble in the middle of the night.

Lassiwalla

Nathu's

One of the most popular meeting points in Delhi, Nathu's is good value, reasonably clean, with comfortable seating and prompt service. The food is diverse, from South Indian to Chinese to typical Delhi chaat, along with a varied range of Indian sweets, all under one roof.

Nathu's
Bengali Market
New Delhi
Tel : 3719784, 3717313
Price : Inexpensive
Speciality : Indian Snacks
Timings : 7 a.m. to 10 p.m.

The all-time favourite at Nathu's is Channa Batura garnished appetizingly with spicy boiled potatoes, slivers of ginger, mint and tamarind chutneys, fresh green chillies and onion rings. Those fond of chaat will find the best Pani Puri, Dahi Batata Puri and Dahi Vadas. The portions are huge, and you can make a meal out of the snacks. Fresh fruit juices are sold at one of the counters. Caution the waiter not to add any masala or ice to the juice, to enjoy the true flavour of the seasonal fruit. We tried the pomegranate juice and found it superb.

There are times when you do not feel like a full meal and want a little tasty something without feeling too heavy. Nathu's is the place. It is part of the haphazard grouping of shops, known as Bengali Market, very close to the Museum of Modern Art and Triveni Art Galleries.

New Pishori

New Pishori
Pul Bangus
On the left before the bridge
Delhi 110 006
Tel: 7532285
Price : Inexpensive
Specialities : North Indian
  Fish and Tandoori Chicken
Timings: Evenings only

Two holes in the wall next door to each other on a main traffic thoroughfare would hardly seem the place to rush to after a hard day's work. But people do. One of the, let's call them dhabas, serves only a type of kolivada, deep fried fish (fresh water) lightly coated with masala, and sprinkled with chaat masala. Avoid the green chutney and onions. The one next door handles only the great Delhi favourites, tandoori chicken (no colour) and butter chicken. The food is tasty and fresh judging by the turnover, but a hell of a place to drive to and, worse still, park. Try it only if you are in the area.

New Tera Hotel

A small, unpretentious, pure vegetarian restaurant, situated amidst the down town hustle and bustle of busy Karol Bagh in New Delhi. The restaurant was started by the very pleasant, Gurdeep Singh, a follower of the guru Radhasoami, who advocates a total vegetarian (no egg) diet for all his devotees. Seeing a lack of wholesome, vegetarian fare at prices affordable by the man on the street, he opened this little dhaba fifteen years ago.

New Tera Hotel
4, Ghaffar Market
Karol Bagh
New Delhi
Price : Inexpensive
Speciality : Vegetarian North
    Indian
Timings : 11 a.m. to 10 p.m.

The food may be a little rich for the average palate, as everything is cooked in Govardhan pure ghee—even the bill says so, just in case you did not notice. But it is undoubtedly very tasty and very fresh. The kali dal, slow cooked the whole night through, sits in a large brass handi at the front of the shop, beckoning customers. The paneer is home-made, channa is yummy and rotis are served piping hot with dollops of ghee. Goodness knows how Gurdeep Singh manages to make a profit with the incredibly low prices.

It is advisable to take away, as seating is limited to a few benches cramped together in a small area. Great value for those who love vegetarian food like 'ma used to make' and for those strict vegetarians who are unhappy about eating in restaurants which cook meat in the same kitchen.

Nizam's Kathi Kabab

Nizam's Kathi Kabab
H-Five Plaza Building
Connaught Place
New Delhi 110 001
Tel : 3713078, 3325481
Price : Moderate
Speciality : Muslim
Timings : 10 a.m. to 10 p.m.

Nizam serves just about the best Kathi Kababs in the heart of Delhi. The menu on the wall gives various permutations and combinations possible; single egg, double egg, single chicken, double chicken, depending on your cholestrol level and appetite. After you choose, your order is passed on to chef Mohammed Akram who goes to work over his huge three feet diameter tawa (griddle). First he slaps the dough, flips it onto the tawa, breaks one or two eggs on top, and then spreads them evenly on the roti. Thereafter, the filling of your choice, the most popular being chicken and paneer, are rolled into the roti, and in a few minutes flat, you have one of the most scrumptious hot snacks ever invented. There are other items, like grilled sandwiches, and home-made chicken and tomato soup, which are good, but the kathi kabab is the main attraction.

Nizam's is a small cabin-like restaurant, with small counters where you can stand and eat, or simply order and take away. It is clean, with mirrors and woodwork decoration. The drinking water is purified with an ozonation water filter. The service at peak hours may be a bit slow. You'll have to take a token and wait for your turn. A sign flashes your number as soon as your order is ready; a little inconvenient, but worth waiting for.

Noble House

The Holiday Inn has acquired a reputation as one of the lively new troupe of five-stars, interested in innovation and contemporary planning. The range of restaurants offered here is certainly large by Delhi standards—Baluchi (Indian), the busy coffee shop which spills out on to the lobby, a poolside café, bar, night club, and the two restaurants which we found extraordinary, Noble House and the Grill Room.

Noble House
The Holiday Inn Crowne Plaza
Barakhamba Avenue
Connaught Place
New Delhi 110 001
Tel.: 3320101; Fax: 3325335
Price : Expensive
Speciality : Chinese
Timings: 12.30 to 3 p.m.;
8 p.m. to midnight
Credit cards accepted
Bar licence
Air-conditioned

The ambience in Noble House is distinctly un-Chinese. In fact this large restaurant (seats 120) could well be a smart restaurant in Beverly Hills or Hong Kong, with its black granite flooring, ebony and pink colour scheme and gleaming brass touches. The menu, on the face of it, is interesting enough. Certain dishes have been created by chef Tsering who has now returned to Tea House at the Taj Palace, where he repeats his favourites. However, there are one or two items only available in this restaurant, which are positively worth raving about.

The Prawns in Garlic Butter Sauce is a perfect blend of French and Chinese cuisine. Fresh plump jumbo prawns are stir fried with a classic garlic butter to which cream and spring onions are added. The Chinese have an unfailing and instinctive wisdom where food handling is concerned. They seem to know just when a prawn is cooked enough to retain its juices. This is partly due to their method of preparation, either stir fried for a couple of minutes on a very high burner or simply steamed. Vegetables are blanched for a few seconds in boiling water before they are added to a dish. This preserves their colour and texture. Spinach, stir fried with garlic and chilli in balachung sauce, is a perfect example.

Nice to see a five-star restaurant crowded these days, as is Noble House, even at lunch.

Om Hotel

Om Hotel
16-17 Jangpura Market
Opp Eros Cinema
New Delhi
Tel : 4615057, 4634290
Price : Inexpensive
Speciality : North Indian
Timings : 7 a.m. to 10 p.m.

An up-to-date dhaba-cum-restaurant, Om has its tandoors and huge pateelas, containing the dishes of the day, outside the restaurant, facing the street. Inside, the seating is functional. The cooking is homely and tasty. Almost all the staple dishes here are popular, especially Tandoori Chicken, Butter Chicken, Dal Makhni and piping hot Tandoori rotis. Once ordered, your dish is quickly stir fried, garnished with fresh coriander, and served immediately. The rotis come hot and fresh too.

We found a lot of patrons eating Aloo Paratha, for which the dhaba is well known. Our order of hot Aloo Paratha, cold yoghurt and steaming Makhni Dal, arrived without any fuss or trimmings. The dal had so pure and concentrated a flavour that no trace was left after we demolished every bit of it. Hearty, simple, tasty fare.

Roadside jalebi maker

Orient Express

The Orient Express train ran from London to Istanbul for ninety-four years, and epitomized the Belle Epoque, a style and an era of unparalled grandeur. What a superb idea to establish a fine dining restaurant in its honour.

As you enter the restaurant car, you are instantly transported to the world of glamour and make believe, the world of international movies and racy novels. You are reminded of Peter Ustinov's portrayal of Hercule Poirot, and of Sean Connery's seduction of the Russian spy Tatiana. We love the idea of a set meal where you can choose your courses from a comprehensive, rather than confusing, menu, without being blitzkrieged by prices (there is a set charge for a four-course meal). The seating is intimate and every detail of the original Orient Express restaurant car has been duplicated, without compromise. The crockery and cutlery are elegant, and the glassware has neat, clearly defined lines.

Orient Express
Taj Palace International
2 Sardar Patel Marg
Diplomatic Enclave
New Delhi 110 021
Tel: 3010404; Fax: 301125
Price : Expensive
Speciality : European
   (Continental)
Timings: 12.30 to 2.30 p.m.;
   6.30 p.m. to midnight
Credit cards accepted
Air-conditioned

Starters are divine; both the Smoked Salmon in Champagne sauce, and Fricasse of Assorted Mushrooms, were delicate. Our second course of seafood was followed by a strong, but refreshing duo of sorbets. A pause and several sips of Beaujolais later, came the main course of Lamb in a thyme flower sauce, and Potato Pancakes with Ratatouille. Even if you are not a dessert person, don't miss the Grand Marnier, flavoured apple tart, surrounded by an unctuous caramel sauce and maple ice cream.

Service at the Orient Express is perfectly paced, efficient and yet discreet.

We found the cuisine, on the whole, excellent in terms of quality, but a little dated. It was neither pure classical nor contemporary. However, it remains the best place in the city for that 'special' dinner with that 'special' someone.

Pakwan

Pakwan
Le Meridien
Windsor Place
Janpath
New Delhi 110 001
Tel: 3710101; Fax: 3714545
Price : Expensive
Speciality : North Indian,
  Moghlai
Timings: 12.30 to 3 p.m.;
  7.30 p.m. to midnight
Credit cards accepted
Bar licence
Air-conditoned

As 'luxury' Indian restaurants in the city go, Pakwan is comparable. The decor and ambience is sort of Mughal—a waterfall, traditional arches, a ghazal performance in the evenings, and has touches of the North West Frontier theme, with tandoori items being prepared in the open, glass fronted kitchen.

We suggest that you leave all the Punjabi, Nawabi and Moghlai dishes aside, and go for chef Kochar's innovative tandoori specialities. The Murg tikka lahsuni (garlic flavoured chicken tikka), Noorani Sikh kabab (lamb and mutton mince sheekh), Paneer Birbali with green masala (not exactly new, but done well here) and a new addition to the menu, prawns wrapped in a fillet of bekti and roasted in the tandoor.

In the case of Pakwan, the parts are more interesting than the whole. Worth a visit if you are looking for something traditional.

Pierre

Although this restaurant, situated conveniently off the lobby (as most of the restaurants are in this hotel) is supposed to represent 'the richness of French classical interiors', we felt otherwise. Burgundy carpets, floral upholstery, a ceiling painted like a sky, colonnades; all these things are a little passé, and reflect an impression of France that only exists in the minds of foreigners.

Pierre
Le Meridien
Windsor Place
Janpath
New Delhi 110 001
Tel: 3710101; Fax: 3714545
Price : Expensive
Specialities : Classical French and Flambé
Timings: 12.30 to 3 p.m.; 7.30 p.m. to midnight
Credit cards accepted
Bar licence
Air-conditioned

The decor aside, we were mildly surprised and thoroughly intrigued to find that the man behind Pierre, chef Devinder Kumar, is not only a francophile to the core, but speaks the language, to boot. He spent two years in France, working in restaurants up and down the country, until he opened Pierre in 1985.

The menu is an ambitious one, drawing mostly from classical French cuisine. It achieves a high rate of success mainly due to the vast amount of imported ingredients (around 150 items), and undoubtedly to this very talented and highly creative chef. We started with an Assiette Gourmand, a credible cold seafood feast, and our usual yardstick for European food, consomme. We also tried a vegetarian option—fresh home-made Tagliatelli with a deliciously creamy parmesan and cheddar sauce. Judging by the other imaginative dishes on the menu, the vegetarians have nothing to fear, considering that this is primarily a flambé speciality restaurant.

The flambé, although a rather dated concept, is extremely well done. True to the original recipes, the meats, etc., are set alight in cognac, removed from the fire, and the accompanying sauces are created in front of you from the pan juices. The Crepes Suzette is the best we have tasted in India, with just that right amount of orange zest for that extra oomph.

An unexpected 'winner' in the heart of Delhi.

Potpourri

Potpourri
Nirula's 1st floor level
L–Block, Connaught Circus
New Delhi
Tel : 3322419
Price : Moderate
Specialities : Salad Bar and
  North Indian
Timings : 7.30 a.m. to
  midnight
Credit cards accepted
Air-conditioned

Probably the best place to eat in Connaught Place, the food is consistently fresh, tasty, well presented and served quickly in clean and pleasant surroundings. It has the best salad bar in the moderate price range, which includes the usual cut vegetables, chicken salad and so on, along with more innovative salads like the sliced lotus root lightly spiced with salt and paprika which we found absolutely delicious. The French mayonnaise and honey lemon dressings are good, so are the breads. Traditional 'add ons' like bacon bits, grated cheese and freshly-cracked black pepper are thoughtful additions to this healthy, satisfying meal. A dessert or jelly is usually included. Refilling is allowed, but understandably not sharing.

The à la carte daily specials are also superb, especially the quiches (asparagus and mushrooms) and the fish dishes. Of the Indian dishes try the Dal Urad Makhni, served with a tandoori roti or naan, a perfect vegetarian meal. For the non-vegetarians and tandoori brigade, the tandoori sampler offers an assortment of kababs and tikkas at Rs 69. Potpourri serves chilled beer and cocktails.

The decor is tasteful and casual, with easy cane chairs and money plant creepers, rather like a green house. The eaterie has large glass windows overlooking the busy Connaught Place intersection.

Nirula's is also famous for their ice creams. You could eat your dessert at the Potpourri or pick up a cone of your favourite flavour on your way out from their busy ice cream parlour on the ground floor level.

Nirula's is also the most successful fast food chain in Delhi today, serving slightly Indianized burgers, pizzas and the rest. The Connaught Circus branch, next to the new Wimpy's, is unfortunately not the best or most spacious branch. Still, a great first for indigenous fast food.

Sagar

It's strange that in a city like Bombay, and of course the whole of South India, you will find an 'Idli-dosa' joint on almost every street corner. Even in luxury hotels the idli and dosa have today replaced the traditional English breakfast of eggs and bacon, and opened up a Pandora's box of possibilities and choice for vegetarians. South Indian food in Delhi has been slow to catch on, for whatever reason—lack of authentic cooks, ingredients or the more conservative North Indian palate.

Sagar
18 Defence Colony Market
New Delhi
Tel : 4617832, 4621451,
 4698374
Price : Inexpensive
Speciality : South Indian
Timings : 8 a.m. to 11 p.m.

This modest little set up in the hub of Defence Colony market serves good, standard South Indian fare—Idli, Vada, Dosa, Uttapam and decent enough South Indian coffee. We found it difficult to believe that people queue for hours on Sundays to get in, until we saw it for ourselves. Delhiwallas are obviously starved of good, clean, cheap vegetarian food in what is basically a kabab city. Another Sagar has opened in Lodhi Gardens, which we believe is bigger, better and even more popular than this one.

Sardar Inderjit Singh Ka Dhaba

Sardar Inderjit Singh Ka
  Dhaba
33/34 Azad Market
Near Ram Mandir
Delhi
Price : Inexpensive
Speciality : North Indian
Timings : Noon to 10 p.m.
Closed on full moons and
  Navratras

Tucked away in Azad Market, this little dhaba, spilling onto the pavement, serves the most delectable mutton chops in Delhi. During the day Sardar Inderjit Singh, who cooks and serves the food personally, dishes out Meat Pulao, Mutton Curry and roti, by the full or half plate. Everything usually gets sold out by 5 p.m. He then starts preparing for his *pièce de résistance*, a mutton 'chap', the likes of which we have never tasted before. Despite the fact that we only came here to 'taste', not really eat a full meal we could not resist the chops, and even took some back to our hotel.

The Lamb chops are first marinated in freshly ground spices (we could taste the jeera, dalchini, black pepper, clove, cardamom, etc.), stuffed with minced meat on both the sides, covered with bread crumbs, dipped into egg batter and deep fried quickly until golden brown in colour. It is served with onion rings and green pudina chutney.

No doubt the place is a little unkempt. You don't expect a dhaba to be spotless, but you will be delighted with the chap. It deserves to be eaten there on the spot, hot and sizzling, as it comes out of the frying pan.

Sitaram Diwan Chand Prasidh Chole Bhature

This hole-in-the-wall eatery has been titillating the palates of Delhiites for the last fifty years. For the cost of a soft drink, you get two bhaturas and a heap of soft black channa, topped with spicy chunks of potatoes, carrots, amla pickle, green chilly and onion rings. The channa has a perfect balance of jeera, elaichi, black pepper, anardana (dry pomegranate seeds), and ginger, and the bhatura is richly stuffed with fresh paneer. What a simple, delightfully satisfying meal. As with most dhabas, you should carry your own drinking water, and don't expect great hygiene. There is no seating. You may be lucky and find a place on the two makeshift tables set up on the pavement. Or better still, use the bonnet of the car (not necessarily your own) parked next to the shop. It is a totally good trip, nothing more.

Sitaram Diwan Chand
  Prasidh Chole Bhature
Paharganj
New Delhi
Tel : 739588
Price : Inexpensive
Speciality : Indian Snacks
Timings : 8.30 a.m. to 4 p.m.

'*Hum chane bhature theek neeyat se banate hain*,'(we make our food with total honesty) the young Diwan told us. We agreed.

Tea House

The Tea House
The Taj Palace
2 Sardar Patel Marg
Diplomatic Enclave
New Delhi 110 021
Tel: 3010404; Fax: 301252
Price : Expensive
Speciality : Chinese
Timings: 12.30 to 2.45 p.m.;
  7.30 to 11.45 p.m.
Credit cards accepted
Bar licence
Air-conditioned

The Tea House of the August Moon takes its name from the Pulitzer Prize winning play which was later made into a film with Marlon Brando and Shirley Maclaine. The Tea House is an integral part of any Chinese community, a place where people meet for dimsum (hot little snacks, often steamed or fried) and tea. This one is massive. It seats 180 people and comes complete with an impressive decor worthy of its namesake. You have dragons, a pond with goldfish, a bridge and a bamboo grove. The upper floor looks like a Chinese pagoda and the magnificent green, gold and red colour scheme is repeated throughout the restaurant.

If you feel like dimsum in Delhi, the Tea House is undoubtedly the place. A trolley of about eight or ten delectable treats, steamed in authentic bamboo baskets, is wheeled to your table. Chef David spent six years in Hong Kong as a company chef, and though not trained in Dim Sum alone, is giving the city a welcome change. For seafood fans, the Steamed Shrimp dumplings are as good as you would find abroad. And you can't stop eating Kothe, moon shaped parcels of chicken, dipped in one of the interesting Dim Sum relishes on the table. Along with a Minced Chicken and Coriander Soup, and maybe the delicious crispy Spinach Pepper Salt, this was a completely satisfying meal. We believe that all the 'salt pepper' items on the menu are immensely popular. Deep fried until crisp and then stir fried, these are great alternatives to the 'gravy' dishes which are the usual favourites in Chinese restaurants in India.

Apart from the dimsum, the menu is fairly 'traditional' by five-star standards. For those with a yearning for beancurd, the Tea House has several creative preparations. This is by no means a cheap way of snacking away in the afternoon, but certainly a very enjoyable one. Attentive service.

The Grill Room

How refreshing it is to see a warm, cosy atmosphere return to five-star dining. The Grill Room is our perfect evening out. It is unpretentious, warm, with a wooden parquet flooring and an impressive teak bar. It also has a great view of the city from every table. It reminds us of a British Gentlemen's Club (minus all the pomp and formality), crossed with an elegant American Grill restaurant.

The menu is a comprehensive choice of less than half-a-dozen items for every course, and is thankfully not over ambitious. Everything we ordered was delightful. It is surprising how many

The Grill Room
The Holiday Inn Crowne
  Plaza
Barakhamba Avenue
Connaught Place
New Delhi 110 001
Tel: 3320101; Fax: 3325335
Price : Expensive
Speciality : European
  (mainly grills)
Timings: 12.30 to 3 p.m.;
  7.30 p.m. to midnight
Credit cards accepted
Bar licence
Air-conditioned

inadequate chicken consommes we have tasted on our travels. Go for this one, it was perfect. Although it had no lettuce, my salad Nicoise was freshly tossed, with the right amount of dressing, and for a change, the right vegetables. It was simply presented, as it should be, without any silly tomato roses or fanned cucumber garnishes. The pepper steak was flambéd at our table with great style, although the preparation differed from the norm (a basic pepper sauce was kept ready, rather than being prepared from the pan juices). However, the quality of the steak was excellent. Crepes Suzette ended what was for us a magnificient dinner.

An understated, small (seats forty-two), quiet yet elegant place to dine.

The Village Bistro

The Village Bistro
  Restaurant Complex
12, Hauz Khas Village
Near Deer Park
New Delhi 110 016
Tel: 6853857, 665445,
  6852226, 6852227
Price: Moderate
Specialities : Indian, Chinese,
  tandoori, South Indian,
  Coffee shop
For timings check with
  individual restaurants
Credit cards accepted
Partly air-conditioned

By no means a gourmet's mecca, this complex of restaurants in the trendy, designer Hauz Khas Village is, however, still worth a visit for a casual bite with friends. Both the Village Darbar, on the second floor, with its black contemporary wrought iron furniture and ikkat upholstery, and the Top of the Village barbecue, have breathtaking views of the lake and the woods that extend forever.

They are both open in the evening only. Khas Bagh, on the first floor is open for lunch and dinner, serves basic tandoori and kababs and has quite a view, too. The restaurants on the ground floor can be avoided—Mohalla (curry), the Great Wall (Chinese), Dakshin (South Indian), and Al Capone (the strangest coffee shop we've ever seen, with Rajasthani decor and wandering folk minstrels!)

None of the restaurants here are particularly cheap, nor do they constitute fine dining. However, one must at least congratulate MP Suresh Kalmadi and fashion enterpreneur, Bina Ramani on the innovative idea of creating a dictionary of restaurants in very pleasant surroundings.

Dinner here is preferable to lunch, although the shops and studios are closed in the evening. Enjoy the scenery and take in the fresh air. Look forward to an informal, relaxed evening of barbecue and beer.

Triveni Tea Terrace

This has always been one of our favourite snacky places is Delhi, at the far end of Triveni Art Gallery. You can sit indoors in the small, spotless restaurant which has black wooden tables and low rope stools, or outdoors, overlooking the impressive amphitheatre and the exquisite bougainvillaea draped walkways. The atmosphere is casual, quiet and full of young budding artists, theatre people and ladies in ethnic minority saris, with large bindis painted (not stuck) on their foreheads.

Triveni Tea Terrace
Triveni Kala Sangam
205, Tansin Marg
Opposite the Museum of
  Modern Art
Price : Inexpensive
Speciality : North Indian
Timings: 10 a.m. to 6 p.m.
Sundays closed

It's the perfect place to size up local arty folk, while munching robust Alu Ka Paratha washed down with a glass of lassi. The lunch menu is limited to some kind of mutton or kheema, shammi kababs, a vegetable like palak paneer and pullav and chapattis. Snacks like hot pakoras and sandwiches are available throughout the day. The ideal place to stop, think and snack in central Delhi, without burning a hole in your pocket.

Wenger & Co

Wenger & Co.
A-Block Connaught Place
New Delhi 110 001
Tel : 3324373, 3324403
Price : Inexpensive
Speciality : Indian Snacks
Timings : 10 a.m. to 8 p.m.
Air-conditioned

A pastry shop, Wenger also serves wonderful snacks which could take the place of a meal for those in a rush. Wenger's Shammi Kabab is both substantial and tasty. Two of them could satisfy even a big eater. The mushroom, mutton and chicken patties are of a high quality, as are the sandwiches (tomato, chicken and cheese). The Paneer Roll was delicious and so was the vegetable cutlet. All snacks are priced below Rs 10 (all inclusive). Those with a sweet tooth will find a treasure trove in the pastry and cake section at reasonable prices. Worth a visit.

Goa

Goan cuisine has a casual vivacity that matches its people. It conjures up images of sun soaked beaches, palm lined coastline and paddy fields, pounding waves and non-stop music. Food and fun go as naturally together as fish curry and feni. What's more, the relaxed locals seem to enjoy their stress-free paradise as much as visitors do. A word of advice, never be in a hurry or expect city efficiency, they are concepts unheard of here.

Goa is rampant with decent little places to eat at every glance, and usually a taverna on every corner, where you can sample generous pegs of feni, fresh urrak in season (first distillation), or any other drink, at incredibly low prices, compared to the rest of the country. Those who love seafood and pork will have a ball, but vegetarians get a sore deal as options are limited.

Although the Portuguese left in 1965, after 451 years of rule, this territory of 700 square kilometres, is still very different from the rest of India. And so is its cuisine. The Portuguese, with all their Catholic fervour, came to Goa well before the British or even the Mughals came to India, and left well after. They cocooned Goa into isolation. Hence Goan (Christian) food developed distinct flavours, which made full use of local ingredients like coconut, kokum (a souring agent used for fish), locally grown red chillies, rice and toddy vinegar. Some dishes were adapted from recipes brought in by the Portuguese from the homeland, or from their other colonies, like Cafrael from Africa, and Piri Piri from South America. It was also the Portuguese who introduced the chilli into India via Goa.

Goan Hindus usually eat fish, but not beef or pork, and they do not use vinegar in their preparations. Most restaurants, however, are run by Catholics, serving home style food.

A typical Goan meal would start with maybe Fried Mussels with drinks. The first course would be what is commonly called a 'side' or 'dry' dish of sausage or Beef Chilli Fry. It may even be a delectable Oyster Pie or Fried Fish with Reichade Masala, or even Prawn Balchao, a spicy, tangy pickle. A gravy dish, like sorpotel, a stew of pork, marinated in a mountain of finely ground masalas, vinegar and pig's blood, is served with Sannas, rice cakes fermented with toddy. Fish or prawn curry and rice always ends the feast. And you cannot leave Goa without trying their famous sweet, Bebinca (pronounced bibink), made with coconut milk, eggs and flour.

Eating out in Goa is always a memorable experience. People are generally friendly and informal, both in dress and in manner, and almost everyone speaks English, in preference to Indian languages with which they are at a total loss. Certain dishes like **Prawn Stuffed Papad, Choriz pau** (local sausage stuffed into a roll), and **Stuffed Crabs**, made famous by certain restaurants, are now available everywhere.

Prices, on the whole, are reasonable, and food even in the most modest of restaurants, will always be fresh. In the inexpensive range, there can be no doubt about the excellent quality of food at Florentine's, tucked away in Saligao. The best Goan specialities at moderate prices are always available at the ever reliable Mandovi Hotel in Panjim. For a full range of excellent dishes near the beach, there's no place like Ronil's.

For the spendthrifts, you can swear by the Goan cuisine, under the expert guidance of Chef Rego, at the Beach House, Taj Village. When you have had just about enough masala, the Banyan Tree, again at the Taj Village, headed by Chef Angelo Collaço, serves mouth-watering Thai cuisine. The Riverside Wharf at the Leela, in South Goa, with Chef Vijayan Parakkal at the helm, is your best bet for European.

Night life in Goa is continuous, especially from November to March. Most hotels have bands, and there are even parties on the beach. Besides all this is the Haystack, an outdoor floor show and dance, held every Friday night (on the road to Anjuna), which also serves excellent Goan food. A branch has also recently opened in South Goa.

For a lasting taste of Goa, you have to visit Mapusa Market on Friday, and the famous old-time store in the market complex, Pedro Vicente Vaz, where you can buy some interesting home products, wines, and beautifully bottled feni.

Watch out for the food served in shacks on the beach in Goa. They may look romantic, but cleanliness is not a high point. If you like seafood, spice and coconut, Goa is a gourmet's paradise.

A meal for one person
Inexpensive: under 100 rupees Moderate: 100 to 250 rupees Expensive: over 250 rupees

21 Coconuts

An up-market shack run by two Swiss designers, smack on the beach. Great if you're staying at the Taj or in Candolim itself, but a pain to find if you're not. You can get to it via the approach road opposite Canara Bank at Candolim, or from the Candolim Health Club. Once you get there, 21 Coconuts is a real breath of fresh air, a delightful European style oasis in a sea of fish curry and rice.

21 Coconuts
On the beach
Candolim
(5 minutes from Taj)
Bardez, Goa
Price : Moderate
Speciality : European
Timings : 8 a.m. to 11 p.m.
Only open in season (October to March)

The original decor of this restaurant was completely off the wall—Irani, marble-topped tables and original colonial furniture. Apparently, everything was on loan and was taken back one bright morning. It has now been replaced with stark black furniture designed by Sonja and Thomas themselves.

21 Coconuts serves a daily menu, chalked up on the blackboard, with two or three choices for every course. Mouth-watering cakes and desserts, breakfast to order and juices complete the offerings. The cuisine is fresh and simple, like home-made noodles with pesto sauce, Quiche, Carrot and Raisin Salad and Fish Steak in butter, with a healthy accent on light, vegetarian dishes and western style seafood. All the raw vegetables are washed properly, so the tossed salads are perfectly safe for sensitive stomachs.

A tropical 'Cuisine Legere' on the beach.

Bob's Inn

Bob's Inn
Main Candolim road
About 1 mile from the Taj
Bardez, Goa
Tel: 277312
Price : Moderate
Specialities : Goan,
 Continental
Timings : Noon to 3 p.m.;
 6 to 11 p.m.
Bar licence

Whatever you do, don't argue with the management. The owner, Bob, spends most of his time propping up the bar, and hates to be disturbed. This aside, Bob's is a great place to size up the local hippy and expat scene. The welcoming scent of 'grass' fills the air, and heavy discussions on existentialism take place in the intimate little nooks and corners, where you can huddle and whisper. This is also a great place to have crab (jumbo) in any style; xacuti, plain boiled, in a soup or in a salad. Ask the waiter in the tight shorts for daily specials. Go for the seafood and more 'European' sounding dishes on the menu.

This used to be a very cheap place, but is slowly becoming expensive, by local standards. A good meeting place as everybody knows it.

Cajueiro (Cashew Tree)

It isn't often that one finds a foreign returned Goan entrepreneur, ready to risk his savings in a venture of this kind. But John Lobo, who for many years worked for Saudi Airways as their Catering Manager, did just that. His main problem is that he has still not been granted a liquor licence, which, he says, would give the restaurant a boost. However, Lobo does seem to have created a rather relaxed, clean place, decorated in a Goan fishing village style, with a thatched roof, fishing nets and terracotta pots.

Cajueiro (Cashew Tree)
Alto Betim
Off the Panjim-Mapusa highway, between the Catering College and the Zuari bridge
Bardez, Goa
Tel: 217375
Price : Moderate
Specialities : Goan, North Indian
Timings : Noon to 3 p.m.; 7.30 p.m. to 11 p.m.

The menu is unusually extensive, ranging from Goan Continental, Tandoori to Chinese. We have never quite tasted squid prepared the way they do it here. Tiny calamares are stuffed with a prawn mixture and coated with a 'brown' sauce, which is refreshingly un-fishy. The Chicken Cafrael, Masala Mussels (a little heavy on the red masala) and Fish curry (served with the dried prawn relish, Kismur) are highly recommended. The fish curry, incidentally, is also served with Goan pickles, made by Lobo's wife, and a Red Chowli Bhaji, a local vegetable at last! Our six-year-old son assured us that the tandoori was the best he had had in Goa.

Plans for the future include a lobster tank with a more free style of cuisine: 'You catch it and we'll cook it whichever way you want.'

Captain Lobo's

Captain Lobo's Beach
  Hideaway
Cobra Vaddo
Baga Road
Calangute
Bardez, Goa 403 516
Tel: 083227-6103
Price: Moderate
Specialities : Goan,
  Continental
Timings : 8 a.m. to 11 p.m.
Bar licence
Air-conditioned

Unfortunately, this is no longer the hideaway that ex-seaman Lance Lobo, had envisaged. His Spanish-style villas are part of the hacienda complex which he shares with Colonia Santa Maria (CSM). Lance's set up revolves around a small poolside restaurant, and a rooftop open terrace dining-hall, which is quite exquisite. Lance's chef, when he is sober (which is most of the time in season), is a whiz in the kitchen. You'll find all the Goan staples here; wonderfully succulent, grilled Morzo fish, Fish Curry and rice, pomfret grilled to perfection, great sorpotel, Goa sausage and very fresh tiger prawns. But meet Lance, a very likeable and ready to please hunk of a man, for daily specials and unusual requests. If you do not find him on the premises, he will probably be on the beach, picking up the day's catch from the local fishermen or wandering around Tinto market for something to flatter the palate.

Casa Portuguesa

One of the most expensive (outside the five-star brigade) and most beautiful little restaurants in Goa. Casa Portuguesa is what it claims to be, an old Portuguese house, with furniture and music (Portuguese fado) to match. The whole theme is handled with a great deal of taste and style.

On a good day, the food is memorable, especially the Portuguese-inspired cuisine, and 'natural' dishes like a simple bowl of boiled prawns in their shells, the stuffed crabs and Guisado, a delicious fish stew. The Chateaubriand, medium rare, is simple perfection. Don't make the mistake of asking for it rare, it really does come, unlike elsewhere in India, quite raw.

You can take your own wine and sit either in the intimate dining-room indoors, in the garden, or on the veranda. We prefer to sit on the veranda, listen to the sound of Amalia Rodrigues, and enjoy a simple, perfect dinner in candlelight. Some nights, Francisco, the wayward owner, has been known to bellow out a few tunes with his guitar. He probably has the most out of tune voice in Goa, but his effort is commendable. A wonderful place for a special night out, but expensive compared with other restaurants in Goa.

Casa Portuguesa
Baga Road
Baga Beach
Goa
**Price: Moderate/
   Expensive**
Specialities : Goan,
   Continental
Timings : Noon to 3 p.m.;
   7.30 p.m. to 11.30 p.m.
Bar licence
Only open in season (October
   to March)
Air-conditioned

Crosshill Bar

Crosshill Bar
Dona Paula
Perched on the left of the
main Dona Paula
roundabout
P.O. N-10
Cross Hill Road
Dona Paula
Goa 403 004
Price : Inexpensive
Speciality : Goan
Timings : 10 a.m. to 11 p.m.
Bar licence

Nelson, a quiet, unassuming sort of chap, owns this very conveniently situated bar, at the junction before you turn left for Cidade de Goa. The decor is really like any other modest establishment in Goa, simple tables and chairs on a small, breezy veranda. If you are lost, pop into this bar perched on the left of the roundabout. There is nothing hair-raising about it, except that the food is fresh and good, and the booze cheap. Fried fish, Mussels and Squid make great pre-lunch snacks, and the famous Goan Choriz Pau (spicy Goan sausage, fried and stuffed in a fresh bread) is hard to beat here. Nelson does a very reasonable cheese and vegetable sandwich, which is about all you'll get if you are vegetarian, but accepts orders for any special request a day in advance.

Florentine's Bar and Restaurant

In one sentence, Florentine's, with its limited menu and home-style way of functioning, probabaly serves the best and the cheapest Goan food in Goa today. Run by the young, smiling Florencio Caithan, this is a family business worth talking about. With very little catering background, Caithan, dressed always in shorts, T-shirt and slippers, is a real whiz in the kitchen, which is opposite the restaurant. You can sit in the old restaurant itself, either on the ground floor, which is a little dark, on the first floor, or outside in the makeshift thatched enclosure. Make no mistake, there is no hint of sophistication here. Tables and chairs are the folding variety and the clientele, mostly locals.

Florentine's Bar and
  Restaurant
Next to the Cottage
  Industries Emporium
Saligao
Bardez, Goa 403511
Tel: 278249
Price : Inexpensive
Speciality : Goan
Timings : Noon to 3 p.m.;
  6.30 to 10.30 p.m.
Mondays closed
Bar licence

It's a wonder anybody can find this taverna, which is down the alley next to the Cottage Industries Emporium, on the main Candolim-Panjim road. We were introduced to it one late monsoon evening by Lance Lobo of Captain Lobo's Hideaway. After an evening of heady bar hopping, we needed food badly, and as it was off season, most restaurants had shut early or altogether. 'You'll get the best Chicken Cafrael in town here,' boasted Lance. Unfortunately, by the time we staggered in, Caithan was closing up, but after a reasonable amount of begging, he very generously gave us one of the chickens he had saved for his own family dinner. The hot, pan fried bird, smothered in a sauce that one can only describe as, 'near to heaven as is possible', captured our hearts and taste buds for life. Cafrael is a recipe brought to Goa by the Portuguese (from Africa), the base of which is green masala and black pepper. The chicken is marinated overnight. A weight is then put on top, and the next day, it is pan fried. We returned to Florentine's on several occasions and in several different seasons, to find the quality of the chicken, and everything else on the menu, as magnificient as the first time.

Everything on the menu here is fresh. We went for the Prawns and Mussels, mildly spiced and pan fried with a gentle coating of rawa; and the Pomfret and Lady Fish Recheide, stuffed very lightly with the most gentle red masala East of Suez. Soft pau (local bread) is served with all the dishes, but a very interesting fried rice is available if you are still hungry. Washed down with copious amounts of home-made feni (Rs 2 a peg!) or beer, a hearty meal for two will probably cost you less than Rs 150 (all inclusive).

Happy eating

Goenchin

Standard Chinese lanterns and the familiar smell of soya sauce and vinegar greet you as you walk into this small, dimly-lit (in fact downright dark) restaurant, which is part of the Mandovi hotel, though nowhere near it.

Goenchin
Mandovi Apartments
Dr Dada Vaidya Road
Panaji
Goa 403 001
Tel : 45718
Price : Moderate
Speciality : Chinese
Timings : 12.30 to 2.45 p.m.;
  7.30 to 10.45 p.m.
Credit cards accepted
Bar licence
Air-conditioned

The food, like the decor, is very average, but if you are in the mood for Chinese while in Goa, this is your best bet. Start with any of the Chef's Special Soups. Ho Kum, an egg drop soup, rich with goodies like meat balls, mushrooms (tinned) and bamboo shoots, with, thankfully, no glutinous corn starch, is well worth trying. The Pork Spare Ribs came highly recommended, but we were presented with pork chops, overdone at that, in disguise.

However, try the Stir Fried Prawns with cashew nuts, or the Hai Nyuk Chang Theu Ha Yin, prawns and tender pea pods topped with a fresh crab sauce. These go well with Singapore Fried Mei Foon (rice noodles), and maybe a dish of Chinese black mushrooms in oyster sauce.

It is refreshing to find subtle flavours in a restaurant of this kind, and dishes marked with a chilli not really all that spicy. Be warned, however, portions are small, and most dishes are floating in sauce, unless specified on the menu or by you. Once you order an extra dish or two to compensate for this fact, you could well wind up paying Rs 250 a head, which we frankly found a little over the top for this calibre of Chinese restaurant.

La Gondola

La Gondola
Leela Beach Goa
Mobor, Cavelossim, Salcette
 Goa
Tel : 6363, 6373. Fax : 6352
Price : Expensive
Speciality : Italian
Timings : 12.30 to 2.45 p.m.;
  7.30 to 10.30 p.m.
Credit cards accepted
Bar licence

Our only reservation about this Italian, trattoria type restaurant is its location. Situated in the Leela lobby, in full view of coach loads of hot, sweaty tourists, regimentary garlanding and general lobby activities, it should probably be a Coffee Shop. In fact it is, more often than not, mistaken for one.

All this aside, the Italian cuisine, again in the capable hands of chef Vijayan Parakkal, is exemplary. Start off with an assortment of Antipasti—Seafood Salad with squid, fish, clams and prawns; Minced Shrimp in chilli mayonnaise; and Roasted Peppers in olive oil and garlic. Or plum for a fragrant Neopolitan Clam soup. All the pasta is home-made from local wheat, and generous with fresh herbs from the Leela Nursery. The Spaghetti with pesto sauce, made us feel we were really in Liguria, Northern Italy, where the dish originates. The Lasagne was creamy, with a sprinkling of crisp fried basil—a nice touch. This was followed by an amazing feni and lime sorbet, to clean and refresh the palate before the meat course. We tried the Pork fillet (the leanest pork we have had in Goa), served with onion-like green beans and sage butter.

Sweet things are more standard; Italian Tiramisu, Lemon Cheese cake and a rich, rounded Sabaglione—all beautifully presented.

Pity about the lobby, but definitely try the food.

Kamat Hotel

A must for all vegetarians and those who love South Indian food, in a land with few options for low budget, vegetarian fare. Kamat is the oldest South Indian restaurant in Panjim, situated very conveniently in the centre of town. Like other Kamats, this one too is simple, with two sections, both identical. Each one has basic wooden tables and Rexine covered benches. The place is spotless and crockery and cutlery is stainless steel. Good South Indian staples like upma, idli, vada and a variety of dosas are all available. The

Kamat Hotel
Church Road
(near main Panjim Church)
Panjim, Goa
Tel.: 46116
Price : Inexpensive
Speciality : South Indian
  Vegetarian
Timings : 8 a.m. to 9 p.m.
Partly air-conditioned

Thali, a steal at Rs 15 is much recommended, with three fluffy puris, two freshly prepared vegetables, rasam, sambhar, yoghurt, pickles and papad. For dessert, try the superb Gulab Jamun, polished off with aromatic South Indian coffee.

Service is very fast which is handy as this is not the kind of place you can hang around for long. A nice, clean always reliable restaurant of the Kamat chain. Although new South Indian restaurants have recently opened in Panjim, this remains the pure vegetarian flagship of Goa.

O Coqueiro (Coconut Tree)

O Coqueiro (Coconut Tree)
Alto Porvorim
Bardez, Goa 403 521
Tel : 217217, 217344, 217806, 217427
Price : Moderate
Speciality : Goan
Timings : 11.30 a.m. to 3 p.m.; 7.30 to 11 p.m.
Credit cards accepted
Bar licence

O Coqueiro has been described as a 'Road house', Restaurant and Pub. Is that where road hogs go? We would describe this more on the lines of a Spanish 'venta', a kind of dhaba which serves home cooked food to locals. The establishment is large, with an outdoor dining-hall, a smaller indoor one, which is less inviting, and a bar. The furniture is basic but the hospitality warm and generous.

The colourful owner of O Coqueiro, Gines Viegas, opened this restaurant in October 1972 when there was no bridge across the river (you had to cross by ferry), and no five-star hotel in this part of Goa. He started off, serving a buffet at Rs 7.50 per head. Prices are just as reasonable today. In fact, O Coqueiro has enjoyed an unparalled success for a restaurant of this kind, due largely to its good food and earthy prices.

Viegas once told us a story of a Sikh gentleman who came to sell him Goan sausages. With a burst of laughter and arms in the air, Viegas asked, 'How can a Sikh make Goan sausages? He was mixing pork and beef with artificial vinegar!' On that basis, Viegas, a real foodie and a great cook himself, serves only what he knows best, his own native cuisine. 'To make good Goa sausages,' he continued, 'we start in September. Firstly, we make our own toddy vinegar, which is kept for six months in wooden vats.' The other essential factor is the drying of the sausages in the sun. If they are not dried properly, they lack that essential flavour and will spoil quickly.

Other specialities of the restaurant, of which there are numerous, are prawns stuffed papad, nowadays available in many Goan restaurants, but actually invented by Gines Viegas. Cooked, spiced prawns (or crabs) are wrapped in a small piece of freshly roasted papad, and then deep fried: a wonderful example of hybrid cuisine responding to local tastes. Viegas' Mole (pickled fish), Para (dried fish pickle), Dried Prawn Curry, Wild Boar Vindaloo, Salt Tongue and Suckling Pig, are all a must for those interested in a real epicurean adventure. His Peixe Guisado, a delicate Portuguese stew of fish and potatoes gently simmered in a broth of onions, tomatoes and green chillies, cloves and garlic, and Chicken Cafrael are also highly recommended.

Viegas loves to meet foodies, so don't feel shy to ask for him if there is something special you would like to have.

Goa at a glance

Palmera

Palmera
The Bogmalo Beach Resort
Goa
Tel : 8345, 2191-2
Fax : 8345, 2510.
Price : Expensive
Speciality : Indian,
 Continental, Goan
Timings : 12.30 to 2.45 p.m.;
 8 to 10.45 p.m.
Air-conditioned

A small set up for a five-star hotel, all the eating areas—the restaurant, the veranda, bar and poolside, are within staggering distance of each other. We would recommend the veranda or poolside, with the wonderful sea breeze and splendid view of Bogmalo Bay. Make a point to speak with chef John Thomas, a normally reserved chap, who comes alive when he finds a friendly foodie. We would recommend the barbecue; the grilled lobster gently smeared with mustard, pomfret, kingfish and squid. The Stuffed Crabs are prepared in yet another Goan style. No red masala in sight, the crab meat is removed, mixed with a hint of onion, green chilli and curry powder, put back in the shell and deep fried. A great snack with a glass of beer. Of the Goan specialities, go for the unorthodox Prawn Balchao made with the most superbly soft prawns in Goa. The Balchao 'pickle' is prepared in advance, with the addition of onions tomatoes and garlic, and the prawns are added at the very last minute to preserve their texture and flavour. The Pomfret Reichade is also excellent.

A neat little oasis, perched on a rock, overlooking one of the most beautiful bays in Goa. And the only five-star restaurant near (ten minutes from) Dabolim Airport.

Pinto's Bar And Restaurant

You can't miss this little bar on the main road to South Goa. Despite the vague address, it is the only Goan taverna worth its sausage, for miles around. Whatever you do, don't go into the ground floor bar, which is dark and dingy. Opt for the first floor terrace, which is also tiny but where you will probably rub shoulders with card sharps and eat some honest to goodness, down to earth, Goan home cooking at unbelievably low prices.

Pinto's Bar And Restaurant
Varca
(Corner of the main road to Leela and turning before Ramada, on the right)
Salcette, Goa
Tel: 245353, 220566
Price : Inexpensive
Speciality : Goan
Timings : 10 a.m. to 3 p.m.; 6 to 11 p.m.
Bar licence

Start off with Fish Cutlets, made by Anthony Pinto's mum, in her house just behind the bar. Then opt for a half or full plate of Goa Sausage, either in a bread roll (choriz—pau) or plain grilled. The sausage is particularly good here, as it is served quite dry. We like spare parts, and so ordered the Salt Tongue, a family dish which you rarely find in Goan restaurants. The Roast Beef and Beef Chilli Fry are also recommended. For fish eaters, both the Masala Fish and Reichade Pomfret were tasty. Avoid the Pork Vindaloo, which was fatty. Don't overlook the home-made mango pickle and vegetables pickled in brine, lying on the table. If you are desperate, the Fish Curry and rice is standard and spicy, but we would recommend that you stick to the dry items. A mini feast for two with drinks came to around Rs 100.

Even if you have to make a detour, stop at Pinto's. You won't find food of this quality and at these prices anywhere in the area.

Riorico

Riorico
Mandovi Hotel
D. B. Bandodkar Marg
Panaji, Goa
Tel : 46270
Price : Moderate
Specialities : Goan, North
  Indian, Continental
Timings : 12.30 to 3 p.m.;
  7:30 p.m. to 11 p.m.
Credit cards accepted
Bar licence
Air-conditioned

Few large hotels in India, fewer still in Goa, can boast of decent 'home' style cooking. The Mandovi Hotel situated in the heart of Goa's capital city is a welcome exception. Panjim, or Panaji as it is now called, is a working town, with real Goans, many of whom steadfastly lunch or dine regularly at the Mandovi Hotel. The expression 'Old World Charm' may sound clichéd, but it describes the experience here. Originally started in 1952 to cater to Goan and Portuguese dignitaries, the Mandovi has an impressive record of having catered to all the Indian Prime Ministers. It also has the highest Food and Beverage sales in Goa today.

Although Panjim is bursting at the seams with quaint little tavernas, the High Tide Bar, on the first floor of the Mandovi hotel, overlooking the vast expanse of river which the hotel is named after, is as good a place as any to begin a venture with Goan cuisine. The Goan and Continental food here is simply superb. Heading the four Goan chefs is Caridad Aphonso, a portly man of few words but much magic, who has been with the hotel since its inception. His specialities include Fish or Prawn Balchao, Stuffed Mussels, the devilishly (spicy) tasty Fish Amotik, and the best Fish or Prawn curry (served with a dry prawn relish called Kismur) in town.

The quality of the Continental dishes took us quite by surprise. The fried fish fillet, simple but well prepared, the Galantine of Turkey (only available at Christmas) and the Caldo Verde, a freshly-made potato and spinach soup are highly recommended. In fact, this is the first restaurant in India where we had, not only tender, but delectable turkey.

Desserts were good, but not earth shattering. The ice cream and chocolate sauce, Crepe Mandovi stuffed with coconut and dripping ice cream, chocolate sauce and nuts, and the flambé Alaska, are among the best.

Much of the success of Mandovi's kitchen is the no-nonsense, good quality ingredients, prepared as freshly as they are in Goan homes. Masalas are ground every day, and nothing is carried forward or frozen. Prices are high by Goan standards, but well below five-star. It is worth every penny.

Riorico is a large restaurant with elegant wooden furniture, chandeliers and exemplary service. Many of the waiters, like the chefs, have been faithfully serving here since the hotel opened over forty years ago.

Bogmalo Beach at sunset

Riverside

Riverside
(On the bank of the river
which flows into the Baga
Bay)
Baga Beach
Calangute
Bardez, Goa
Tel : 6062, 6186
Price : Moderate
Specialities : Goan,
Continental
Timings : Noon to 2:30 p.m.;
7:30 to 10 p.m.
Bar licence
Open only in season (October
to March)

Quite an amazing location for this home-run little hotel and restaurant. It is within walking distance of all the 'in' places in Baga, and yet affords the great luxury of seclusion too. The rooms are modest, unlike the food, which ranks among the best in the area. The daily menu is chalked up on a blackboard, and usually includes simple home cooked specialities like Spaghetti with Mussels, fish in garlic sauce and maybe a plate of delicious grilled sardines. It is advisable to book in advance, unless you are staying there, as a limited amount of food is cooked every day. A couple of dining tables have been placed on the sand outside the veranda, because of the growing popularity of this restaurant.

Special requests are welcomed, if ordered in advance, and if possible ask for a table by the window in the main dining-room. All the windows frame an exquisite view of the river.

Riverside Wharf

An elegant, underrated restaurant away from the main resort complex, serving delicate Goan Cuisine and fresh Seafood (on display). Dinner here is magical, with the palms swaying just outside the windows and the boats passing by. You cannot get more 'riverside' than this. The food is no less. The Crab Soufflé, the chef's creation served in the shell, with a topping of light whisked egg white, is deliciously creamy. The pan fried Pomfret with a tomato coulis, and Prawns with a warm hollandaise sauce, were worth hefty praise. But our confirmed favourite and something we would drive all the way to South Goa for again, were the Lobster medallions with a fresh dill sauce.

Among the Goan specialities, we would recommend the Prawn Balchao, Mackerel Reichado and Red Pumpkin Mergor. Incidentally, there is plenty of choice for vegetarians, despite the accent on seafood.

Vijayan Parakkal, executive chef of the Leela is undoubtedly one of the few, inspired, young chefs in India today. After several years of experience in luxury hotels in the Middle East, he came back to India and was selected one of the five best chefs of India in 1991, which he clearly deserved. His creativity, versatility and experimentation is clearly what gives him the edge.

A riverside table is recommended, but watch out for mosquitoes, or ask for an anti-mosquito coil to be placed under your table.

Riverside Wharf
The Leela Beach Goa
Mobor Cavelossim
Salcette, Goa 403731
Tel:246363,246373
Fax : 246352
Price : Expensive
Speciality : Seafood (Goan and Continental)
Timings : 12.30 to 3 p.m.; 7.30 to 11 p.m.
Reservation recommended
Air-conditioned

Chef Vijayan Parakkal

Ronil Beach Resort

Ronil Beach Resort
Baga Calangute Road
Bardez, Goa 403516
Tel : 27-6101, 6099
Price : Moderate
Specialities : Indian, Goan,
  Chinese, Continental
Timings : 7 a.m. to 11 p.m.
Credit cards accepted
Bar licence

Not to be confused with Ronil Royale next door, this is probably the most efficiently run hotel of this type in the Baga-Candolim area. Outside the five-star hotels, this is one of your best bets in luxury dining. You can eat in the open dining-room, around the pool or on the veranda. All the cuisines served here are first rate. Of the Goan specialities, the Squid stuffed with prawns and Prawn Balchao are a must. However, this is the place you should come when you really need a change from Goan red masala. The Chinese menu is extensive and alarmingly good, considering the lack of ingredients available in Goa. Of the Continental dishes, the Grilled Fish (try the local Morzo, a succulent fillet from a large marine creature weighing no less than ten kilograms) with garlic sauce, and Tiger Prawns are excellent. We also recommend the tandoori section, especially the hot tandoori rotis with a bowl of simple Palak (spinach).

Much of the success of both the hotel and the excellent restaurant is due to the Resident Manager's input. A great foodie himself, Rui Madre Deus, is always dashing around looking for all kinds of new ideas to improve or extend his menu, even if they are only daily or seasonal specials.

In season, a different live band plays almost every night by the pool. A great plus point is that the hotel and restaurant are open throughout the year, even during the monsoons, when they offer very attractive low season discounts. The food is consistently reliable.

Seaview Bar And Restaurant

There is nothing extraordinary about this modest family owned-and-run bar except that it represents Goa at its earthiest best. We had tripped across this place on the way back from Dona Paula a few years back. You get to it (it is signposted) via a dirt track which runs to the sea on the main Miramar-Dona Paula road. All we could remember was the sound of the sea, the superb yet simple location on the waterfront, the faint smell of freshly pulled in

Seaview Bar And Restaurant
Aivao Beach
Caranzalem (on the way to
   Dona Paula), Goa
Price : Inexpensive
Speciality : Seafood
Timings : Noon to 3 p.m.;
   7 p.m. to midnight
Bar open the whole day

fishing nets and the large shots of feni. This was enough to warrant another visit.

We discovered the Rodrigues family. Pa is a fisherman by profession, who once owned trawlers in Mozambique and now spends his time making special fishing nets. Ma does all the cooking using her own special blend of stone-ground masalas. And son, Diago, a pleasant, calm sort, who goes out fishing himself, runs the place.

On the surface, this is your run-of-the-mill bar, but once you taste the food and the feni, overlooking the calm blue sea, this may as well be heaven. The secret is undoubtedly the freshness of the seafood. Specialities include Chonak (from January to the end of May), a delicious, soft creamy textured fish which is caught in brackish waters, near rocks which you can see on the other side of the bay. Fried Mussels, Chilli Fried Squid, Red Snapper and a special red Prawn which is only available during the rains (June to August) are other delicacies to look out for.

Diago takes orders for special requests, including Lobster, Tiger Prawns, etc., at a day's notice. Although a teetotaler himself, he goes all the way to Sankerin near Bicholim in North East Goa, to select his Cashew Feni and Urrak (first distillation of feni available in April and May), which he sells by the peg and by the bottle.

A must for all those who love the simple pleasures of life.

Sousa Lobo

Sousa Lobo
Calangute Beach
Bardez, Goa
**Price : Inexpensive/
Moderate**
Speciality : Goan
Timings : 11 a.m. to 3 p.m.;
7 to 10.30 p.m.
Bar licence
Only open in season (October
to March)

Sousa Lobo is the Goan equivalent of the corner bistro, the only difference being that it is smack on the busiest stretch of the Calangute Beach. You'll find everybody and anybody in this modest family-run restaurant, but especially Goans, from all over the world, who yearn for family favourites like Beef Chilli Fry and Sorpotel, at very reasonable prices.

Sousa Lobo reminds us of all the wonderful Goan ladies that we know, who, through the years, have managed to perfect a few everyday dishes, which are their trademark. At Sousa Lobo's, you'll get Salt Tongue as tender as Aunty Bella's (not her own), Prawn Balchao almost as good as Gilda's, and Potato Chops (with a stuffing of mince), which, on a good day could rival Ophie's.

This is primarily an eating place, inside or on the long veranda overlooking the sea. But don't expect swaying palms. There is no greenery on this part of the beach, which is actually beginning to look as tatty as Bombay's Chowpatty. The decor and seating is basic, and the restaurant often quite crowded, but this is a good place to size up the local scene.

St Anthony's

This superbly located beach restaurant and bar remains unchanged and untarnished by its popularity. We love sitting on the benches overlooking the beach and wriggling our toes in the sand. After all, this is what Goa is all about.

St Anthony's is open from very early in the morning (for breakfast) to very late at night (they close when you're ready to quit). We feel the best time to enjoy St Anthony's is at sunset when most of the lunch crowd has disappeared. You can have a wonderful sultry afternoon swim in Baga Bay, and then enjoy a long cool drink to the sounds of Ella Fitzgerald. 'Eats' at St Anthony's would not stretch to gourmet fare, but are still excellent quality, especially the seafood. The daily lunch and dinner menus, chalked up on a central blackboard, always feature both Goan specialities like Shark Amotik, Pomfret Recheide, and European type dishes like Shrimp Cocktail and Lobster Thermidor. Our favourites are the Chilli Fry Calamare (squid), Mussels in Goan masala, and plain boiled Baby Crabs.

Breakfast is a treat here, with a whole range of freshly squeezed juices and waffles with honey.

An unpretentious, very relaxed, and still a very reasonable place to 'hang out', but packed, at meal times, during season. Service can be atrocious if there is a crowd.

St Anthony's
Baga Beach
Bardez, Goa
Price: Inexpensive/ Moderate
Speciality : Goan, Continental
Timings : 8 am. to 11 p.m.
Bar licence

St Francis Xavier's Trattoria

St Francis Xavier's Trattoria
Taj Fort Aguada Beach Resort
Sinquerim
Bardez, Goa
Tel: 276201–10
Price : Expensive
Speciality : Italian
Timings : 12.30 to 2.30 p.m.;
  7.30 to 10.30 p.m.
Credit cards accepted
Bar licence

With a view like this, you need little else. The easygoing, relaxed mood of the Trattoria, with its checked tablecloths and superb setting, overlooking miles of sandy coastline, is Goa in a nutshell. Yet five-star comforts are close at hand. The Trattoria is a stone's throw from the pool, the barbecue and the buffet. The menu is fairly standard and unambitious, but well prepared and presented. You must start with the Tribale di Melanzane Nicoise, a wonderfully tasty aubergine pâté, which is served with crisp garlic toasts. The pasta is either home-made or imported, and cooked, as it should be, al dente. Both the Spaghetti alla Romana, tossed with generous amounts of olive oil, mushrooms, garlic and parmesan and the classic Fettucine Carbonara, with cream, egg and bacon bits, were delicious.

But the *pièce de résistance* was undoubtedly the grilled Baby Bekti marinated with garlic and lemon, and basted with olive oil. Choose from any of the fresh seafood on display in the barbecue area, or ask the chef for his suggestions. The evening we dined here, there was exceedingly fresh mullet, lobster, tiger prawns, squid and kingfish (surmai) displayed. We would call it a day here, but if you feel like being a pig, then go for the Tiramisu or the Carved Fruit Platter.

The Banyan Tree

Like the Beach House, the success of this restaurant is due mainly to its chef, Angelo Collaço, who treats his food with an almost meditative quality. Situated under an enormous old banyan tree, this Thai eating house, with its temple-like structure, spacious verandas and exquisite flora and fauna, is probably the most elegant place to dine in Goa. At night the whole place is lit up which makes it quite magical. We like to sit on the veranda, overlooking the water which surrounds the restaurant. There is also an air-conditioned section in the centre of the structure, but you frankly need only go there in May. The decor is stylish, with cane and blue matting and tall green palms everywhere.

The Banyan Tree
Taj Holiday Village
Sinquerim
Bardez, Goa 403515
Tel: 276201–9 Ext. 583
Price : Expensive
Speciality : Thai
Timings : 12.30 to 2.45 p.m.;
7.30 to 11 p.m.
Credit cards accepted
Bar licence
Partly air-conditioned

The cuisine is authentic to the core. Collaço did his Thai training at the Oriental Hotel in Bangkok, and is helped in his task by the Thai herb garden on the premises.

The yardstick by which Thai cuisine can be judged is the famous soup, Tom Yam Goong. This version is not red with chilli oil, as is more common, but is almost a cloudy fragrant consomme of Thai herbs and milky white prawns. The cold starters are all masterpieces of preparation—Yam Ba Mee Koong (spiced prawns with glass noodles), Laab (minced lamb with mint and lime) and a truly exquisite Som Tham Malagow, a raw papaya salad. Other winners are Migrob, a sort of Thai bhelpuri, red curry served with prawns and poached cucumber, and the most soothing spinach, simmered in coconut cream. Our undisputed favourite was the fresh Steamed Mussels, topped with a creamy coconut sauce.

Chef Angelo Collaço

A great escape from Goan cuisine, if you are in an exotic and luxurious frame of mind. Wonderful service.

Chef Rego and his smoked fish

The Beach House

For those who want to taste great Goan food in the lap of casual luxury, this is undoubtedly the place. You can just about see the beach from this restaurant, which goes well with the relaxed mood of this five-star resort. Chef Rego serves an imaginative selection of Indian, Goan and Continental dishes, but it is undoubtedly his 'Ghorchen Jevon' (Goan food) which reigns supreme. The Crab Xecxec, Clams in coconut, and the traditional Fish Curry with unpolished Goan rice are superb. For those with a taste for splendid things, tiger prawns and lobsters are always available in season. Despite this being a five-star restaurant, all the Goan masalas, a different one for each preparation (xacuti, cafrael, sorpotel, vindaloo, etc.) are stone ground. Poisson à la Raiza (named after Rego's daughter), poached fillets of fish on a bed of spinach, topped with shrimps and an unctuous creamy curry sauce is a wonderful option in the Continental section.

The Beach House
Taj Holiday Village
Sinquerim
Bardez, Goa 403519
Tel: 276201–10
Price: Expensive
Specialities : Goan, Indian and Continental
Timings : Noon to 3.30 p.m.; 7.30 to 11.30 p.m.
Credit cards accepted
Bar licence

If toddy takes your fancy, then Anthony Noronha, the resident toddy tapper, will be sent up a coconut tree to pamper your request. And if it's smoked fish you feel like, don't be surprised to see Rego himself fanning a bunch of hay at the back of the kitchen. What is charming about the Beach House is the ambience; casual, yet clean, efficient yet relaxed. Dark stone flooring, terracotta pots and serving utensils, shells—are nonchalantly scattered around to remind you where you are. An expensive deal for Goan food, but well worth it if you feel like spoiling yourself.

The Bougainvillea

The Bougainvillea
Grandpa's Inn
Anjuna, Goa 403 509
Tel: 273271; Fax: 274370
Price : Moderate
Specialities : European,
  Indian
Timings : 12.30 to 3 p.m.;
  7.30 to 11.30 p.m.
Bar licence

What was previously a beautiful restaurant and ancestral home, Grandpa's Inn, has been carefully transformed into an efficiently-run little hotel with a delightful garden restaurant. Micha Zell, an enterprising young German, with the help of some of his countrymen, has kept the charm and grace of the house intact, added a swimming pool, and 'spruced' up the gardens. The black wrought iron and cane furniture, black crockery and red and black decor, complete the picture.

The menu is a daily affair, which changes according to what is available and fresh in the market every morning, always a smart move in Goa. It is an interesting exercise, if unintentional, in fusion cuisine. Curries and kormas, mildly spiced and without a trace of oil, appear alongside 'Chinese inspired' dishes and simple grilled items. What we especially liked was that each dish is pre-plated, beautifully presented and was a complete meal in itself. The Kolhapuri Pomfret, for example, was tasty with a hint of spice, and served with an elegantly rolled papad, rice, naan and salad. We especially enjoyed the Chicken Pâté, a gallantine of chicken, cashew nuts and kishmish, served with brown bread and fresh green lettuce, and the Cold Chicken, served with a curry sauce in half an avocado. Desserts are deliciously light, and almost always served with fruit.

This is by no means gourmet cuisine, but an amazing effort to produce something original and well presented in spotlessly clean, charming surroundings.

A little off the beaten track, if you do not have your own transport, but well worth a visit.

Venite

Another little taverna whose quality has somewhat deteriorated because of tourism. Venite's location is prime, and the ambience reminds you of the side lanes of a sleepy Portuguese village. Tables for two are perched at narrow windows with sun soaked wrought iron balconies, overlooking the street below. The bare wooden floor and empty bottles hung around haphazardly, bear testament to great wild days where one would munch from twelve to five in the afternoon, soak in the street life and be brought plates of delicious Goan snacks and seafood. Today Venite is still high on atmosphere, but Lewis, the owner of this successful little establishment, wants to become a fisherman. We don't blame him. The menu, though fun to look at and reasonably priced, is clearly catering for the foreign tourist. Everything goes with chips and salad, and the portion of the main dish itself, besides the chips and salad, has greatly shrunk in size and quality. The best way to feel whatever magic is left, is to avoid the food and stick to a drink, the view and maybe a snack.

Venite
Dr Cunha Gonsalves Road
  (2nd turning left after the
  GPO when heading into
  Panjim)
Panjim, Goa
Tel : 45537
Price : Moderate
Speciality : Goan
Timings : Breakfast–8 a.m. to
  noon; Lunch–noon to 3 p.m.;
  Dinner–7 to 10 p.m.
Bar licence
Sundays closed

White House

White House
Dona Paula
Left at the Cross Hill Bar
 crossroads, first left up the
 hill
Goa 403004
Price : Inexpensive
Speciality : Goan
Timings : 11 a.m. to 3 p.m.;
 7 to 11 p.m.
Bar licence

A little out of the way, but the White House has the most spectacular view imaginable of the Mandovi river, miles of coconut palms and clear blue skies. It is really something straight from a picture postcard. There is usually an adequate breeze, as the restaurant is perched on the edge of a hill, but when there isn't, it can get a little stifling, with enormous windows on three sides which let in the bright sun.

The food is down to earth, nothing to write home about, but fresh. The fried Goa Sausage, rawa fried Mussels and Masala Fish, are good nibbles with drinks. The Fish or Prawn curry is home-made in the kitchen downstairs. The Pomfret Guisado, a fish stew with onions, tomatoes and green chilli was novel, but a little heavy on the haldi.

A basic eating place with a terrific view. Don't forget the camera.

Hyderabad

This is one city where rulers have influenced the cuisine to such a degree that you almost forget that you are in South India, a predominantly Hindu region. The days of the grand Dastarkan dinners may be over, but the memory lives on. After all, it wasn't just the opulence that will be remembered, but also the expression of a feudal lifestyle, a lavish 'haute cuisine' which was both rich, painstakingly laborious and entailed hours of tedious marination, fine grinding and slow cooking.

Unfortunately, the traveller is unlikely to find any trace of traditional Hyderabadi food outside homes and at weddings. More than the Kormas, Kababs and Biryanis are dishes like Tomato ki Kut, Mirch ka Salan and Khatti Dal which are particular to this city alone. They represent a synthesis of the rich ingredients of Moghlai food, like almonds, saffron and khoya (reduced milk) tempered by local condiments such as coconut, tamarind and green chilli.

A typical Hyderabadi dinner would be several courses, starting with Shikampuri Kabab, a pattie of finely-ground mutton stuffed with a delectable chutney made with hung curd, mint, coriander and a hint of green chilli. The main courses may begin with Dalcha, a mixture of dals cooked with mutton and pumpkin and seasoned with tamarind, jeera and red chillies. There would be at least one formidable chicken dish like Dum ka Murg and a mutton one such as Pathar ka Gosht, where the meat is traditionally slow cooked on a granite stone fired by coals. Somewhere in between would be what is called a 'fusion' vegetable like Baghare Baingan or Tamater ki Kut, an aromatic dish of fresh tomatoes perked up with tamarind, garlic and curry leaves followed by the Biryani. Desserts in Hyderabadi homes are legendary. In restaurants all you are likely to get are Khubani ka Meetha, stewed apricots with malai and Dubbel (bread) ka Meetha, a heavenly royal bread pudding. In homes, if you're lucky, you might find yourself confronted with Unday ki Piyosi, a rich diamond shaped sweetmeat made with almonds, egg yolks, sugar and khoya or even Badam ki Jaali, an almond halwa lined with the real silver leaf, varak.

We dragged ourselves to the Char Minar very early one morning to experience the traditional breakfast, Nahari, a thin, slow cooked soup of trotters and tongue. Maybe our expectations were too high, but we were truly disappointed. The prohibitive cost of the raw materials and the amount of time and energy needed for authentic Hyderabadi dishes make it impossible for any restaurant, outside the five-stars, to reproduce the dishes well. If you are invited to a Hyderabadi home for dinner, never refuse. The next best is the one at the Krishna Oberoi, which is tastefully decorated and serves some excellent Hyderabadi specialities.

What is left of the 'old days' are numerous bakeries, all producing wonderfully soft sheermal and kulchas, and the makers of varak, who can still be heard thumping away at their little pieces of silver, near the Mecca Masjid in the old city.

Local Andhra cuisine can be deadly if you eat at any of the dingy, roadside haunts. For a touch of real Andhra, as hot or as tempered as you wish, head for Abhiruchi in Secunderabad and Dakhni at the Gateway Hotel.

Whatever you do, don't waste your time looking for the 'real', or old Hyderabad in restaurants. It is so far from present reality that it may as well be a fairy tale.

A meal for one person

Inexpensive: under 100 rupees
Moderate: 100 to 250 rupees
Expensive: over 250 rupees

Abhiruchi

As we are not sold on red chilli, the prospect of trying what we heard was a fiery cuisine (Andhra), did not delight us. But after visiting Abhiruchi, Andhra food shot up in our esteem. We began to appreciate the subtleties of each herb and spice, when used in correct proportions. We arrived too early for lunch, and were told the non-vegetarian items were still not ready (a good sign that everything is fresh) and that we could only be served the vegetarian thali.

Abhiruchi
Sarojini Devi Road
Secunderabad
Tel: 811900
Price : Moderate
Speciality : Andhra
Timings : 11 a.m. to 4 p.m.;
  7 to 11 p.m.
Air-conditioned

We quite liked the no-nonsense atmosphere of this functional, but neat and clean eatery, comfortably air-conditioned with a sparkling clean kitchen and filtered drinking water. So we went ahead and ordered one vegetarian thali (Rs 19) and struck gold. We were served five little bowls, overflowing with assorted chutneys and pickles, papads, yogurt, rasam, sambhar (rich with fresh vegetables including drumsticks) and a mountain of fluffy white rice. A plate of fried red chillies, which we initially looked at with suspicion, accompanied the thali. Bhupendra, the head waiter educated us on possible combinations, and soon we were tucking into rice, first with sambhar, then with rasam (superb), then each of the dry chutneys (to be pre-mixed with a teaspoonful of pure ghee), and finally rice with home-made full fat yoghurt on which you break a couple of fried red chillies.

By this time, the crab curry and the fish fry was ready. Hyderabad is not a place to eat seafood, being miles away from the sea. The only exception is a local sweet water fish called murrel, which is sold live in tanks. At Abhiruchi you can safely order fish and crab, and be sure that you are getting fresh stuff at a reasonable price. The crabs were small, but heavy with flesh, and the fish curry, a masterpiece. We could not possibly run through the whole menu, but looking at the other diners, we could see that other items like chicken ginger, mutton masala and chicken biryani, looked equally fresh and delicious. The food at Abhiruchi left a certain memory on the tongue that will not be easily forgotten. Truly a mecca for both vegetarian and non-vegetarian foodies.

Toddy tapper

Dakhni

The Dakhni menu takes its inspiration from the traditional, but lesser known specialities of Bidar, Bijapur, Gulbarga, Tellangana and Nellor in Andhra Pradesh. Andhra food is really a cuisine of the soil. The Bidaris use sesame seed, peanut and coconut in their gravies while jaggery is intrinsic to the Bijapuris. Chilli and tamarind are used everywhere in the Deccan along with aromatic spices and herbs. At Dakhni, they also serve traditional (Muslim) Hyderabadi dishes.

Dakhni
Gateway Hotel on the
  Banjara Hills
Road No-1
Banjara Hills
Hyderabad 500 034
Tel : 399999
Price : Expensive
Specialities : Andhra,
  Hyderabadi
Timings : 12.30 to 3 p.m.;
7.30 p.m. to midnight
Credit cards accepted
Bar licence
Air-conditioned

We started with a plate of Shikampuri Kababs (finely ground kheema with a delectable stuffing of dahi ki chutney), a Hyderabadi speciality. The Haleem (pounded wheat and minced mutton, seasoned with spices) served with sheermal was excellent. Although this is available on street corners today, you can't be too sure about the quality. Other specialities worth trying out, are Chicken or Crab Eguru, cooked in a paste of coconut, onions, curry leaves and spices, and Mamsam Vepudu cooked with ginger. Both dishes, infused with pungent, assertive flavours, are guaranteed to wake up your appetites.

For the vegetarians, try the Bendekaya Vepuda (lady's fingers, coated in spice and deep fried), Mirchi Ka Salan, semi spicy green chillies cooked in a paste of coconut and seasame seeds and Baghare Baingan, brinjals in a nutty sauce of seasame, peanuts and browned masala. Finish off with Tamater ki Kut, with steamed rice.

Sweet lovers must try the Khubani Ka Meetha (apricot pudding) or Dabbal Ka Meetha (bread pudding saturated with cream and nuts).

The restaurant is located off the lobby level, overlooking the artificial lake and garden. Service is attentive, and the dining experience a real pleasure.

Firdaus

Firdaus
The Krishna Oberoi
Banjara Hills
Hyderabad
Tel : 222121
Price : Expensive
Speciality : Hyderabadi
Timings : Noon to 3 p.m.;
   7 to 11 p.m.
Credit cards accepted
Bar licence
Air-conditioned

Firdaus is an elegant restaurant, overlooking the gardens and swimming pool area of the luxurious Krishna Oberoi. The decor is almost regal, without being overbearing. Dusk pink and beige brocades, bolsters, original Deen Dayal black and white photos and ornate columns all typify the grandeur of a bygone era. Waiters and Captains are dressed in traditional achkans and the service matches the refined tempo.

The menu, however, is a mix of Tandoori, North Indian, Rajasthani and traditional Hyderabadi. A Hyderabadi consultant has been brought in to ensure the authenticity of the cuisine. For starters, order the Shikampuri Kababs or Luqmi, puffed patties stuffed with mince. Try the Dalcha Gosht, a lamb and dal combination, Dum ka Murg Asifi, chicken baked in a rich sauce of poppy seeds, almonds and saffron, Baghare Baingan, Mirchi ka Salan and the tangy Tomato Qoot, a delicious rendering of the Hyderabadi speciality, especially with white rice. The Achaar Gosht, mutton cooked in pickle spices is excellent with Khurmi Naan (stuffed with tomato and cheese) or Mirch Piaz Kulcha. The Double ka Meetha, a traditional Hyderabadi bread pudding, made with khoya and saffron, is phenomenal, as is Khubani ka Meetha, stewed apricots with cream.

An informal buffet, more in the style of a private dining room, is set out for lunch, but to enjoy the Hyderabadi specialities, dinner is a must.

Haiking Chinese Restaurant

Haiking, now twenty years in business, was and still remains the best Chinese restaurant in Hyderabad. The cuisine is Hakka, which is the name of the inhabitants from the Mei Hsien district of Canton. It is non-spicy and relies on steaming and gentle toss frying to bring out the flavours.

Besides the regular 'Indian Chinese' dishes like Chicken Chilli and Manchurian whatever, you can also get authentic Chinese food, drawn from different parts of China. Owner-cum-chef Mervin Lew, has kept a very high standard of cuisine and cleanliness. The decor, though the usual red and black, is elegant. The tables are covered with fresh linen, and the drinking water is purified. All signs of an owner who cares for the customer.

Haiking Chinese Restaurant
3-6-276-276/1-277/1,
University Road
Himayatnagar
Hyderabad 500 029
Tel : 240911, 235641
Price : Moderate
Speciality : Chinese
Timings : 11 a.m. to 3 p.m.;
  6 p.m. to midnight
Credit cards accepted
Bar licence
Air-conditioned

On the food front, the chicken clear soup was full strength, with chunky cubes of chicken, topped with fresh spring onions. The most striking and enjoyable dishes at Haiking were Woi Yam Kay (boneless chicken marinated in Chinese herbs, wrapped in paper and grilled in hot salt) and Chicken in Lemon Sauce and Shredded Lamb or Chicken with black bean sauce (Kay Chow Tew Ssi). For the vegetarians, Lew has Choisum (Chinese greens) with oyster or soya sauce, mushrooms toss fried with baby corn and best of all, Foong Sao To Fu—fresh bean curd deep fried and then simmered in celery, onions, capsicum and flavoured with Chinese wine. For the health conscious, Lew does wonderful, quick, toss fried bean sprouts. For starters prawn toast and fried vegetable Wonton with garlic sauce were good.

For dessert (we found it unnecessary), you could try date pancakes with lychee ice cream and finally wash everything down with fragrant Chinese tea.

Kabab-e-Bahar

Kabab-e-Bahar
Gateway Hotel
Road No-1
Banjara Hills
Hyderabad 500 034
Tel : 399999
Price : Moderate
Speciality : North Indian
Timings : 7 p.m. to 11.45 p.m.
Credit cards accepted
Bar licence

Nahari in the old city

Kabab-e-Bahar is worth writing about for its succulent kababs alone. However, they are also served in what is perhaps the most romantic setting in the twin cities of Hyderabad and Secunderabad. The open air restaurant has a waterfront location, reflecting the lights of the residential area of the quiet Banjara Hills. The team of chefs, Chamanlal and Mansoor Alam, turn out mouth-watering, melt in the mouth varieties of Reshmi (Boneless chicken) Kabab, Tangri Kabab, Barra Kabab, Sheekh Kabab and Tandoori Bater (quail). The quality of all items is consistently good. The reason perhaps is that everything is freshly prepared everyday. The Kakori Kabab, though not our favourite, was still one of the best we have tasted. For the vegetarians there are Vegetarian Sheekh Kabab, Paneer Tikka and Dal Makhni, to be eaten with roomali or tandoori roti. In fact, it is wise to avoid dessert and concentrate only on the tandoori specialities.

New Baisakhi Dhaba

Situated about ten kilometres from Banjara Hills on National Highway No-7, New Baisakhi Dhaba is, in fact, the oldest of several dhabas, clustered together on either side of the road. It is not difficult to locate them, as they are lit up with huge sign boards. This particular dhaba, which turned out to be an open air garden restaurant, is reserved for families, i.e., a female companion is essential for you to be served here. New Baisakhi Dhaba, is run by owner-cum-chef, the debonair M. A. Naem who claims to be a

New Baisakhi Dhaba
National Highway NH - 7
Hyderabad
Tel : 849854
Price : Moderate
Speciality : North Indian
Timings : 6 p.m. to midnight

grandfather. Naem is the perfect entrepreneur. He blends well with his clientele and pays great attention to their every need. The kitchen is a dhaba-style set up, with the gravies and vegetarian food, already prepared and put into stainless steel utensils, to be reheated and spiced according to the taste of the customer. Meanwhile, the hot tandoor turns out tandoori delicacies and rotis. The specialities range from Dum Ka Murg, Kalmi Kabab and Reshmi Kabab, which are all superb. However, we found his Jeera Chawal (rice) with home-made yoghurt, the best combination. It cooled us down from the heat and excitement of driving all the way from the city. Desserts are missing from the menu but the special tea (ninety per cent milk) was as good as one, and helped wash down the rich food.

The combination of honest to goodness tandoori food and dining under the stars, makes the trip to New Baisakhi Dhaba worthwhile.

Shanbhag Hotel

Shanbhag Hotel
Panjagutta
Hyderabad 500 482
Tel : 313446, 310148
Price : Inexpensive
Speciality : South Indian
  Vegetarian
Timings : 7 a.m. to 10 p.m.

Shanbhag, is one of the most popular, value for money, vegetarian eateries in Hyderabad. Large, bustling and busy, it was also our favourite place in the city for a quick snack like Tomato Bhath (savoury semolina cooked with peas), which was absolutely delicious, or Bisi Bele Bhath, yet another mind-blowing snack made out of lentils and rice. It is no doubt spicy, but we ordered a round of sweet lassi to counter the hot, irresistable kick of the spices. All the other snacks: Idlis, Rava Dosa, Dahi Vadas are equally good. If you feel like a full meal, Shanbagh's South Indian Thali with Rasam, Sambhar, one vegetable, yogurt, papad, rice and pickle, is wonderful value at Rs 13. Last but not least, the freshly brewed coffee is superb, as is their range of sweets, especially Basundi and Son Papdi.

Kheema pau in old Hyderabad

Swad Hotel

If you are missing home cooked vegetarian food, then Swad is the place for you. Everything, including the service, is just like at home. The owner-cum-chef Ganapathi scolds you affectionately if you waste any food. In fact, the chances that you leave anything on your plate is remote, as the food is delicious and satisfying. There is a North Indian menu too, but we suggest that you can either make a meal of the snacks like Bisi Bele Bhath, a spicy combination of rice and lentils, Butter Masala Dosa, or order a Thali Janata (Rs 10) or a special one at (Rs 14). We recommend you select a vegetable of your choice from a range including Capsicum Masala, Alu Palak, Paneer Kofta or Paneer Butter Masala, Gobi Manchoorian(!), a house speciality and combine it with Boondi Raita and plain hot Phulka or Jeera Rice. A perfect meal will set you back well under Rs 50 (all inclusive). Hot Gulab Jamun or Basundi (thick rich cream) yet another house speciality, are recommended.

Swad Hotel
2-2-57/20, Paan Bazaar
Secunderabad 500 003
Price : Inexpensive
Speciality : South Indian
  Vegetarian
Tel : 77043
Timings : 7:30 a.m. to 9 p.m.

Swad looks deceptively like a canteen, with its formica tables and steel chairs, but the general standard of food, service and cleanliness, is well above a great many more expensive, fancy restaurants. There are times, usually after a spate of self indulgence, when one's soul cries out for a simple meal. Look no further than Swad.

"

Jaipur

Jaipur, like Agra, is very much a tourist town, where even local handicraft sellers speak a few sentences of several European languages. Men in colourful turbans, women swamped with bangles, camels and elephants are all part of a Rajasthan which exists outside the Pink City. However, unlike Agra which solely depends on tourism, Jaipur does not. Much of the business in the city is still controlled by the traditional Marwari community, whose cuisine reflects the austerity of the desert and whose loyal patronage to it ensures that it not only continues but thrives. The ingredients are totally vegetarian and centre around a mind boggling variety of dishes made from gram flour (besan), ghee and pulses or legumes (dals and dried beans). Traditionally, no onion or garlic is used. The outcome is both spicy and very rich, with very little imagination or energy spent on presentation. After a while, the textures and colours of the dishes all look the same. This may be partly due to the fact that generally, Marwari food is prepared by brahmin Maharaj cooks, who serve directly from the cooking utensils to the thali, to avoid contamination.

A typical Rajasthani Thali at its simplest, is served at Chokhi Dhani, a mock village set up outside the city, where dinner is served on the floor, in disposable thalis. If driving out of town to sit on the floor and eat with your hands doesn't grab you, then opt for the Jai Mahal Hotel, which serves an excellent Rajasthani Thali, a vegetarian one and one with lamb and chicken. Both contain a good variety of typical vegetarian dishes like dumplings made of Ghatte (gram flour), Aloo Mangodi (dal paste dumplings with potatoes), and a variety of rotis, including misri, made from gram flour, ginger and coriander. The traditional meat speciality served here is Mutton Soola, a boneless kabab cooked over charcoal.

Jaipur is very much a 'snacky' town. Most of the action centres around M.I. (Mirza Ismail) Road, which separates the new city from the old, and in the area around Johri Bazaar, in the old part of town. It is easy to find your way around as the streets, all relatively wide, are at right angles in a grid system. For the plumpest, tastiest kachoris in town, head for RMB (Rawat Mishtan Bhandar), opposite the Apollo Victory Cinema, not far from the Mansingh Hotel. The man who does the frying sits outside, so you can see they are fresh. There are three types, one heavier than the next, onion, dal and mawa (clotted cream). To wash them down, head for the Lassiwalla, Kishinlal Govind Narain Aggarwal, opposite Niro's restaurant, on M.I. Road. He usually sits in his white dhoti on the platform outside his shop, but you must go between 8 a.m. and noon or 4 p.m. and 6 p.m.

This city has a very definite sweet tooth. At the street level, a simple breakfast of Doodh Jalebi (milk with the orange sweet jalebi) is always available at Gheewalon ka Rasta, and Mishri Mawa, in Gopalgee ka Rasta in old Johri Bazar. For those who like their sweets rich and creamy, Chhappan Bhog, the famous Bengali sweetmart, has opened a branch on Sardar Patel Marg, and LMB, in Johri Bazar, still has the creamiest Ras Malai and Kulfi in town.

Although you may want to try Rajasthani food once, after a couple of thalis, you will probably kill for something simple and non-spicy. In the moderate range, Niros is the answer. It offers a variety of well prepared Continental, Chinese and Tandoori items, the staff is exceedingly polite, and the kitchens, spotless. At the top of the range, the Rajputana Sheraton has a wonderful Coffee Shop with excellent food and presentation, and an extensive and very reasonable buffet.

Not a city for foodies, but interesting and relatively clean street snacks.

A meal for one person
Inexpensive: under 100 rupees
Moderate: 100 to 250 rupees
Expensive: over 250 rupees

Chanakya

Chanakya was opened in 1983 to meet the demand for pure vegetarian food, cooked in ghee. This is nothing to rave about, but it is clean, comfortable and always packed. The decor is standard, upholstered chairs and large wooden tables in a relaxed, roomy environment. The place, though, does smell a little of 'curry'. The food is less spicy than elsewhere in the city, but the restaurant still reeks of the familiar smell of 'masala' as you enter. The specialities here are the Paneer (home-made) Butter Masala, Malai Kofta (with a stuffing of dry fruit), and khoya muttar (peas cooked in rich thick cream). For vegetarians who insist on a restaurant where absolutely no non-veg is cooked, this is the most popular place in town.

Chanakya
2 AB-MI Road
Jaipur
Tel: 376161, 378461
Price: Moderate
Specialities: North Indian,
    Rajasthani Vegetarian
Timings: Noon to 11 p.m.
Credit cards accepted
Air-conditioned

Chokhi Dhani

Chokhi Dhani
12 Miles, Tonk Road
Via Vatika
Jaipur
Tel: 550118
Price : Inexpensive
Speciality : Rajasthani
Timings: 6 to 11 p.m.

A new concept in dining out, this combines the experience of a Rajasthani village with a rustic, traditional dinner. The idea is good, clean, indiginous fun for all the family. You are greeted at the entrance by enthusiastic little boys in white dhotis and outsized red pugdis, hailing that well known village greeting, 'Ram Ram'. Inside the man-made village, you have bullock cart rides, boat rides, a village square with crafts people working, puppets, folk dances, musicians, and parents stretching out on charpoys, with some relief, as their children play about.

Dinner is served from 8 p.m. onwards in a large communal hut. It is spotlessly clean, but you do have to sit on the floor and eat with your hands. The food is simple Rajasthani home cooking—chutneys, raw onion, dry vegetables, various lentil preparations (beans and more beans), dal, rotis, rice and a yoghurt-based kadi. The food is served in disposable (environment friendly) dry leaf thalis and katoris, one dish at a time, by the same enthusiastic little boys. Forget dieting, as they urge you to take more, while throwing tiny terracotta pots, full of creamy white butter on to your thali. You can eat as little or as much as you want for Rs 70 per head (a real steal), but leave room for the hot, home-made jalebis.

It is very refreshing to see a totally Indian set up, with no western influence, that is basic but clean. Two more places of this kind have come up around Jaipur, but this one is by far the best. A must if you have children, and great value for money.

The Musician

Gulab Mahal

Gulab Mahal
Jai Mahal Palace Hotel
Jacob Road
Civil Lines
Jaipur 302 006
Tel.: 371616
Fax: 365237
Price: Expensive
Specialities : Indian,
   Rajasthani, Continental.
Timings : Lunch & Dinner
Credit cards accepted
Bar licence
Air-conditioned

Though much smaller than the Rambagh Hotel, this is a much underrated palace hotel, taken over and totally renovated by the Taj group in 1984. One of its major features is the Mughal Lotus Gardens designed by Elizabeth Moynihan, wife of the former US Ambassador to India and an expert in the field.

For fine dining in Jaipur, Jai Mahal is probably your best bet. The main dining hall, Gulab Mahal, retains its royal elegance and stature. Large arches overlook the veranda and the entire restaurant is white marble including exquisite marble latticework. The colour scheme of the restaurant, the upholstery, napkins and table settings is maroon and pink. You can breakfast, lunch or dine on either of the restaurant's two levels or on the marble veranda outside, overlooking the garden.

Chef Sanjeev Sharma is another underrated feature of Jai Mahal. With great modesty and creativity, he puts together a fine menu of both excellent, delicate Continental flavours and Indian cuisine, including the most beautifully presented Rajasthani thali in Jaipur. From the Continental specialities, start with any of his tossed salads. They are basic, but always fresh and pretty to look at. His Consomme is, as one should be, clarified and full of natural chicken flavour. The Roulade of Chicken in a light saffron and white wine sauce was impeccable. Sharma was originally with La Patisserie, the Pastry shop at the Taj Hotel, Delhi. His desserts are a testimony to this, especially the apple tart with a fresh custard and cognac sauce. The Rajasthani thali has a succulent Lahsuni Murg Tikka (garlic flavoured chicken kabab) and typically Rajasthani fare—Aloo Mangodi (heavy dal curry with potatoes), Safed Maans (mutton in a cashew nut gravy), Potli Ki Dumpling (ghatte poached in muslin), and a variety of very interesting rotis - makki (corn), bajra (millet), mìssi (chick pea flour), and baby naans coated with chopped onion, tomato and coriander. Don't miss the dry fruit pullav.

A real feather in the cap of the Taj group.

A Royal Rajasthani Thali

Laxmi Mishthan Bhandar

Laxmi Mishthan Bhandar
Jaipur
Tel: 565644–47
Price: Moderate
Speciality: North Indian,
  Rajasthani, snacks
Timings : 8 a.m. to 11 p.m.
Credit cards accepted
Air-conditioned

LMB, as it is known in Jaipur, is an institution in itself. Started in 1955 by Rajesham Aggarwal to cater to the mainly local, traditional vegetarian population, it unfortunately runs more on the mileage from its reputation, than on its food now. We found the service in this large, packed hall, slow, and the decor very strange, with its space shuttle ceiling and blue and white, marquee type awnings.

The food, as the menu points out, is satvic (simple vegetarian, cooked without onion or garlic), and the cooking medium is Vishuddh desi ghee (pure clarified butter). We tried most of the Rajasthani specialities—Kair Sangri (dried beans with dumplings), Bele Rajasthani (chickpea flour dumplings in a yoghurt-based gravy), and Papad Mogdi soup (papad, the consistency of pasta). Frankly, everything looked the same sloppy mess and was over spicy and too oily.

Go to LMB for the famous Dahi Bhalla, fruit chaat, pakoda and their rich rasmalai with saffron. It is still a good place to check out the local scene, but don't expect miracles in the kitchen.

Niros

This is undoubtedly the best restaurant, outside the five-star circuit, in Jaipur today. It is fun, with its garden look, and is today a landmark on the busy, commercial, M. I. Road. The service is impeccable, the staff well trained, and the kitchen (one chef for every type of cuisine) is clean and run with an almost military efficiency. Though we are generally wary of restaurants which serve all types of cuisine, Niros has to be the exception.

Niros
Mirza Isamail Road
Jaipur 302001
Tel : 371874, 374493
Price : Moderate
Specialities : North Indian,
   Continental, Chinese
Timings: 10 a.m. to 11 p.m.
Credit cards accepted
Air-conditioned

Started by Ved Pardal, who worked with P. L. Lamba of the Kwality chain of restaurants, he branched out on his own and opened Niros in 1949. It was the first restaurant in Jaipur to serve Chinese food (1969). The restaurant is now managed by his sons. Senior, now in his seventies, still comes to work every day, that is when he is not in New York visiting his youngest son who is now with the UN.

We were told that fish is risky business in Jaipur, except during the winter season. Not so; fresh catfish (singada) and river sole were available at Niros. Both the Fried Fish with Tartare Sauce, and Fish with Garlic Sauce (Chinese) were prepared exceedingly well. Most of the people around us (the place was packed, with a queue outside on Saturday night) were eating Indian or Chinese. The Reshmi Kabab was superbly succulent, garnished with red (not coloured) onion rings and lime wedges. The other Indian dishes were thankfully not too spicy nor oily. The Chinese is standard, but for traditional Jaipur tastes, quite exotic.

Breakfast is a real treat—kidney on toast, mushrooms, eggs to order, etc.

When in Jaipur, by all means try the local cuisine. But we guarantee that by the second day, you'll be running to Niros.

Rajputana Palace Sheraton

Rajputana Palace Sheraton
Palace Road
Jaipur 302006
Tel : 62031,68254,72170; Fax
: 67848
Price : Expensive
Specialities : Continental,
Indian, Chinese, Rajasthani
Timings : 12.30 to 3.30 p.m.;
    7.30 to 11 p.m.
Credit cards accepted
Bar licence
Air-conditioned

The rest of the five-star brigade had better watch out. In a few years time, we estimate that this newly opened (1 November 1992) member of the Welcomegroup Sheraton chain will be miles ahead of the competition. The hotel is all a luxurious new five-star should be; large, modern, tastefully decorated, efficient, good facilities etc. Rajputana is pulling out all the stops to grab the tourist traffic. They are catching depressed timings like 'tea time', when a chaat bar is available in the open coffee shop on the ground floor. They will be following this with a late night promotional campaign. Theme parties are catered for and Rajasthani folklore is exhibited at Prakarti, an artisan corner within the hotel complex. There is a jogging track, a very large swimming pool, and the best little buffet in town. The food is innovative, tempting and great value for money.

Chef Sultan Mohuddin creates a buffet of sixty-six very pleasing dishes, every day of the week, which include fifteen hot main courses (Chinese, Rajasthani, Continental, North Indian), hors d'oeuvres, salads and desserts. We even spotted asparagus! At the weekend, you can dine (candlelight) and dance to a Western band. All this for only Rs 125 (plus taxes). It is almost unbelievable.

We found the coffee shop menu creative, and the dishes we ordered—fish and chips (a local favourite we were told, called the 'The British Connection') and chicken pepper steak—excellent quality and presentation. If you are in the hotel or nearby, do not miss the opportunity to try the chef's delicious sweet creation, rum and raisin rolls—a simple swiss roll is filled with vanilla ice cream and chocolate sauce and flavoured with rum and frozen.

Rajputana looks more like a luxurious American condominium, with its brown stone facade and greenery, but it is very definitely a luxury hotel of international standards, with food to match.

Shivir

A contemporary luxury hotel, Mansingh caters mainly to foreign groups, local business and entertaining. The restaurants, bars, twenty-four-hour coffee shop, buffet and extensive banquet and conference facilities, reflects this. Shivir is the lively rooftop restaurant, which does have very pretty views of the city. The decor is soothing terracotta and copper tones, with tassled jhalers on the pelmets and copper tableware.

Shivir
The Mansingh Hotel
Sansar Chandra Road
Jaipur 302001
Tel : 78771; Fax : 77582
Price: Expensive
Specialities : North Indian, Rajasthani
Timings: 12.30 to 2.45 p.m.; 7.30 to 11.30 p.m.
Credit cards accepted
Bar licence
Air-conditioned

The food is well above average and caters to all tastes. The range of thalis, though rich, are extremely tasty. They include, Ameri (traditional Rajasthani), Panna (vegetarian) and Mumal (a royal treat). A vegetarian and non-vegetarian selection of tandoori items served on sizzlers, with Kulcha and Maa Ki Dal, is also available. The popular favourites include a succulent Sulla (mutton) kabab, Kasturi kabab (a chicken tikka marinated with egg and lemon juice), Kakuri Sheekh (finely ground mince marinated with cream), Nawabi Raan (leg of mutton in a cashew nut and cream paste) and Murg Shan-e-Shivir, chicken drumsticks with dry fruit.

Street vendor in Jaipur

A very popular feature of the restaurant are the local ghazal singers who perform every night.

A comfortable, relaxed place to spend an evening.

Surya Mahal

Surya Mahal
Mirza Ismail Road
Jaipur 302 001
Price : Moderate
Specialities : South Indian,
  North Indian Vegetarian
Timings : 8 a.m. to 11 p.m.

Elephants in disguise

A little dark, but nevertheless, a nice clean place on the busiest part of M. I. Road. Service is fast, portions ample and the general ambience cheerful. An open kitchen means that you can judge the standards of cleanliness for yourself.

The food is basic North Indian, with an emphasis on 'snack meals', i.e. Muttar Paneer (cottage cheese with peas) comes with two parathas, Paneer Butter Masala, with two kulchas, etc. You will always find people in the restaurant munching on South Indian dosa. The thalis are a good deal—combining South Indian sambhar and rasam with vegetables, raitha, etc. You even get fusion cuisine here. We saw people eating dosa with paneer! Why not? The pizzas are popular, but conform to local tastes, i.e., cheese, onion, capsicum and pineapple, all on together. Enough to make any Roman throw up his hands in disbelief!

The Rambagh Palace Hotel

Where does one get a chance to live and feel the kind of opulence and grandeur of the lifestyle of the former maharajas? The enormous verandas, magnificent suites, dining-halls and sprawling gardens of the Rambagh Palace, will give you an idea.

'The cuisine at Rambagh was excellent,' recounts the very beautiful Rajmata Gayatri Devi, third wife of polo player extraordinaire, Maharaja Sawai Man Singh II, in her autobiography. Unfortunately, the Taj has not been able to match the lavish and flamboyant food of the former home of the Maharaja. Enjoy the splendour of the setting, a drink at the Polo Bar, English tea, served in real style on the veranda or the excellent Rajasthani thali in the magnificent Suvarna Mahal dining-room. The dining-room itself is a masterpiece of interior design, with an exquisite painted ceiling and translucent marble lamps in the Florentine style, Lalique chandeliers, etc. The 'Royal' silver thali, vegetarian and non-vegetarian, is filled to the brim with all the traditional Rajasthani items, including the most delicious ginger lassi.

Do not expect the usual five-star standards and style of functioning here. Many of the old retainers from the palace have been kept on in their traditional Rajasthani regalia. Service is therefore a little slow and sometimes haphazard, but always warm and ready to oblige.

The Rambagh Palace Hotel
Bhawani Singh Road
Jaipur 302 005
Tel: 381919; Fax: 381098
Price: Expensive
Speciality : Rajasthani, North Indian, Continental
Timings : 12.30 to 3 p.m.; 7.30 to 11 p.m.
Credit cards accepted
Bar licence
Air-conditioned

Madras

We are admittedly partial to South India, with its warm, leisurely pace, and quiet, unassuming people. The food follows a similar pattern. It is simple and yet visually eye catching, with the staples, rice, rasam, sambhar and vegetables laid out against the backdrop of a green banana leaf. And the famous pungency depends entirely on what you add to your basic rice, a light tadka of mustard seeds, chilli and urad dal or chutneys made with coconut, mango or fiery red chillies.

The core of Tamil Nadu cuisine is rice and dal in various combinations. All the possibilities of these two basic ingredients seemed to have been explored, whether they are ground, fermented, steamed or fried. The result is dishes like Curd Rice, Idlis, Dosas, Idiappams, Vadas, etc., which are both delicious and disgustingly healthy too. Don't leave Madras without trying the innocuous Rasam, an indescribable soup of sinful flavours. It may seem like a poor man's dal, but no South Indian meal, however elaborate, is complete without this aromatic combination of clarified dal, perfumed with fresh spices, onion, tomato and coriander.

If you do hanker after meat, fear not, there is life beyond the idli and dosa. The cuisine of the Chettiyar trading community, from Chettinad (around 250 miles south of Madras), centres around a variety of unusual vegetarian, fish and meat dishes, simple in form, but extraordinary in taste. Like the Marwaris in the North, the Chettiyars are a wealthy community who can afford to indulge their taste for fine food. The Raintree Restaurant at the Taj, a real breath of fresh air in the five-star brigade of restaurants, is responsible for popularizing this cuisine in the city. This has spawned a series of smaller Chettinad restaurants in Madras, which are simply not able to duplicate the original, subtle flavours. For variety in Madras, look no further than Dakshin, which serves the entire gamut of South Indian specialities under one roof.

Vegetarian places in Madras, where ever you go, are always excellent quality, terrific value and will almost always serve freshly brewed South Indian filtered coffee, using their own particular blend of beans. In the north, restaurant food is quite different (much heavier, in fact) to what people would eat at home. In the south, it is just the opposite. Food in restaurants is just like the dishes you would eat at home, with an emphasis on vegetables like cabbage, magai (giant cucumber) and pumpkin, rice preparations, yoghurt and sour spicy dals. In the moderate range of restaurants, we recommend AVM Dasa, totally vegetarian which has a Salad Bar as an added bonus, and Coconut Grove, which serves both vegetarian and non-vegetarian dishes. For inexpensive, vegetarian fare, the best places are Saravana Bhavan for 'meals' and Meneka for 'tiffin'.

Although the Idli and Dosa have crossed state boundries to become national favourites, experiencing them in Madras can be a totally new and satisfying experience. Remember, you are unlikely to find an idli at noon, because this is when 'Meals', a full lunch on a banana leaf, are served. Look for the sign 'Tiffin', to indicate that snacks are available.

A meal for one person

Inexpensive: under 100 rupees
Moderate: 100 to 250 rupees
Expensive: over 250 rupees

Ahaar Restaurant

The ever modest Residency and its restaurants offer five-star amenities at three-star prices. The young executive chef, S. Babu, ensures that the food served at all the in-house restaurants is consistently good. We recommend Ahaar for its extraordinary buffet, which includes a mind-boggling variety of soups, salads, four non-vegetarian dishes, ten vegetables, three kinds of rice, pasta, noodles and hot chapattis or appams made on the spot, and a special section for chaat lovers. All this and four kinds of desserts for Rs 80. A quick business lunch is only Rs 55 (non-veg) and Rs 45 (vegetarian).

Ahaar
The Residency
49 G. N. Chetty Road
T. Nagar
Madras 600 017
Tel : 8253434
Price : Moderate
Specialities : Moghlai, South Indian, Continental
Timings : 12.30 to 3 p.m.; 7.30 p.m. to midnight
Credits cards accepted
Reservation essential
Air-conditioned

But it was the creative cuisine that impressed us. The chef turns out over a hundred tasty varieties of rice, flavoured with everything from methi and tomatoes to curry leaves, curd and lemon. While the South specialities are superb, the Hyderabadi and Moghlai dishes are worth trying too. Vegetarians will love the Brinjal in coconut gravy, mushrooms with bamboo shoots, Kabuli Pulao and Fried rice with burnt ginger. Fresh Crab in a smooth coconut gravy is available in season. Whatever you do, don't skip dessert, especially the Pineapple Rava Kesari, a home-made Suji Halwa flavoured with fresh pineapple and saffron.

The decor is modern and the restaurant, bright and cheerful with huge french windows and overhanging plants. Ahaar is a comfortable and elegant place to dine.

Amma Chettinadu Restaurant

Amma Chettinadu
Restaurant
27, G. N. Chetty Road
T. Nagar
Madras 600 017
Tel : 8252242
Price : Inexpensive
Speciality : Chettinad
Timings : 11 a.m. to 3 p.m.;
7 to 11 p.m.
Air-conditioned

What is unusual about this place are the specialities—rabbit, patridge, dove and turkey. Quite esoteric for a restaurant of this kind, or for any restaurant in India for that matter. However, we didn't manage to taste any of them. The marksman had obviously overslept that day, or else he was a pretty lousy shot. We did taste most of their other non-vegetarian specialities though, out of which the Nalli Special Roast (marrow bone meat cooked on the griddle with dry masala) was good and the boneless Crab and Chicken Pepper roast were superb. Not a place for vegetarians, Amma, as its name suggests, offers home cooked food, served on banana leaves in three rooms of an old bungalow, with its fair share of gods and goddesses on the wall. Rasam, heavily flavoured with thick chopped garlic, sambhar, yoghurt and rice are placed before you, no matter what you order. Everything is freshly prepared on the premises.

Amma may not get the first prize for hygiene, but it is a bit better than the rest in the inexpensive price range. Best to carry your own water or order a soft drink.

AVM *Dasa Restaurant*

At AVM Dasa (short for Dasaprakash), we had the most delicious Dosai. Served with mildly spiced, but tasty masala potato, sambhar and chutneys, Butter Dosa 'a la Dasa', took our breath away. A tiny square piece of banana leaf, carrying a pat of white butter, nestled in the fold of the steaming Dosai. A bit expensive at Rs 20 though worth every paisa. Yet another attraction at the Dasa, is Kadubu, a pair of cylindrical shaped idlis, (a Mangalorean speciality), which is a close cousin of the idli and yet with its own texture, shape and flavour.

AVM Dasa Restaurant
806, Anna Salai Road
Madras
Price : Moderate
Specialities : South Indian,
    Salad Bar (Vegetarian)
Timings : Noon to 3 p.m.;
    7 to midnight

Dasa also springs a surprise with its Salad Bar, perhaps the only one of its kind in Madras. The variety included Greek Farmhouse, Chef's Salad, Beansprouts with vegetables, Coleslaw, Tomato with fresh Basil (good), Potato Nest, made with mash potato, tomato, broccoli and leeks (very good) and Pasta and Spinach (excellent). The dressings range from garlic oil and basil to lemon and honey. A choice of eight salads costs Rs 75 a plate (no sharing). Freshly made twice a day by chef Sachin Gomes with vegetables from Ooty, the salads make a welcome change. Dasa serves fresh fruit; juices, and a large variety of their own naturally flavoured ice creams.

The decor is modern with natural stone flooring, cane partitions, and pretty tiffany lamps. An ideal place for a rendezvous.

Chin Chin Restaurant

Chin Chin Restaurant
The Residency
49 G. N. Chetty Road
T. Nagar
Madras 600 017
Tel : 8253434
Price : Moderate
Speciality : Chinese Szechwan
Timings : Noon to 3 p.m.;
7 to 11 p.m.
Credit cards accepted
Air-conditioned

Chin Chin is miles ahead of the other grotty, old Chinese restaurants in Madras and remarkably reasonable. Imagine rich Sharkfin and Crab Soup (the real thing) for only Rs 35 (plus taxes)! We also recommend the Manchow Soup (clear chicken soup with shredded spinach), Steamed Crab Claws and the delicious, deep fried cauliflower in chilli and fresh tomato sauce. Then go on to the exotic and quite sensational Chicken Herbs Honey, cooked with cinnamon, star anise, mustard and red chillies. For those with a modest appetite, just order this dish along with a bowl of steamed rice. Szechwan Fried Baby Corn and Mushrooms Pepper Salt are good vegetarian dishes, accompanied by Burnt Ginger Fried Rice.

Chinese chef Sanu Rai previously worked for China Garden, Bombay, and is quick to adapt to an individual customer's taste. The dessert is best avoided. The decor is Chinese (mirrors and red latticework) but smart, the service superb and the price reasonable. Worth a visit.

Coconut Grove

Coconut Grove serves specialities from Malabar, Chettinad, Godavari, Coorg and Konkan. Coconuts, peppers, cloves, garlic, tamarind, raw mangoes, curry leaves and even fresh toddy is used in various permutations and combinations, in the preparation of the dishes. We tried out Meen Kolambu—Surmai (kingfish) stewed in tamarind juice, chillies and onions, which was excellent. Nandu Kar (softshell crab from the backwaters of Kerala, cooked with fresh ground masala and coconut), was a bit too spicy for our taste, but delicious nevertheless with spongy Appam. Kai Kari Shtew, fresh mixed vegetables in coconut milk, was as delicious as the Thiel (pearl onions cooked in grated coconut masala with heaps of coriander). Both should be eaten with piles of steamed rice. Kari Mezagu is another stunner (cooked with black pepper and jeera) which went well with flaky Malabar paratha.

Coconut Grove
95, Harrington Road
Chetpet
Madras 600 031
Tel : 868800
Price : Moderate
Speciality : South Indian
 Vegetarian and
 Non-vegetarian
Timings : 11:30 a.m. to
 3 p.m.; 7 to 11:30 p.m.
Credit cards accepted
Partly air-conditioned

Coconut Grove, is owned and managed by the great former filmstar, Sowkar Janaki. We witnessed the extent of her popularity when almost all the diners in the restaurant stood up to applaud her as she appeared from the kitchen in her apron and chef's hat. She says that she learned to cook from her mother, who used to send her meals from home, while she was shooting.

The restaurant is tastefully decorated with simple wooden furniture inside and cane seating under a gazebo outside. The outdoor section also has striking redstone sculptures. One relief of a Kathakali dancer on the garden wall is particularly remarkable. You must include this restaurant on your culinary itinerary when you go to Madras. Don't feel shy to ask for Sowkar Janaki herself. Her charm is devastating and so is her home style food.

The chef-proprietor—Sowkar Janaki

Dakshin

Executive chef Mathur who created food for VIP's like Rajiv Gandhi, now oversees the operations at Park Sheraton, in which Dakshin is situated. As with the other restaurants in the Hotel (especially the amazing buffet at the Residency), Mathur's signature is evident—the freshness of food, extravagance, flamboyance and superb service.

Dakshin is an elegant, creative, designer restaurant. Care and attention has been lavished on the smallest detail, from the traditional Urli at the entrance, to the waiters in traditional Dhoti Kurta. The food, courtesy of chef Praveen Anand, lives up to the terrific ambience.

In one corner, chef Sundaram A.M., conducts a counter of visual theatricals, turning out lacy Iddiappams (string hoppers), mouth-watering Dosais and Veleappams (flying saucer shaped white dosais, the dough of which is fermented with toddy overnight to obtain that fluffy belly in the middle).

As starters go, South Indian first courses are sheer tongue teasers, that seek not only to appease the palate, but induce a relaxed mood of bonhomie and anticipation. Rasam did the trick. The main courses came in the form of Dakshin Yera (deep fried prawns in ginger, garlic and chilli), a Tamil Nadu speciality. The prawns were expensive at Rs 250 (plus taxes), but worth it. Mirupakai Kodi (chilli chicken) was yet another stunning dish.

For the vegetarians, we recommend Vegetable Stew (in coconut and grated onion), Keerai Kotu (spinach and lentils with cumin seeds) and the ever popular Avial (vegetables in coconut milk). All the dishes go well with steamed rice and Appam. The dessert Semiya Payasam

Dakshin
Park Sheraton Hotel & Towers
132, T.T.K Road
Alwarpet
Madras 600 018
Tel : 4994101
Price : Expensive
Speciality : South Indian Vegetarian and Non-vegetarian
Timings : 12.30 to 3 p.m.; 7.30 to 11:30 p.m.
Reservation recommended
Credit cards accepted
Bar licence
Air-conditioned

(Seviyon vermicelli, in sweetened cardamom milk) was excellent, and so were the silver foiled paans served in an elegant dish, at the end of the meal. The coffee (freshly brewed) was aromatic and served by chef Sundaram who theatrically poured it from one tumbler to another before presenting it.

Though expensive, eating out at Dakshin is a total visual and gustatory experience.

Kapiliswarar Temple

Kalpaka Restaurant

Green and yellow steps lead up the narrow gangway to the first floor of an old building. Two rooms of a flat have been converted into a very basic restaurant which, despite the modest surroundings, serves home-made Kerala food. The specialities include Kerala Syrian Beef cooked with slivers of coconut and dry masala. We found this quite unusual considering that most Keralite specialities in restaurants revolve around fish, vegetables and dal. The Fish (surmai) Fry was fresh and non-greasy. The Fish Masala was more akin to a North Indian preparation, in a rich gravy made from cashewnuts, khuskhus, green chillies and tomatoes. The utterly delicious fish curry was typically Keralite, in a light sauce of coconut milk and green chillies. Buttermilk, rasam and a bit of diced salad consisting of lightly cooked tendli and beet root in coconut chutney are served as appetizers, along with an assortment of pickles and chutneys.

Kalpaka Restaurant
318, Mowbrays Road
Madras 600 014
Price : Inexpensive
Speciality : Kerala
Timings : 11 a.m. to
   3.30 p.m.; 7.30 to 10.30 p.m.
Partly air-conditioned

The vegetarian lunch (Rs 14 plus taxes) comes with rice and vegetables. The non-vegetarian dishes have to be ordered separately. Chapattis come piping hot from the griddle.

Kalpaka is home away from home, if you are from Kerala, that is. The restaurant has an air-conditioned section which costs ten per cent more.

Meneka Restaurant

Meneka Restaurant
Hotel Palm Grove Adam
5 Kodambakkam High Road
Madras 600 034
Tel : 8271881
Price : Moderate
Speciality : South Indian
  Vegetarian
Timings : 7 a.m. to 10 p.m.
Air-conditioned

For the best idli in town head for Meneka, named after a dancing temptress from Hindu mythology. Somewhat like Chinese food, South Indian snacks are easy on the stomach, as most of them are prepared from fermented rice. If you have brunch instead of breakfast, as we did, you can then try out the whole range of breakfast specials, all of which are fresh and superbly cooked. Start with a fluffy soft idli, with a dash of coconut chutney. Move on to Upma (made of steamed semolina, curry leaves, cashew nuts etc). It really does not need any chutney as it is moist enough on its own.

Finish off with Rice Pongal, a mixture of rice, yellow moong dal, cumin seeds and whole black pepper. Do not discard the full black pepper, they lose their sting in cooking, but not their flavour. Pongal eaten with sambhar is a complete meal. Sambhar here has a treasure of vegetables including pearl onions, drumsticks and lady's fingers.

Meneka also serves fresh grape juice. The coffee, an aromatic South Indian brew, made rich with buffalo milk and sugar, is a must to wash down the delicious brunch. Being sweet, it also takes the place of dessert.

The plastic decor is functional and clean, and the service, excellent. Ask for waiter Ramraj, he is not only attentive, but will also answer all your queries about the large variety of dishes available at different times of the day.

Palimar Restaurant

Specializing in 'heavy' snacks, which can easily substitute for a lunch or a dinner, Palimar is popular for its daily specials. We liked the Adai Malabar, a kind of hot 'melt in the mouth' dosa, made of green moong dal, coarsely ground black pepper and red chilli. The accompanying chutneys and sambhar were equally memorable. Other specialities worth trying, are, the Sunday Special, Bisi Bele Bhath (a torrid mix of rice, dal and spices), and the Thursday Special, Rava Onion Bhath. Full lunches are also served. The special Madras meal is Rs 35, while the special Bombay meal is Rs 45 (plus taxes), both inclusive of chapatti and dessert. The giant Butter Paper Dosa, as light as a feather, was served with potato onion vegetable and assorted chutneys.

Palimar Restaurant
48, Ground floor
Parsn Manere
602, Anna Alai
Madras 600 006
Tel : 8279718, 8279713
Price : Moderate
Speciality : South Indian
  Vegetarian
Timings : 11 a.m. to 11 p.m.
Sundays 9 a.m. to 11 p.m.
Credit cards accepted
Air-conditioned
Non-smoking

Unlike other eateries in Madras, Palimar has no pictures of gods and goddesses on the walls. Instead, there are over twelve colour TV sets fixed in every nook and corner of the restaurant, relaying different channels of Star TV, Doordarshan and CNN. The volume is, mercifully, low, which keeps the customers both happy and occupied. The decor is 'modern' with black formica-topped tables and marble flooring. The place is sparkling clean. The Manager, Sripathi, was most helpful, and the service was excellent.

If ever you want to catch up on the current episode of *Santa Barbara*, or watch your favourite team play football, while you crunch and munch on well made South favourites, then Palimar is the place for you.

Peshawri

Peshawri
Chola Sheraton
10, Cathedral Road
Madras 600 086
Tel : 880101
Price : Expensive
Speciality : North Indian
Timings : Noon to 3:30 p.m.;
   7:30 to 11:30 p.m.
Credit cards accepted
Bar licence
Air-conditioned

Inspired by Bukhara in Delhi, Peshawri does as well as the original restaurant. Chef Suraj Singh's speciality is Kadak Sheekh Reshmi, a chicken kabab, crisp on the outside and soft inside (made with minced chicken, cheese, saffron, elaichi, garam masala, green chilli, and fresh coriander). It tasted wonderful rolled up in a roomali roti. The Sheekh Kabab and the Sikandari Raan were superb. The vegetarian specialities include Karela Kabab (bitter gourd) served in the evenings only and Paneer Tikka, which are both perfectly cooked in the open tandoor.

Desserts include Gulab Jamun, heated for a short time in the tandoor, making the outer coating hot and crisp while retaining the fragrant syrup inside. This was a little master touch worth taking note of. Peshawri is the best place in Madras for tandoori food in the deluxe category.

Raintree Restaurant

We were a bit apprehensive about dining out in the open air, not out of a dislike of the great outdoors, but because we thought we would be spending the better part of the evening fighting off mosquitoes, rather than enjoying Raintree's famous Chettinad cuisine. Fortunately, nothing of the sort happened. Obviously, the Management at the Connemara Hotel had already taken all the necessary precautions to ensure a peaceful, pest-free evening.

Executive chef Anand Reddy, and his right hand man chef Mahadevan, have successfully reproduced the original flavours of Chettinad cuisine without compromise, and succeeded in

Raintree Restaurant
Connemara Hotel
Binny Road
Madras 600 002
Tel : 860123
Price : Expensive
Speciality : Chettinad
Timings : 7.30 to midnight
Credit cards accepted
Bar licence

elevating the status of these pure and simple local specialities to fine dining.

Even though vegetarian and non-vegetarian thalis are available, we would recommend that you order à la carte, to be able to appreciate and savour individual flavours. First prize jointly goes to Karuvepellai Yer (Jumbo prawns cooked with curry leaves) and Erachi Melagu (Black pepper chicken). Both are strikingly different from anything we had ever tasted before. Eat these with Appam or special Chettinad dosa. A unique, milder dish was Kozhi Vellai Kurmah (chicken simmered in coconut milk with a dash of fresh mint). Another favourite here is 'canon balls chettinad' (Kola Urundai Ko Zhambu) made from ground mince, in a thick, spicy gravy. A superbly crafted dish not to be missed by those who enjoy mutton.

Vegetarian delights include the excellent Vegetable Stew cooked in soothing coconut milk and Vendakai Melagu, a robust dish of lady's finger (bhindi) cooked with fresh peppercorns. Though there is a variety of Appams, Dosai and Iddiappams to choose from, we recommend Appams and Dosai to mop up the wonderful Chettinad gravies.

For dessert order Paruppu Payasam, a fine combination of lightly mashed lentils and jaggery, with nuts.

The restaurant is situated in a rectangular courtyard, flanked by an open passage, which is supported by pillars, beams and a tiled sloping roof. The enormous rain tree in the middle of the lawn gives the restaurant an extraordinary ambience. The trio of flute, violen and mridang add to the whole dining experience.

Chettinad spices

Saravana Bhavan

Where in the world could you get the following for Rs 14, service included: unlimited helpings of steamed rice, green vegetable (spinach), dal, sambhar, raita with boondi, lassi (buttermilk) garnished with rose petals, rasam (curry water), sweet seera (dessert), papad, pickles and a fried chilli?

Saravana Restaurant
209, N.S.C. Bose Road
Georgetown
Madras
Tel : 587766
Price : Inexpensive
Speciality : South Indian
  Vegetarian
Timings : 6 a.m. to 10 p.m.
Partly air-conditioned

A favourite with the rich as well as the rickshaw pullers, six branches of Saravana Bhavan spread throughout the city of Madras, serve consistently good vegetarian food from 6 a.m. to 10 p.m. non-stop. For under Rs 20, you can run through the whole gamut of South Indian breakfast delicacies: Idli, Medhu Vadai, Pongal, Poori Masala, Sada Dosai all served with an assortment of chutneys, rich sambhar packed with assorted vegetables, dry chilli (nicknamed 'gunpowder'), with a bowl of pure ghee to spike up the routine. You can also have a small breakfast called Mini Tiffin, consisting of six mini Uttapams (rice pancakes) served with the same range of chutneys and sambhars, for Rs 8.50, all inclusive.

We found the green vegetables cooked in channa dal, the tastiest of the lot. For those who like spicy food, they could try the rough and robust combination of the dry, fried chilli with curd and rice. Puttu, a dessert made from lentils, coconut and jaggery was terrific, and the coffee was the best we had in Madras. No wonder the place simply packs them in.

The branch we went to had huge pictures of gods and goddesses on every inch of the wall on all three floors of these spotlessly clean dining-rooms. The owner, S. Subbiah personally supervises the daily marketing, cooking, service and cleanliness. The drinking water is treated through a Zero B filter.

At the ground floor level, Tandoori (Punjabi) vegetarian food of exceptional quality is served. There is also a Chinese menu. But it is undoubtedly the South Indian meal which should be the highlight. Served to you on a banana leaf with love and devotion by soft tempered waiters, holy ash smeared on their foreheads, this restaurant is also tremendous value for money. When we left a tip, the waiter politely returned it whispering, 'Sir, tips are not accepted here.'

Larger than life

Varandah Restaurant

After all our aggressive adventures into fiery Chettinad cuisine, the Varandah was a bit of a relief. Ask for chef Balindralal Barua and he will whip up dream dishes from his Continental repertoire, not only superb in style, taste and content, but also comparable to the best of Europe. His Steak and Kidney pie was a masterpiece, as was his Chicken Picata, served with Sali (wafer-thin) fried potato chips. But the *pièce de résistence* was the Stuffed 'fried' fish (Ravas). Not a drop of oil is used, as the fish is actually baked, then filled with a stuffing of prawns and mushrooms.

Barua also specializes in traditional Parsi dishes, like Patra Ni Machhi, Chicken Farcha (cutlet) with a hot tomato garlic sauce, and Mutton Kid Gosht, which was delicious with hot tandoori rotis. We cleaned up every bit of it. Though some of these dishes may not be on the menu, chef Barua would be glad to russle them up, if given sufficient notice. He has cooked for Queen Elizabeth and the Late Marshal Tito.

While at Varandah, try the chef's special, Cheese Puffs, A La Reddy, spiked with green chilli.

Varandah has a pleasant decor and comfortable seating, overlooking the swimmimg pool and palm trees. It was previously a veranda which has now been enclosed with picture windows and air-conditioning. A perfect setting for an excellent cuisine.

Varandah Restaurant
Connemara Hotel
Binny Road
Madras 600002
Tel : 8520123
Price : Expensive
Specialities : North Indian, Continental
Timings : Round the clock.
Credit cards accepted
Bar licence
Air-conditioned

Woodlands Drive-in-Restaurant

Woodlands
Drive-in-restaurant
Agri-Horticulture Gardens
30, Cathedral Road
Madras 600 086
Tel : 471981
Price : Inexpensive
Speciality : South Indian
   Vegetarian
Timings : 6 a.m. to 9 p.m.
Air-conditioned

Not to be confused with the main Woodlands Hotel which has a similar menu. This one is far more pleasant, since it is set in the Horticultural Gardens on Mount Road. Woodlands serves a superb quality of tiffin at very reasonable prices. A plate of idli with accompanying sambhar and chutney costs only two rupees (all inclusive). Aromatic, freshly-brewed coffee is Rs 3.50.

Specially recommended, at any time of the day, are Tomato Bhath, (Semolina uppama flavoured with fresh tomatoes, curry leaves and mustard seeds), Idli (melt in the mouth variety) crisp Dosai, and traditional Pongal. The freshly squeezed black grape and lemon juice and badam kheer, a nourishing almond milkshake, are wonderful alternatives to a fizzy drink. Ice creams are from Dasa Prakash.

The main restaurant is situated in two large halls which look like a clean, white aeroplane hanger, divided up by orange mechano type partitions. Overhanging tiffany lamps and private niches create a more personal tone. Polite bearers in white mini lungis serve with alarcity. No menu card. Everything is displayed on the board as you enter.

The huge open kitchen is spotless. Lots of parking space. Food is also served to you in your car, as the name suggests.

Nepal

KATHMANDU

Kathmandu is basically a tourist city which attracts trekkers, campers and those who love the mountains. There is no distinctive style of cooking in Nepal. The food is, by and large, very similar to Indian, but with less spice. The closest to local food here is Tibetan cuisine, which specializes in dumplings, called Momos, and a warming soup, known as Thukba. Most of the ingredients are imported, and transport is always a big problem. Certain foodstuffs disappear altogether or become exorbitant. Local dairy products like milk, yoghurt butter and the utterly delicious Yak cheese are always in plentiful supply, and a number of bakeries, including the German Bakery, make sure that nobody ever goes hungry.

In the Sixties, Kathmandu was invaded by hippies. Some came to visit, but were so taken with the friendly folk, the climate and the blend of Hinduism and Buddhism, that they stayed on. Since then the city has attracted foreign tourists. The core of activity, restaurants and hotels, is in Thamel, at the north end of the Old City.

For some reason, Italian food seems to be very popular and very good in the city, with Alfresco, at the Oberoi, leading the field. La Dolce Vita is your best bet in the moderate price range. Chinese is also a sure shot here—Saino, though it specializes in Indian and Continental as well, is best for its Chinese dishes.

Restaurants keep opening and closing all the time in Thamel, so it is difficult to keep track of which are the best at any particular time, and which are likely to stay that way. But Western food is definitely your best bet in Kathmandu.

A meal for one person

Inexpensive: under 100 rupees
Moderate: 100 to 250 rupees
Expensive: over 250 rupees

Alfresco

Alfresco
The Soaltee Holiday Inn
  Crowne Plaza
Tahachal
Kathmandu
Nepal
Tel : 272555 Fax : 272205
Price : Expensive
Speciality : Italian
Timings : 12.30 to 2.30 p.m.;
7:30 to 11:30 p.m.
Credit cards accepted
Bar licence
Air-conditioned

Who needs a library when you have as enticing a menu as Alfresco's to read. Chef Sanjay Malkani has worked hard to reproduce the earthy flavours of Southern Italy all over again. His sense of balance and texture is remarkable. He manages to coax delicious flavours out of light seasonings. All the raw materials used are authentic, from the pastas, cheese and extra virgin olive oil.

We started with Crema di Funghi alle Erbe Aromatiche, a bowl of clear mushroom soup, scented with herbs. It was both robust and elegant in its understated simplicity. Pizza 'La Bella Contessa', a thin crusty variety, loaded with goodies like olives, sweet peppers, cheese, ham, salami, mushrooms, etc., is tremendous. We followed this with the bread and butter of Italian cuisine, the pasta, Fettucchine con le Melanzane e Pomodoro ai Formaggi. This simple dish of home-made, flat noodles tossed with fresh tomatoes, aubergine, chilli and parmesan, was again superb. In fish, go for the Poached fillet of Bekti, mildy favoured with Italian herbs. Vegetarians will be delighted with the range of pizzas, pastas and exotic vegetables like Artichokes and Asparagus.

For dessert try the Zuccotto, a liqueur soaked cake, filled with chocolate whipped cream and nuts, or the home-made Cassata ice cream, with candied fruits and nuts. Finish off with an espresso coffee.

The decor is a reflection of the luminosity of the Mediterranean. You come away feeling lifted in spirit, bodily satisfied and totally delighted with the experience.

As the book goes to press, we have been informed that the Hotel has been taken over by the Holiday Inn Crowne Plaza group, and chef Malkani is now with the Oberoi in Delhi. However, we have been assured that the quality of this restaurant will not change despite the take over.

Al Pollo E Pizzeria

Open right from breakfast through lunch and dinner, Al Pollo has its own following of loyal foodies, who flock here for down to earth, authentic Italian pasta and pizzas, at a very reasonable price. The restaurant was started by the present owner's father, Hariprasad, who learnt his craft while working as a chef in the USA. We ordered a Spaghetti con Tonno e Funghi (spaghetti with tuna fish and mushrooms), followed by a simple grilled (beef) steak, with spinach and mashed potatoes. Both were excellent. The other specialities of Al Pollo are Pizza al Prosciutto (Ham, cheese and tomato pizza), and the Mexican dishes, Taco de Pollo, Taco De Vegetable and mushrooms, and Enchilada Carne (minced meat in a soft pancake). The home-made caramel custard, was generous as well as tasty. Two can easily share one portion.

Al Pollo E Pizzeria
Thamel
Kathmandu
Price : Moderate
Speciality : Italian
Timings : 8 a.m. to 10 p.m.
Credit cards accepted
Air-conditioned

A no-nonsense eatery run by the owners themselves, Al Pollo is situated in the courtyard of an old house. We like its honest homely cooking and atmosphere.

Arniko Room

Arniko Room
Hotel De L'Annapurna
P.O. Box No 140
Durbar Marg
Kathmandu
Nepal
Tel : 2-21711
Price : Expensive
Speciality : Chinese
Timings : Noon to 2:45 p.m.;
7 to 11.30 p.m.
Credit cards accepted
Bar licence
Air-conditioned

Yet another restaurant in Durbar Square serving mouth-watering Szechwan cuisine. Chef Jitendra Bhatnagar has created his own specialities, using local ingredients. The crisp fried Chilli Honey Potatoes, unheard of in China, were unforgettably delicious, and make a great starter. We have heard that the Chinese consider garlic an essential ingredient in the kitchen, both for flavour as well as its inherent healing properties. At Arniko they obviously adhere to this belief as every dish reeks of the stuff. Bear this in mind when tucking into the Chicken Hong Kong style and the Shredded Lamb in hot garlic sauce. They are both devilishly tasty, but not for the likes of Dracula.

Of all the dishes, we liked the sliced steak, stir fried with oyster sauce. Vegetarian options are standard but the Beancurd with vegetables and the ever popular Vegetable Manchurian are safe bets.

The decor is no great shakes, but comfortable and obviously Chinese (red dragons, lanterns, etc.).

Boris' Room

Boris' Room is named after the famous Russian ballet dancer (who at one time danced with Diaghalev's Ballet Russe) who turned into a chef, and made Nepal his home in the Fifties. The restaurant, now run by one of his sons, is situated on the second floor of a pretty house at the north end of Thamel. Look for the sign 'Sanghmitra' (meeting place) which leads into a courtyard, and then to the two restaurants upstairs. Red velvet curtains and memorabilia of Boris's extraordinary life never let you forget what old Russia stood for. Neither does the food, which is a mix of Russian and classic European.

Boris' Room
Opposite Hotel Marshyangdi
Thamel
Kathmandu
Tel : 411611
Price : Moderate
Speciality : European
Timings : 11 a.m. to 10 p.m.
Tuesdays closed

The famous Russian beet root soup Borstch, Chicken Liver Pâté, Beef Stroganoff and Shashlik are all excellent, as are the Chateaubriand, Pork Chops baked with Apple and Guinea Fowl Marechal (stuffed with pâté). Finish off with either Yeti's Delight, crepes with cream and Kahlua (Mexican coffee liquer), or a platter of Yak cheese.

More than a restaurant with fine food, eating here is a real experience.

Ghar-E-Kebab

Ghar-e-Kebab
Hotel De L'Annapurna
P.O. Box No 140
Durbar Marg
Kathmandu
Nepal
Tel : 221711
Price : Expensive
Speciality : Moghlai
Timings : Noon to 2.45 p.m.;
   7 to 10.30 p.m.
Credit cards accepted
Bar licence
Air-conditioned

One of the most popular Moghlai restaurants in Durbar Square, Ghar-e-Kebab makes no bones about its meat specialities. Chef Vishal Kapoor has mastered the art of blending strong, almost firework like flavours. On top of the list, is his Mutton Malai Kabab, a magical mixture of mutton mince, ginger, green chilli, coarse ground black pepper, khoya and finally cream, to balance the fiery masalas. The result is sublime, in fact pure self-indulgence. For chicken lovers, there is the popular Reshmi Kabab, made with chicken mince and seasoned with ginger garlic, green chilli paste, nutmeg, cardamom, coconut powder, cream, saffron and fresh coriander. For vegetarians, there is Haryali Kabab.

Big chunky fish like Rawas, Gol and Bekti, which keep fresh for longer (brought frozen from Calcutta), are used for the Jal Pari Ke Tikke. Bekti fish steaks are minced along with curds, ajwain, ginger-garlic paste, saffron and cream, shaped into kababs and broiled over charcoal to produce a dish worth waiting for.

For the main course, try the Boti Kabab Masala or the Achar Gosht, both aromatic gravy dishes. We went gaga over the Chooza Kali Mirch, tender spring chicken simmered in yoghurt and coarsely ground black pepper. For the vegetarians, the Khumb Palak, a semi dry combination of fresh mushrooms and spinach, was interesting as was the Punjabi Kadi, a richer version the Gujarati one. Another speciality is the Bawan Patti Paratha, a multi-layered paratha close to Lachcha, but bigger in size. For dessert, try the Kesari Kheer, garnished with pistachios. You need a massive appetite to enjoy and appreciate all the specialities.

The decor is quite tacky, with a mirrored ceiling, and heavy turquoise carpet, which tends to absorb the 'curry' aromas. However, the delicious food and good service make up for it.

Helena's

Located right in the heart of Thamel, what looks like a hole in the wall turned out to be a good eatery, that leads from one room to another like a cosy house. The seasonal menu is chalked up daily on the blackboard, and the dessert usually either a Carrot Cake (in summer) or a Lemon Meringue (in winter), is displayed in the window. The speciality of the house is Chicken Kiev (breast of chicken filled with butter, rolled and deep fried). Watch out for the butter spurts into your face as soon as you prick the chicken with a fork! For the vegetarians, there are excellent options like the Lasagne (eggplant, yak cheese, white sauce and parmesan cheese), and the Moussaka (made with beans, potato, onion, tomato and cheese). Salad Nicoise too is a meal in itself (they will gladly omit the egg and tuna for the vegetarians).

A homely, lively, fun restaurant, recommended for good value.

Helena's
Thamel
Kathmandu
Tel : 412135
Price : Moderate
Speciality : Continental
Timings : 7 a.m. to 10 p.m.
Credit cards accepted
Air-conditioned

Kathmandu Temple

Him Thai Restaurant

Him Thai Restaurant
Him Thai Plaza
Thamel
Kathmandu
Nepal
Tel : 226277
Price : Expensive
Speciality : Thai
Timings : 12.30 to 3 p.m.;
    7.30 to 11.30 p.m.
Credit cards accepted
Bar licence

An old cottage, set in a pomello (pink grapefruit) fruit orchard, Him Thai is one of the most picturesque restaurants in Kathmandu. At night, the garden resembles fairyland, as every table glimmers with candlelight. Uchai Manenlot the Him Thai executive chef is from Bangkok. It is no wonder then that the Tom Yam Koong soup tasted strikingly similar to the best we have had in Thailand. Som Tam Mala Ko (raw papaya salad) was scrumptious. Goy See Mee (crisp fried noodles with chicken and bamboo shoot) was also excellent. These are the house specialities and the most popular items on the menu. Fish is best avoided, as fresh fish is not always available. There is a reasonable but not extensive choice of vegetarian dishes, including a vegetable Tom Yam soup, vegetables in a green curry (Kang Kiew Warn Kab Pak) and fried as well as crispy noodles.

Him Thai, with a menu that looks suspiciously like the Thai Airlines one, is definitely more expensive than other restaurants in Thamel, but still good value, as the Thai cuisine is authentic and prepared with imported ingredients. If you need a change of cuisine in an elegant ambience, then Him Thai fits the bill beautifully.

Mike's Breakfast

There is really no difference here between an English breakfast and an American one, except that the American portions are huge, and can easily be shared. We ordered the Mike's special, which consisted of an omelette made with three eggs, mushrooms, onions, mozzarella cheese and herbs, cooked together into a huge cake. Fresh home-made, whole wheat muffins, butter, jam, freshly ground (Nepali grown beans) coffee makes up the rest. Everything was delicious, especially the muffins which went exceedingly well with the aromatic black coffee. For small eaters it is advisable to avoid the eggs and stick to muffins jam and butter, which together with coffee will cost you only Rs 65 as against Rs 120 for Mike's special.

Mike's Breakfast
1, Seto Durbar
Durbar Marg
Kathmandu
Nepal
Tel : 227834
Price : Moderate
Speciality : American
Timings : 7 a.m. to 4 p.m.
5 p.m. to 9 p.m. pizzas
(not everyday)

For lunch, the all-time favourite here is the Quiche served with a Tossed Green Salad and whole wheat bread. The sandwiches (grilled or plain) are substantial and good value. Try the Cheese and Chutney, or the Cheeseburger; all fresh and good value. For health freaks, Mike's Breakfast also serves granola with milk or yogurt.

Mike's Breakfast is located inside a beautiful old mansion, which has been converted into a restaurant. Each nook and corner of this house is filled with tables and surrounded by plants. The best place to sit is in the balconies overlooking the rose garden, or in the garden (weather permitting) under the gazebo. A charming place to visit for a late breakfast or brunch.

La Dolce Vita

La Dolce Vita
P.O. Box No 4477
Thamel
In front of Kathmandu Guest
  House
Kathmandu
Tel : 419612
Price : Moderate
Speciality : Italian
Timings : 11 a.m. to 11 p.m.
Reservation recommended
Credit cards accepted
Bar licence
Air-conditioned

Originally started by Tony Mantora, an Italian, in 1986, La Dolce Vita is now managed by Sagar Shreshta, and still retains its original charm and cuisine. La Dolce Vita is decorated beautifully in stark black and white. The walls display original (now collectors' items) posters of Fellini's famous film of the same name, starring Sofia Loren. To grab your attention further, there are two striking paintings of nubile Italian nympets in tight black evening dresses, saying 'wow' to plates of spaghetti. These are original works by the resident Italian artist, Giorana Carugo. Philipino San Miguel beer and European Tuborg beer (bottled in Nepal) flows freely in the bar on the second floor.

Indra Tamang, the present Nepali chef, has learned his craft (well) from Tony Mantora and turns out excellent Pasta. Gnocchi di Patate al Formaggio (potato dumpling with melted mozzarella, cheddar cheese and double cream sauce) wins our first prize. The vegetarian Lasagne overflows with freshly sautéed mushrooms, fresh tomato sauce and buffalo mozzarella, with a generous dash of olive oil. Rich, creamy, very tasty, and great value. Melanzane Alla Parmaziana, was another vegetarian masterpiece, with layers of aubergine, smothered in tomato sauce and cheese, and then baked. Finally, the thin crust Pizza, cooked in an authentic, wood fire pizza oven, was the best in Thamel. The Steaks and Veal Escalope, simply grilled, were also excellent.

The Gelato al Liquor, Nirula ice cream doused with Nepalese whisky, makes a fitting finale to a good meal.

La Dolce Vita is a large restaurant, situated on the first floor of a rambling old house. Although it seats nearly 200 people, the bar area included, do not go without a reservation.

Saino Restaurant And Bar

What attracted us to Saino was the magnificent antique wrought iron street-lamp which sits in the middle of a small pond. Surrounding this is a well kept garden in which you sit and eat. Thank Heavens for open air restaurants. This one is made all the more delightful, by its little red and white checkered tablecloths. For those who do not hanker for the great outdoors, there is additional seating on the first floor, where you squat around low red tables.

Chef Tilak Karki, a Nepali, learnt his craft from hotels in India, and is proficient in both Indian and Chinese cuisine. His Ginger Prawns and Manchurian Chicken, were typically 'Indian Chinese', but tasty and good value. The best dish was Mixed Vegetables with Mushrooms and Bamboo shoots. This is eaten with a bowl of steamed fluffy white Basmati rice. We were informed that the chef's speciality is the Steamboat (hot chicken consomme served from a samovar type hot pot, in which you cook prawn, chicken, eggs, meat, mushrooms, noodles, etc. yourself).

Like most of the restaurants in Nepal, Saino serves three cuisines, and the menu is quite extensive. From what we tasted, we feel that the general standard of this newly opened restaurant is very good.

Saino Restaurant And Bar
Darbar Marg
Kathmandu
Tel :230682
Price : Moderate
Specialities : Chinese, Indian, Continental
Timings : 11 a.m. to 10 p.m.
Bar licence

Tashi Deleg

Tashi Deleg
Thamel
Kathmandu
Price : Inexpensive
Speciality : Tibetan
Timings : 7 a.m. to 10 p.m.

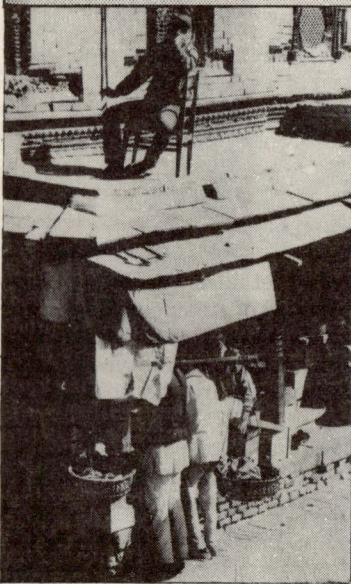

Street life in Kathmandu

The speciality of Tashi Deleg is the Tibetan Momo—a steamed dumpling, similar to their Chinese cousins, with freshly ground beef, to be eaten with sauces of mustard, tomato and green chutney. Momo can also be prepared with chicken or vegetables. We found this speciality utterly delicious, and very filling. Good value for those on a budget.

The restaurant is honest-to-goodness, with red formica tables and plastic orchids in little vases, but reasonably clean and well looked after. Everything is freshly cooked, so you have to wait a while for service. The music system plays the local FM radio station, relaying a strange mix of Indian, Nepalese and European music.

Other specialities of the restaurant are Rhichossi, momo in steaming chicken soup (excellent for the Nepalese winter), and Thupka noodles, fried with vegetables. It is advisable to carry your own drinking water or order a soft drink. There are Chinese and Italian dishes on the menu, but Tashi Deleg is best known for Tibetan dishes.

Pune

Pune is often described as the 'Soul of Maharashtra', although Bombay is the capital. This is not entirely fair, since the city is one of the most cosmopolitan places outside Bombay, made up of many different communities, and diverse historical influences. The latest outside influence to hit it is the Osho Commune, the nerve centre of a worldwide movement which follows the teachings of Bhagwan Osho Rajneesh. Many of his followers, of which a large percentage is foreign, live in and around the beautiful Commune, in the residential area of Koregaon Park. The others visit from October to March, when there are often 10,000 visitors a day in the area. In fact, the Commune is today India's largest tourist draw, attracting more rupee spending visitors than the Taj Mahal. Consequently, the restaurants that have popped up in the area, sometimes run by sanyasins themselves, serve mildly spiced Indian food and an imaginative variety of European alternatives. The German Bakery, for example, is an oasis serving health foods, cakes, bread and snacks. You'll get the most authentic Italian Pizza (though vegetarian) in town at La Pizzeria, at Hotel Sriman. Deccan and what is referred to as 'the City', is where you will find the much talked of 'Soul'. Maharashtrian food is characterized by simplicity and restraint. It is satisfying, visually appealing, and a great deal of thought goes into the skilful blending of the basics to retain the individual colour, texture and flavour of the main ingredients. Quantities are usually ample, but excess and over indulgence is usually frowned upon.

There are three distinct cuisines in the state: the fiery, rich vegetarian and meat dishes of the Maratha (warrior) community; the subtle flavours of the Saraswat Brahmins; and the unique seafood preparations of the Konkan coast. Outside homes, traditional food is served only in simple Thali hotels, which cater to a mainly local clientele. Shreyas, in Deccan, will give you an adequate glimpse into a vegetarian Maharashtrian Thali, with sweet, salty, hot and sour combinations all served together, without offending the palate. Jaggery, peanuts, coconut and sabudana (sago) are used in every second dish, including dal (amti). On special occasions, Puranpoli, a roti stuffed with a sweet channa dal mixture, is a real treat. Though Shreyas does not serve Bakri (traditional rotis made from millet or javar), you should grab the opportunity to try them in other restaurants.

The Camp side of town is the area once occupied by the British. It combines the rest of the hotch potch in Pune. This is reflected in eating places, which range from sizzler restaurants, like the Place, to the famous Parsee Dorabjee's (who also caters to almost every big Parsee function in town) to Bhelpuri wallas.

The only factor that links both sides of town is price. Pune is not a city for big spenders. The popular restaurants are reasonably priced, but more than them, many roadside stalls and small, snack places have a loyal patronage. The smarter snack shops are Marz O Rin, on Main Street (M. G. Road), which serves a variety of home-made sandwiches, cakes and soft drinks. The Spicer College Shop, in Wonderland Shopping Arcade, specializes in Health Foods and produce from their farm. Café Naaz, at the end of Main Street, opposite Aurora Towers Hotel, serves simply the best masala chai and brun we have ever tasted. The ABC Farms shop, off M.G. Road is a dairy specializing in an amazing variety of cheeses and organic farm produce, like brown rice.

You cannot talk about roadside eating without mentioning the second generation panipuri wallas, the Aggarwal brothers in Pudumjee Park, who, besides panipuri, enchant you with mouth-watering Kachoris and Mirchi Pakodas. Sadashiv Peth, in the City, is crammed with little snack bars, some less flea-ridden than others, where an outsider is stared at with some degree of suspicion. Maruti is a hole in the wall serving ussal and misal for no more than the price of a Thums Up.

Shopping for Pune's specialities is also a local pastime. The city is of course famous for its bakeries, especially Kayani on East Street, for their all-butter Shrewsbury biscuits and fantastic Mawa Cakes, Royal and City Bakeries (owned by the same family), for their all butter Cashewnut biscuits, Flaky Hearts, crusty brun bread and Plum Cake and Empire on Sachapir Street for their naan and paratha breads and rawa cake. For mithai, the only places in town are either of the Karachi's, run by different branches of the family. The original is on Sachapir Street and the more modern one, on the ground floor of Aurora Towers Hotel. Try the Angir (fig) and Mawa varieties. Chitale in the city is famous for all its quality milk products, especially the Pedas and bakarvadi, a Gujarati inspired fried snack which Chitle senior has slightly adapted to Maharashtrian tastes.

For cheese lovers, you must stop at ABC Farms, situated conveniently in the middle of M.G. Road, where you can pick up an enormous variety of cheeses and organic farm products like Bio rice and ice berg lettuce.

Finally, you cannot leave the city without picking up a packet or two of Laxmi Narayan Chevda, from their mini factory cum outlet in Bhavani Peth.

Pune is definitely not for the luxury category of diner, but it does have some interesting nooks and corners which are worth exploring.

A meal for one person

Inexpensive: under 100 rupees
Moderate: 100 to 250 rupees
Expensive: over 250 rupees

Abhiruchi

Abhiruchi
Cottage Restaurant
Bhide Baug
Near New Bombay-Bangalore
  Flyover Bridge, Vadgaon BK
Pune 411 041
Tel: 424588, 436683
Price : Inexpensive
Speciality : Maharashtrian
Timings : 8 a.m. to 9 p.m.

You cannot beat this for a cheap, wholesome family outing. Abhiruchi, which means 'preference', is certainly long overdue in a city like Pune, with its many unexploited green spots. Set in twenty acres of farmland, this newly opened rustic eating spot is very near the heart of the city (fifteen minutess by car from Deccan), yet sufficiently far away to escape the noise, traffic and people.

You park your car at the entrance next to their plant nursery and farm shop and walk right in to either a hut, sit under a gazebo near the children's playground or park yourself under the shade of a guava tree. Your meal is served to you wherever you choose to sit. Hot bhajias are first brought to you, followed by unlimited quantities of freshly cooked, but slightly oily, vegetables, Dal (amti), Pitla (besan relish), Raita and pickles, all made in a central, open kitchen. There is a choice of javar, bajra and ordinary wheat rotis, and plain white rice, or a very interesting unpolished pullav. Avoid the sweets. Take a walk around the farm instead, pluck your own vegetables, or, if you are too lazy, go on a healthy shopping spree at the farm shop.

There is a large central kitchen which is functional and friendly, with lots of ladies making fresh rotis and frying bhajias.

There is a playground and ducks to keep the children busy. Great value for money at Rs 35 per head (all inclusive), and you can stay as long as you like. Free for young children, even if they nibble.

Angaraj

Called a 'holiday resort' because of a few cottages, Angaraj, a little out of town, past the village of Kondhwa, is one of the newest eating establishments on the scene. To call it a restaurant would be an understatement. People do definitely come to eat here, but they can also take a walk on the wild side, around the miniature zoo, watch the train, go for a swim or simply snack, lunch or dine.

Angaraj
Kondhwa Budruk
Dist Pune
(On the road to Kondhwa from M.G. Road, past Lullanagar on your left about 1 km after the village)
Tel : 672135
Price : Moderate
Specialities : North Indian, Chinese
Timings : 11 a.m. to 11 p.m.
Bar licence

The decor is made up of tree house structures, using local materials like bamboo, cane and stone. In fact, all it lacks is Tarzan swinging around. The place is enormous, and service, though pretty efficient, must be a nightmare. You can eat in any one of the garden sections, in the central, mosaic tiled hut, by the poolside, in the open Coffee Shop or in private 'tree top' dining areas.

The menu is extensive, with the standard mix of Tandoori, Chinese and Continental. We liked the Tandoori Chicken, Naans, Palak Chicken and dal. The children ate Chinese which, although it was 'Indian Chinese' was good, especially the soups and noodle dishes. We would avoid the heavy Moghlai fare like Rogan Josh, Navratan Korma, Kheema and Pullav, which although it looked fine, is not our cup of tea when we come to a place where for once we can enjoy a little nature with the kids.

There is an interesting bar which you must take a peep into. It looks straight out of a Hindi movie, with a statue of a voluptuous dancer in the centre!

However, avoid the bathrooms, which are really not up to the mark for a restaurant of this kind.

Ashoka Hotel

Ashoka Hotel
2163 B, Peshwa Park
(near Neelayam Talkies
Cinema)
Pune 411 030
Tel : 433444
Price : Inexpensive
Speciality : Gujarati Thali
  Vegetarian
Timings : 11 a.m. to 3 p.m.; 7
to 11 p.m.

Another inimitable Thali restaurant, based on a Gujarati style, but in much more plush and cleaner surroundings (marble fountain in the centre!) than most of its counterparts. The service is quiet, the washbasin discreet, but without adequate towels or paper napkins. The food is unusually well balanced for a Thali joint, with emphasis on fresh, seasonal vegetables. The Potato Bhaji is particularly tasty, as is the home-made Mouli relish. The quantities are unlimited, service very fast, and portions generous. Both chilled lassi and soft drinks are available. Worth going all the way into the city (around the corner from the zoo).

Roadside temple

Badshah Cold Drink House

A sister concern of the original home of juices and milk shakes opposite Crawford Market in Bombay. This one is far more comfortable, with a small seating area outside too. The juices, made even more tempting by the fresh display of fruits, are squeezed on order and very clean. The faludas are legendary.

Snacks include bhel puri, sev batata puri, good sandwiches, pizzas, burgers and home-made kulfi in tiny terracotta pots.

Ice creams are churned the old-fasioned style. Try the fresh strawberry and sitaphal.

A nice place for a snack even though it is situated on the busy East Street. Service is attentive.

Badshah Cold Drink House
7, Dr. Coyaji Road (East
  Street)
Opp Victory Cinema
Pune 411 001
Tel : 662667
Price : Inexpensive
Speciality : Snacks
Timings : 7.30 a.m. to
  midnight

Blue Nile

Blue Nile
4 Bund Garden Road
(Opposite Pune Club)
Pune 411 001
Tel: 625238
**Price: Inexpensive/
  Moderate**
Specialities : Irani, North
  Indian
Timings : 11.30 a.m. to
  midnight

A fierce competitor of Dorabjee's, the Blue Nile, with the 1947 Plymouth parked outside, has been in existence for as long as anyone can remember. The menu has been expanded to include Moghlai, Punjabi and Chinese dishes, in addition to the standard Irani fare. We can recommend, with some degree of certainty, the Brain Fry, Baghdadi Chicken, cooked in egg and cream, red hot Kohlapuri mutton and the inimitable Mutton Biryani. The Tandoori Chicken is always good especially if you ask for the one without colour. Avoid the caramel custard at all costs.

Chandni

We were taken to Sagar Plaza, one of Pune's newer luxury hotels, one rainy evening, for a fish called bekti (or betki as it is known in its native Bengal). Fish? During the rains? We were genuinely worried.

Chandni is the rooftop restaurant, open to the sky with live music playing, when it doesn't rain that is. As we went in June, the roof of Chandni was covered, which transformed it into a relaxed dhaba, with an open kitchen (always a good sign) in one corner. Chandni's menu varied slightly from the norm, and the quality was, surprisingly, very good. The Fish Tikka in question (made from fresh bekti) came piping hot straight from the tandoor. It was succulent, medium spiced and simply mouth-watering, with no hint of that awful red colouring one sees everywhere.

Chandni
Hotel Sagar Plaza
1, Bund Garden Road
Pune 411001
Tel : 622680
Price : Expensive
Speciality : North Indian
Timings : 7.30 p.m. to
  11.30 p.m.
Credit cards accepted
Bar licence
Air-conditioned

Chef Saeed Allahuddin, now no longer with the hotel, perfected the recipe. The secret is the blend of just a few, rather than too many, carefully selected spices—haldi, jeera, dhania and chaat masala. A clever coating of eggs with lemon juice keep the tikka intact.

The Reshmi and Kalmi Kababs are equally succulent and successful. Of the main courses, the Balti Gosht is an innovative addition to the menu. It is slow cooked in a copper handi and served in a rather sweet little copper bucket.

Other items on Chandni's menu, more familiar to Indian clientele, like the Murg Saagwala and Kachche Gosht Ki Biryani, are all above average. Service is reasonably quick, attentive and very polite. A breath of fresh air in the five-star restaurant brigade in Pune.

China Town

China Town
Blue Diamond Hotel
11 Koregaon Road
Pune 411 001
Tel:625555
Price: Moderate
Speciality: Chinese
Timings:7.30 to 11 p.m.
Credit cards accepted
Bar licence

This is clearly the best Chinese restaurant in Pune, and is under the supervision of the knowledgeable chef Arora. The decor is decidedly un-Chinese, with the standard, comfortable furniture and subtle trimmings, as you would expect in a luxury hotel. The menu has taken an up-market turn, including fresh lobsters and tiger prawns, specially brought in from Bombay on a daily basis. Chinese vegetables, though, are still unimaginative.

The seafood soup to start with is more akin to an egg drop one, slightly milky in texture and thankfully without the usual amount of cornstarch. Pla na Prik, a Thai name but more 'Thai' inspired, is a dish of pomfret fillets topped with a translucent sauce made with lemon grass and a hint of green chilli. Lobster in salt and pepper and even in a sweet-and-sour sauce, are fresh and well presented. The flesh is removed from the shell, stir fried and then returned to the shell. We preferred the medium sized prawns to the large variety, done in a garlic sauce. This Indo-Chinese dish is very common in Chinese restaurants in India, but done particularly well here. The Lemon Chicken is also worth trying. All the usual staples like sweet corn this and that, spring rolls, fried rice and noodle dishes are available and competent.

This is by no means a trip down the Yangtse, but for Pune, it ranks pretty well. The service is good.

Chetana

Chetana is considered the King of Gujarati thalis in Pune. Only for the adventurous, as this hotel cum restaurant is in the heart of the city, right next to the red light area. As you walk into this dingy hotel, you buy a coupon and walk down a flight of stairs to the spotless restaurant which is in the basement. The decor is basic with functional tables, chairs and steel crockery and cutlery.

There are two types of thalis—normal (spicy), and without salt and chilli. Kachoris, steaming Dokhlas (you get an array of farsan with the thali), several vegetables, rotis, rice, etc. The chutneys are quite extraordinary, especially the tamarind chutney made with tamarind, jaggery, red chilli and garlic, and the red hot garlic chutney. The home-made shrikand (one portion is enough for three) is deliciously yellow with kesar, and not colouring. Try the Rose Barfi which is their speciality.

Chetana
884, Budhwar Peth
Near Vijayanand Talkies
Pune 411 002
Tel : 475454, 475455
Price : Inexpensive
Speciality : Gujarati Thali
Timings : 11.30 **a.m.** to
    2.45 p.m.; 7.30 to 10 p.m.
Air-conditioned

Bounty of vegetables

Coffee House

Coffee House
2, Moledina Road
(Between Manney's Bookshop
and Dorabjee Sons)
Pune 411 001
Tel : 664974, 667716
Price : Inexpensive
Speciality : South Indian
Timings : 8 a.m. to 11 p.m.

Here's Pune's melting pot. You once saw Parsis in Bombay bowters eating eggs and bacon. Today sanyasins from the Osho Commune nibble on paneer and fruit salad, students tuck into vadas the size of tennis balls, and the aroma of South Indian Coffee permeates.

Renovated by Sitaram Shetty, this one-time Parsi eatery is now a smart restaurant in cane and marble. Although it now serves the ever popular Chinese and Moghlai dishes too, Coffee House's reputation is still based on their mouth-watering South Indian snacks. Never have you tasted a Mysore Masala dosa quite like this one. A large, standard plain dosa is stuffed with green chutney, coconut chutney, grated coconut, soft potato sabji, topped with cashew nuts and folded into a triangular envelope to seal in the steam.

Other standard South Indian delicacies are equally good: Upma, Rava Dosa, Uttapams (not the stodgy mass one often finds) and Fried Idli. Try the Malgapudi Idli, served with dry red, 'gun powder' chutney which you mix yourself. Of the continental items, the Vegetarian Fish Pickle (actually soft fried paneer) and Creamed Spinach with potato cutlets, are unbeatable. Be warned, proportions are hog sized, and Nair, the ever-helpful little headwaiter, is the first to suggest that you share. He also recounts in true filmi style, how Raj Kapoor used to come here after the races and order everything on the menu!

Dorabjee & Sons

If you haven't already heard of this Pune institution, Marazban Dorabjee, the charming uncle of the clan, will tell you how he is the third generation Parsi to run it, since it opened nearly a hundred years ago. The food is practically legendary. The Kid Roast (a huge knuckle of succulent young goat) and Khara Roast (the same knuckle in a thin mutton soup) are good enough to kill for. The Mutton Biryani is well known, and the best time to have it is just before midday, when the patila is opened for lunch. Apart from the excellent quality of meat and subtle masalas, we believe that the extra oomph is only possible because of slow cooking on natural wood fires. The cutlets, Brain Fry and deliciously soft liver and kidneys, are also among our regular orders. Steaming hot Paya (goat trotters) is available in the evening only. Kheema and Akuri, masala scrambled eggs, are the breakfast specials. You cannot leave without tasting the Custard Pudding, the secret of which is the reduced milk and desi, not English, eggs and, of course, the wood fire on which it is made. This must be the only restaurant in Pune that shuts when it runs out of food, which is pretty often. Not high on ambience or decor, this is a place strictly for hogging. An added attraction is Marazban's son Darius, a veritable hunk, who often sits at the counter.

Dorabjee & Sons
845, Dastur Meher Road
Pune 411 001
Price : Inexpensive
Specialities : Irani, Parsi
Timings : 9 a.m. to 11 p.m.

No toilet and very basic washrooms. Take away is recommended. 'There is no phone as I don't want to waste half of my day speaking to finicky Parsi ladies,' says Dorabjee.

Good old Dorabjee's

Golconda

Golconda
Lt Col Tarapore Road
Sub Area Shopping Complex
Next to KV School
Pune 411 001
Tel : 666167 (Residence)
Price : Moderate
Speciality : Hyderabadi,
     North Indian
Timings : 7.30 to 11 p.m.

A strange place for a restaurant, but the ever energetic Bina Chandra pulled it off. Golconda, an outdoor (covered) dhaba serving Mathur Kayasth, Hyderabadi cuisine, is situated bang in the middle of a military complex, but is open to the public.

Opened in June 1992, Golconda became an instant hit during the 1992 horse-racing season in Pune, when hungry punters, eager to find somewhere new and not too far from the Turf Club, chanced upon this establishment. The decor is no doubt 'basic', as is the cutlery, crockery and napkins. The food is honest to goodness and home style, with a Hyderabadi inclination. The specialities include Bhuna Bheja (brain masala), Tomato Methi Gosht (mutton pieces in a tomato and fenugreek gravy), Biryani and Dum Ki Murg (baked masala chicken). Recent additions to the menu are the Salan Raan and Chippa Chicken (cooked in a Hyderabadi earthen pot on coal). Vegetarian options are limited, but seafood is available on order. No doubt the cuisine is on the spicy side and is sometimes a little oily too, but the quality of the ingredients is exemplary. The kheema, for example, is hand chopped which makes all the difference. Traditional sweets include Khubani Ka Meetha (stewed apricots with cream) and Shahi Tukra (rich bread pudding), although Lemon Pie and Gulab Jamun are also available.

A special 'Racegoers brunch' is open during the Racing season only (June to October), with Hyderabadi staples such as Nahari, Paya and Bheja. It's a wonder that anyone makes it to the Turf Club after all that !

Like all one-man (or woman) operations, Golconda is a very personalized restaurant. The food here does have that extra oomph when the owner-chef is around, and sometimes lacks it when she isn't.

No beer or liquor licence.

Jaws

Situated on the ground floor of an old, run down, Pune mansion, this is a basic fast food joint, with lots of scope for the future. Jaws serves a very satisfying and extremely cheap, basic hamburger and its offsprings—the Jaws Burger, Deluxe Burger, Cheese Burger, Chicken roll, Frankies, all bursting at the seams with a variety of relishes. Recent additions to the menu include Kathi Kababs and Grilled Sandwiches. There is ample seating outside, but most of the business is take away. The atmosphere is always charged with young energy. You can watch MTV while you wait, or even play table tennis.

Jaws
No-7, Castellino Road
Pune 411 001
Tel : 662621 (Residence)
Price : Inexpensive
Speciality : Fast food
Timings : 9 a.m. to 11 p.m.
Self-service

The bread of life

Kabab Corner

Kabab Corner
Amir Hotel
15A, Vaswani Road
(Near Pune Railway Station)
Pune 411 001
Tel : 621846-9
Price : Moderate
Speciality : North Indian
Timings : 7.30 to 11.30 p.m.
Credit cards accepted
Bar licence

Finding good food at a luxury hotel nowadays is rare. The Kabab Corner at Pune's Amir Hotel, is an exception. The decor is 'South Seas come to the Indian village': thatched huts, wooden tables and a bangle maker at the entrance. There is even a log fire for those cold Pune evenings, and cosy, discreet corner tables if things hot up. The menu is printed on wooden boards, and consists of the usual tandoori and standard Indian fare. Although we usually avoid Butter Chicken, it must be said that this one is the best one we have tasted in Pune; huge chunks of marinated chicken are swamped in a true butter and cream (not tomato, sugar) sauce. The Dhingri Kaju Muttar and Paneer Saag are musts for vegetarians, and the Murg Ke Tikke and Tangri Kabab for meat eaters.

The service is attentive. There is a full bar service which helps the mood along. With its subdued lighting, waterfall and open tandoori barbecue, this is certainly a good bet for a relaxed evening out.

La Pizzeria

Puneites have been slow to catch on to 'real' pizza. Until a few years ago, the fast food 'Ketchup variety' hogged the limelight. That is, until an enterprising Italian from the nearby Osho Commune saw the need for genuine pizzas, only they had to be vegetarian, in keeping with Osho's wishes. In fact, La Pizzeria is generally thought of as a 'sanyasins only' restaurant, because of the sheer number of Osho's maroon robed followers, who flock here after their evening discourse, but it is open to the public.

La Pizzeria
Hotel Srimaan
361/5 Bund Garden Road
Pune 411 001
Tel : 622857
Price : Moderate
Speciality : Italian
Timings : Evenings only
Home delivery

The menu, however, has been tailor-made to suit the largely sanyasin clientele. Do not be put off by the strange names of the pizzas—Zorba, Zen, etc., which are obviously just targeted at the maroon brigade. On a good day, you think you are in Rome, but unfortunately, the quality is not consistent. All the pizzas are freshly made, with mozzarella, olive oil, oregano, etc. We are also very fond of their home-made tagliatelle, with garlic and olive oil. The salads are a little disappointing. Most foreigners in India are advised not to eat raw vegetables in restaurants, so it's a case of boiled vegetables thrown together.

Wonderful ambience, simple and cheerful decor, and candlelit tables. There is, unfortunately, no liquor licence, but you can check with the Management about bringing your own bottle.

Mirch Masala

Mirch Masala
Hotel Saras
Nehru Stadium
Near Saras Baag
Pune 411 030
Tel : 420245
Price : Moderate
Speciality : Goan, North
  Indian
Timings : 11 a.m. to 3 p.m.;
  7 p.m. to midnight
Credit cards accepted
Partly air-conditioned
Full bar licence

Mirch Masala is the second venture of Dr Suhas Awchat, after Goa Portuguesa in Bombay. This is a strange place to start a restaurant of this type—within the somewhat shabby Nehru Staduim, and next door to one of the busiest bus and coach stops in the city. Despite this, it is proving popular with the local Puneites, starved of culinary variety.

All the seafood is brought in fresh from Bombay and Goa. The Lobster Piri Piri was fresh, but the 'piri piri', a little fiery. Crab Masala, again very fresh, was a cross between the spicy xacuti and more coconut based xecxec, but worth getting your fingers dirty for. In season, (November to May), try the Mussels in green masala and Coconut Clams. Round off with the Bebinca and ice cream.

We would recommend the seafood, but order it as near to the natural state as possible, i.e., avoid heavy masalas and cheese toppings. A big plus point is the full bar licence, including some interesting feni based cocktails. Good service and a relaxed atmosphere. Live band on weekends and holidays.

Portico

This up-market restaurant and bar, with black granite flooring, brass railings and crystal glassware, looks more like something out of a James Bond movie than a restaurant in downtown Deccan.

Portico
Dealing Chambers
J. M. Road
Deccan Gymkhana
Pune 411 004
Tel : 322503
Price : Expensive
Speciality : North Indian
Timings; 11.30 a.m. to 3 p.m.;
  7.30 to 11.30 p.m.
Reservation recommended
Credit cards accepted
Bar licence
Air-conditioned

The interiors are designed by Chandrashekar Kanitkar, who has also done the very tasteful Blue Diamond Hotel Bar, Casablanca. 'I wanted this to be Pune's really posh restaurant,' says Prem Tiwari, the Managing Director, who was previously with Hotel Natraj in Bombay. Portico is everything one would expect of five-star dining and most of the staff are from Bombay. There is even a car parking service. The food, though, is average compared with the lavish decor. Specialities include Amritsari fish, Mali Machli Tikka, fish in a mustard marinade, and Murg Methi Malai, chicken simmered in cashew nuts and yogurt, flavoured with methi and freshly ground masala. The Indian dishes, on the whole, with the exception of the barbecue, which is on the spicy side, are preferable to the highly overrated continental fare, like roast chicken in green and red pepper sauce, or vegetables au gratin.

Tiwari, a keen racegoer himself, was the first to introduce OCBC (no, not a new pop group, but an Off Course Betting Centre), in the restaurant itself, which is linked directly by computer with the R.W.I.T.C (Royal Western India Turf Club).

Sahare

Sahare
Near Sadhu Vaswani Chowk
Opposite GPO
Camp
Pune 400 001
Tel : 623776
Price : Inexpensive
Speciality :Gujarati
  Vegetarian Thali
Timings : 11 a.m. to 3 p.m.;
  7 to 10.30 p.m.

A relatively new thali eatery opposite the GPO in Pune. This one is spotlessly clean, large and roomy with granite splurged here and there, wooden tables, mock Irani chairs and the usual steel thalis. The Thali is Gujarati with a touch of Rajasthani on certain days. We found that the thali lacked green vegetables, but that may be due to the fact that we went during the rains. However the hot, mini bajra rotis smothered with ghee compensated for any complaint we may have had. Both the dals were excellent, a sweet one with peanuts and a savoury whole moong one. Of all the sabzis and curries, we liked the delicious spicy and sweet karela (bitter gourd) masala. For Rs 32, all inclusive, you get unlimited amounts of everything including a farsan (the special dahi vada is available only on Thursday and Sunday), papad, pickles, rice and chaas (buttermilk). Sweet (amras, shrikand, fruit salad) is Rs 10.

Very good value. A good place for a thali in Camp and very close to the Railway Station too.

Sanghmitra

A newly opened 'meeting place' on the ABC Farms dairy, deep at the end of Koregaon Park. Run by the gentle Darshan, a sanyasin from the nearby Osho Commune, who learnt his skills from his famous father, Boris Lissanevitch, an ex-ballet dancer who made his name and fame in Nepal. Many of Darshan's recipes come straight from his father's kitchen, like the Ukranian Borstch, served with the traditional garnishes of dill, onion and sour cream. Other dishes are a blend of European, with an emphasis on Health foods.

Sanghmitra
ABC Farms
Koregaon Park
Ghorpadi
Pune 411 001
Tel: 676555 (pp)
Price : Moderate
Speciality : European
    Vegetarian
Timings : Breakfast 8 a.m.
    to noon; Dinner 5.30 to
    11 p.m.

We especially liked the Miso Soup with Tofu, Guacamole (Mexican avocado dip), Stroganoff, Chilli (kidney bean stew) with Tofu and Pasta à la Maison, fresh noodles in a creamy mushroom and asparagus sauce. What we also liked were the add ons: parsley, potatoes, organic brown rice and delicious brown bread. The Apple Pie, Lemon Cheese Cake and Chocolate Pie, are also recommended. Fresh juices are squeezed to order. At the time of opening, the menu was totally vegetarian, but a separate non-vegetarian kitchen is planned for the near future.

Seating is in the garden or in the cosy indoor section, Japanese style, on the floor. We liked the quiet charm of Darshan and his band of Nepalis. The food is simple and straightforward, with no adulteration, heavy sauces or overpowering spices.

Shabri

Shabri
F. C. Road
Near Fergusson College
Pune
Price : Inexpensive
Speciality : Maharashtrian
  Thali Vegetarian
Timings : 11.30 a.m. to
  3 p.m.; 7 to 11 p.m.
Partly air-conditioned

You walk under a canopy of lilac flowers and find a thali restaurant which goes a step further than most. Shabri provides a rare commodity in inexpensive dining: ambience. The garden and waterfall, beautifully designed by Pune based landscape artist, Sumitra Awchat, may not be as well maintained as they could be, but the effort is commendable. Outside is seating for forty around heavy wooden tables. The decor is reminiscent of the old village restaurant in Worli Bombay. Twenty-five can eat in the make-believe village indoors, which is air-conditioned.

The fare is a standard Maharashtrian (slightly spicy) thali. Unlimited quantities of bhakri (javar or bajra rotis), spicy and sweet dals, Pitla (thick besan relish), fried snacks and vegetables, with a lashing of pure ghee over the whole lot. As with most thali restaurants, service is swift, and the surroundings clean and tidy.

Shreyas

The only place in Pune where a woman can go in a pair of shorts and be totally ignored. At Shreyas, people are too busy eating one of the best Maharashtrain (Brahmin) thalis in town to notice who you are or what you are wearing. Ignore the fake waterfall and the plastic chairs at the entrance (Shreyas, like Shabri, is also a hotel) to find a spotlessly clean dining-hall and matching waiters. The thali, sweetish and unlimited, ranges from good to divine depending on the day. The Usal Amti (sweet dal, usually made with sprouts), baingan with jaggery, coconut and peanut, and grated beet root salad are some of the treats in store. Rice is hot and fluffy (ambemor), and served with pure ghee, and the fried snacks exceptionally welcome. Some of the sweets are made on the premises; the shrikand is worth a try if you have any room left. Try and get to Shreyas early as it is jampacked an hour after opening.

Shreyas
1242 B, Apte Road
Deccan Gymkhana
Pune 411 004
Tel : 321024, 322023
Price : Inexpensive
Speciality : Maharashtrian
  Thali Vegetarian
Timings : 11.45 a.m. to
  2.30 p.m.; 7.45 to 10.30 p.m.

Copper and brass sellers

Shri Upakar Griha

Shri Upakar Griha
794, Sadashiv Peth
Pune 411 030
Price: Inexpensive
Speciality : Maharashtrian
 Vegetarian
Timings : 10 a.m. to 9 p.m.

Atul P. Bhide and his wife run this hole in the wall (literally) in the heart of the city. Outside, the menu is chalked in Marathi on a wobbly blackboard. Inside, men in pyjamas sit elbow to elbow on benches chomping away to glory on traditional Maharashtrain snacks. The kitchen, visible from wherever you sit, is amazingly orderly considering its shoe-box size. On one side, plates of Misal, the Maharashtrain answer to bhelpuri, are lined up ready for eating squad outside. On the other, Sabudana Vadas are fried, tossed on to a plate, topped with grated coconut and served with mild green coconut chutney. Other snacks include Sabudana Khichdi (a full meal), Samosas, Vadas and Sample, a thin red vegetable curry, which is served with all snacks, the poor man's staple diet. The bill for four all-time hoggers never exceeds Rs 50. Don't look for a romantic encounter here, or any kind of encounter for that matter. This is no more than a local family kitchen. Expect to be stared at if you wear anything other than working class Maharashtrian clothes.

The Charcoal Pit

A little known 'tandoori' restaurant, way up above M.G. Road (Main Street). Why this restaurant is not popular escapes us. Maybe it is because M.G. Road is primarily a shopping area which is deserted at night. The Charcoal Pit serves decent Tandoori rotis and relatively unoily vegetarian food at very reasonable prices. The service is quiet and sensitive to the clients' needs. I asked for kabab without any food colour, and although had to wait a little longer (understandable, as the chicken had to be cooked from the raw state), was well worth it. The plain Saag (spinach) was like good, simple home cooking. Simple but straightforward food in a clean, dhaba like atmosphere.

The Charcoal Pit
Roof Top Restaurant & Bar
Tej Regency Hotel
5 M.G. Road
Pune 411 001
Tel : 641570
Price : Moderate
Speciality : North Indian
Timings : 7 to 11.30 p.m.
Credit cards accepted

The Coffee Shop

The Coffee Shop
Hotel Blue Diamond
11, Koregaon Road
Pune 411 001
Tel : 625555
Price : Moderate
Speciality : Snacks
Timings : 24 hours
Credit cards accepted
Beer licence

Undoubtedly the best little coffee shop in the city. We are generally not covering coffee shops, but when we feel there is a desperate vacuum, which is filled by one, we mention it. The Coffee Shop certainly doesn't compare in terms of lavish decor, style and pizazz, with its cousins in bigger cities, but it does serve the best grilled sandwiches and filtered coffee, in town. The South Indian snacks, accompanied by a tangy tomato rasam (not on the menu anymore, but can be russled up), are great value. Other reliable staples include the Fish and Chips and Pizzas. You also get the most delicious, thick fresh orange juice (no additives or sugar) here, and on a cold winter night in Pune, there is nothing to beat their Hot Chocolate.

It is the kind of place where a woman would feel comfortable dining alone. Excellent service and incredibly reasonable prices for a five-star hotel.

The Coffee Shop

The German Bakery

Not a restaurant in the strict sense of the word, the German Bakery sells and serves the best sour-dough brown breads in India. They also cut them, top them with sumptuous relishes, and serve them as snacks. The Spring Bread with Garlic Herb Cheese, Country Bread with Cashewnut Butter and half a roll with feta, olive oil and herbs are all delicious. Other items worth their dough, are Honey Almond Slice, Peanut Cookies, Apple Crumble and Pie and a range of lunch-time snacks like the Mushroom Patty and Wholewheat Pizza. Our sons swear by the Cold Chocolate Cake.

The German Bakery
North Main Road
291 Koregoan Park
Pune 411 001
Price : Inexpensive/ Moderate
Speciality : Continental, Health Food Vegetarian
Timings : 9 a.m. to 11.30 p.m.

This is a no-nonsense, basic place, which caters mainly to the maroon robed sanyasins from the nearby Osho Commune. Signs on the wall tell you which breads contain no wheat, that the juices contain no added sugar, and that the tea is made with honey and mint. For those on a caffeine free diet, try the heady Nepalese Kam Bu Cha Fungus Tea; for those who are not, the German Bakery serves the best Capuccino in town.

Seating is on low wooden chairs, nursery school style, under the awning outside. All German Bakery's products are kept in glass fronted display units, away from flies and other unwelcome insects, so you can be sure of the hygiene. The place is nearly always packed, so prepare to queue. Klaus (Woody), the man behind the operation, has also opened branches in Kathmandu and Goa (near Anjuna flea market).

The Place

The Place
Touché the Sizzler
7, Moledina Road
(Near Manneys Bookshop)
Pune 411 001
Price : Moderate
Specialities : Continental,
    Indian, Sizzlers
Timings : 8.30 a.m. 11 p.m.
Beer licence
Air-conditioned

The Synagogue

The most successful sizzler restaurant in town, the Place has been run by Shahrookh Erani and Farida since 1971. His father, Feroz, started the concept of sizzlers in Bombay and was also a partner in the successful restaurant Touché at Breach Candy. The Place's specialities remain their Sizzler Steaks, Garlic Mushrooms, and for those with an appetite, the special Mixed Grill (pork chop, chicken, ham, steak, sausage, kidney, liver and egg with chips and vegetables). The salads, especially the Seafood Salad and the Green Salad tossed with a real discovery, a wonderfully refreshing anisette dressing, are both healthy alternatives to the sizzler selection. We also liked the Smoked Tenderloin, and Smoked Fish. From the Indian section, there is nothing to beat the Chicken Tikka Palak with a hot tandoori roti.

A casual, dining out experience, with guaranteed good food.

Vaishali

With its modest entrance one wouldn't think that Vaishali is the 'in place' in Deccan. Started in the Sixties to cope with Fergusson College students, it has remained a favourite with all ex-students (especially on Sunday mornings) and locals. One of the waiters, Lingu, nicknamed the 'Go Between', confessed that he has faithfully been passing on messages from boyfriend to girlfriend and husband to wife for over twenty years. The food is standard South Indian, and is always good and fresh; Dosas, Vada, Uttapam, Idli, and excellent South Indian coffee.

Vaishali
F C Road
(Opposite British Library)
Pune 411 004
Tel : 321244
Price : Inexpensive
Speciality : South Indian
Timings : 7 a.m. to 11 p.m.

The great plus point at Vaishali is its well-maintained, simple outdoor garden. Expect to have to wait for a table, and maybe even queue on weekends.

Zamu's Place

Zamu's Place
169, Sangamwadi
Off Dhole Patil Road
Pune 411 001
Tel: 623610
Price : Moderate
Specialities : Sizzlers,
  Continental, Indian
Timings : 9 a.m. to 3 p.m.;
  6 p.m. to midnight
Beer licence (including
  draught beer)
Air-conditioned

It is unfortunate that the partners of the Place, on Moledina Road, had to split up. The result is Zamu's, named after the owner's two sons. It therefore has a similar menu to the Place, with interesting daily specials. The mainstay is, however, the sizzlers—Kobe Steak, Chicken, Pork Chop, etc. Here too, the Garlic Mushrooms, crumb fried and served with a home-made Thousand Island dressing, are a treat. Salads and soups are reasonable, but the home-made dried apricot ice cream is phenomenal.

The decor is reasonable with cane furniture which looks better than it feels (i.e., the chairs). There is also an outdoor, covered section.

Index

A meal for one person
Inexpensive: under 100 rupees Moderate: 100 to 250 rupees Expensive: over 250 rupees

Memories of China : Chinese : Expensive, 33
Nagarjuna : South Indian (Vegetarian and Non-vegetarian) : Inexpensive, 34
Paradise Island : Oriental, Indian, Continental : Moderate, 35
Queens Restaurant : North Indian : Inexpensive, 36
Samrat Restaurant : South Indian Vegetarian : Moderate, 37
Sana : Middle Eastern : Inexpensive, 38
The Farmhouse : Continental (European) : Moderate, 39
The Only Place : Continental : Moderate, 41
The Tamarind Tree : Cuban/Mexican : Moderate, 42
The Schezwan Court : Chinese Schezwan : Expensive, 43
Tycoons : Continental, Indian : Moderate, 44
Woody's : South Indian Vegetarian : Inexpensive, 45

Bombay

Amritsari Fry Centre : North Indian : Inexpensive, 52
Anantashram : Malvani (Coastal) : Inexpensive, 53
Apoorva Restaurant & Bar : Mangalorean : Moderate, 54
A. Ramnaik's Udipi Shri Krishna Boarding : South Indian Vegetarian Thali :
    Inexpensive, 55
Bade Mian : Muslim kababs : Inexpensive, 56
Bagdadi : Persian : Inexpensive, 57
Bharat : Mangalorean seafood : Moderate, 58
Bombay A-1 Restuarant : North Indian : Inexpensive, 60
Candies : Snacks : Moderate, 61
Chawla's : North Indian : Moderate, 62
China Garden : Chinese : Expensive, 63
City Kitchen : Goan : Inexpensive, 65
Copper Chimney : Moghlai : Moderate, 66
Delhi Darbar : Moghlai : Inexpensive, 67
Fountain Inn : Mangalorean Seafood : Inexpensive, 68
Gajalee : Malvani : Inexpensive, 69
Gaylord Restaurant & Bar : Continental, Indian : Moderate, 70
Goa Portuguesa : Goan : Moderate, 71
The Golden Dragon : Chinese : Expensive, 72
Gomantak : Malvani : Inexpensive, 74
Gupta Restaurant : North Indian : Inexpensive, 75
Haji Tikka Corner : Muslim : Inexpensive, 77
Ideal Corner : Parsi : Inexpensive, 78
Indian Summer : North Indian : Moderate, 79
Jeff Caterers : Bohra Muslim : Inexpensive, 80
Kailash Parbat : Sindhi Punjabi : Inexpensive, 81
Kamling Chinese Restaurant : Chinese : Expensive, 83
Khyber Restaurant : Moghlai : Expensive, 84
Kobe Sizzlers : Steaks and Hamburgers : Moderate, 85
Kool Corner : Parsi : Inexpensive, 86
La Rotisserie : French Grills : Expensive, 87

Leopold Café : Irani, Continental, Indian, Chinese : Moderate, 88
Ling's Pavilion : Chinese : Expensive, 89
Mahesh Lunch Home : Mangalorean : Moderate, 91
Mela : North Indian : Expensive, 92
Ménage à Trois : European : Expensive, 93
Nanking : Chinese (Cantonese) : Moderate, 95
Nish : Chinese : Expensive, 97
Olympia : Muslim : Inexpensive, 99
Only Fish : Bengali (Seafood) : Expensive, 100
Pal's chicken Corner : North Indian : Inexpensive/Moderate, 101
Pancham Puriwala : North Indian Vegetarian : Inexpensive, 102
Paradise : Parsi Continental : Moderate, 103
Pizzeria Uno : Italian Pizzas : Moderate, 104
Pradeep Gomantak Bhojanalaya : Goan : Inexpensive, 105
Purohit : Gujarati Vegetarian Thali : Inexpensive, 106
Rajdhani : Gujarati Vegetarian Thali : Inexpensive, 107
Revival : Indian and Continental Vegetarian : Moderate, 108
Ritz : Italian : Expensive, 109
Saayba Hotel : Mangalorean Seafood : Inexpensive, 110
Sabar Dining Hall : Gujarati Vegetarian : Inexpensive, 111
Samovar : North Indian Snacks : Inexpensive, 112
Sardar Refreshment : Pau Bhaji (Vegetarian) : Inexpensive, 113
Sarvi : Muslim : Inexpensive, 114
Sea Lounge : Snacks : Expensive, 115
Sheetal Restaurant And Bar : North Indian, Chinese : Moderate, 116
Sheetal Samudra : Seafood and Tandoori Specialities : Moderate, 117
Sher-e-Punjab : North Indian : Moderate, 118
Sriram Boarding House : Konkani : Inexpensive, 119
Star of Asia Restaurant : Muslim : Inexpensive, 120
Swati Snacks : Gujarati Vegetarian : Moderate, 121
Tanjore : North Indian : Expensive, 122
Tewari Brothers Mithaiwala : North Indian: Inexpensive, 123
Thai Pavillion : Thai : Expensive, 124
Thaker Bhojanalay : Gujarati Vegetarian Thali : Inexpensive, 126
Thali Restaurant : Gujarati Vegetarian Thali : Inexpensive, 128
La Brasserie : Continental : Expensive, 129
The Great Wall : Chinese : Expensive, 130
The Outrigger : Polynesian : Expensive, 131
The Waterfall Café : Continental : Expensive, 132
Trattoria : Italian : Expensive, 133
Trishna Restaurant & Bar : Mangalorean Seafood : Moderate, 134
Under the Over : American, Continental : Moderate, 136
Vintage : Hyderabadi : Expensive, 137
Vithal Bhelwala : Maharashtrian Vegetarian Chaat : Inexpensive, 139
Wayside Inn : Continental : Inexpensive, 140
Yoko Sizzlers : Continental Sizzlers : Moderate, 141
Zodiac grill : Continental : Expensive, 142

Calcutta

Aheli : Bengali : Moderate, 150
Amber Bar & Restaurant : Moghlai : Moderate, 152
Aminia : Moghlai : Inexpensive, 153
Chinoiserie : Chinese : Expensive, 154
Kafulok Restaurant : Chinese : Moderate, 155
Lakhanlal Hotel : North Indian Vegetarian : Inexpensive, 156
Nizam's Restaurant : Tandoori, Moghlai : Inexpensive, 157
Rotisserie : French : Expensive, 158
Royal Indian Hotel : Moghlai : Inexpensive, 160
Shiraz Golden Restaurant : Moghlai : Inexpensive, 161
Siddheshwari Ashram : Bengali : Inexpensive, 162
Suruchi : Bengali : Moderate, 164
The Dhaba : North Indian : Inexpensive, 165
The Sonargaon : North Indian Bengali : Expensive, 166
Zaraanj : North Indian : Expensive, 167

Delhi

Al Kauser : North Indian : Moderate, 174
Baan Thai : Thai : Expensive, 175
Basil & Thyme : Continental : Moderate/Expensive, 177
Bukhara : North West Frontier (Indian) : Expensive, 178
Captain's Cabin : Seafood, Continental : Expensive, 180
Casa Medici : Northern Italian : Expensive, 181
Chor Bizarre : North Indian Kashmiri : Moderate, 182
Coconut Grove : South Indian : Moderate, 183
Colonel's Kabab : North Indian : Moderate, 184
D's Biryani Corner : Muslim : Moderate, 185
Dehli-ka-Aangan : North Indian : Expensive, 186
Dum Pukht : Avadhi : Expensive, 187
El Arab : Middle Eastern : Moderate, 188
Frontier Samosa Shop : Indian Snacks : Inexpensive, 189
Ganesh Restaurant : North Indian (fish only) : Inexpensive, 190
Gulati Restaurant : North Indian : Moderate, 191
Gulu Meatwala : North Indian : Inexpensive, 192
Karim's : Muslim : Moderate, 194
La Piazza : Italian : Expensive, 195
Minar Restaurant : North Indian : Moderate, 197
Moti Dhaba : Muslim : Inexpensive, 198
Nathu's : Indian Snacks : Inexpensive, 199
New Pishori : North Indian : Inexpensive, 200
New Tera Hotel : Vegetarian North Indian : Inexpensive, 201
Nizam's Kathi Kabab : Muslim : Moderate, 202
Noble House : Chinese : Expensive, 203
Om Hotel : North Indian : Inexpensive, 204

Orient Express : European (Continental) : Expensive, 205
Pakwan : North Indian, Moghlai : Expensive, 206
Pierre : Classical French and Flambé : Expensive, 207
Potpourri : Salad Bar and North Indian : Moderate, 208
Sagar : South Indian : Inexpensive, 209
Sardar Inderjit Singh Ka Dhaba : North Indian : Inexpensive, 210
Sitaram Divan Chand Prasidh Chole Bhature : Indian Snacks : Inexpensive, 211
Tea House : Chinese : Expensive, 212
The Grill Room : European (mainly grills) : Expensive, 213
The Village Bistro : Indian, Chinese, Tandoori, South Indian, Coffee Shop :
    Moderate, 214
Triveni Tea Terrace : North Indian : Inexpensive, 215
Wenger & Co : Indian Snacks : Inexpensive, 216

Goa

21 Coconuts : European : Moderate, 221
Bob's Inn : Goan, Continental : Moderate, 222
Cajueiro (Cashew Tree) : Goan, North Indian : Moderate, 223
Captain Lobo's : Goan, Continental : Moderate, 224
Casa Portuguesa : Goan, Continental : Moderate/Expensive, 225
Crosshill Bar : Goan : Inexpensive, 226
Florentine's Bar and Restaurant : Goan : Inexpensive, 227
Goenchin : Chinese : Moderate, 229
La Gondola : Italian : Expensive, 230
Kamat Hotel : South Indian Vegetarian : Inexpensive, 231
O Coqueiro (Coconut Tree) : Goan : Moderate, 232
Palmera : Indian, Continental, Goan : Expensive, 234
Pinto's Bar and Restaurant : Goan : Inexpensive, 235
Riorico : Goan, North Indian, Continental : Moderate, 236
Riverside : Goan, Continental : Moderate, 238
Riverside Wharf : Seafood (Goan and Continental) : Expensive, 239
Ronil Beach Resort : Indian, Goan, Chinese, Continental : Moderate, 240
Seaview Bar And Restaurant : Seafood : Inexpensive, 241
Sousa Lobo : Goan : Inexpensive, 242
St Anthony's : Goan, Continental : Inexpensive/Moderate, 243
St Francis Xavier's Trattoria : Italian : Expensive, 244
The Banyan Tree : Thai : Expensive, 245
The Beach House : Goan, Indian and Continental : Expensive, 247
The Bougainvillea : European, Indian : Moderate, 248
Venite : Goan : Moderate, 249
White House : Goan : Inexpensive, 250

Hyderabad

Abhiruchi : Andhra : Moderate, 255
Dakhni : Andhra, Hyderabadi : Expensive, 257

Firdaus : Hyderabadi : Expensive, 258
Haiking Chinese Restaurant : Chinese : Moderate, 259
Kabab-e-Bahar : North Indian : Moderate, 260
New Baisakhi Dhaba : North Indian : Moderate, 261
Shanbhag Hotel : South Indian Vegetarian : Inexpensive, 262
Swad Hotel : South Indian Vegetarian : Inexpensive, 263

Jaipur

Chanakya : North Indian, Rajasthani Vegetarian : Moderate, 269
Chokhi Dhani : Rajasthani : Inexpensive, 270
Gulab Mahal : Indian, Rajasthani, Continental : Expensive, 272
Laxmi Mishthan Bhandar : North Indian, Rajasthani : Moderate, 274
Niros : North Indian, Continental, Chinese : Moderate, 275
Rajputana Palace Sheraton : Continental, Indian, Chinese, Rajasthani :
    Expensive, 276
Shivir : North Indian, Rajasthani : Expensive, 277
Surya Mahal : South Indian, North Indian Vegetarian : Moderate, 278
The Rambagh Palace Hotel : Rajasthani, North Indian, Continental :
    Expensive, 279

Madras

Ahaar Restaurant : Moghlai, South Indian, Continental : Moderate, 285   •
Amma.Chettinadu Restaurant : Chettinad : Inexpensive, 286
AVM Dasa Restaurant : South Indian, Salad Bar (Vegetarian) : Moderate, 287
Chin Chin Restaurant : Chinese Szechwan : Moderate, 288
Coconut Grove : South Indian Vegetarian and Non-vegetarian : Moderate, 289
Dakshin : South Indian Vegetarian and Non-vegetarian : Expensive, 291
Kalpaka Restaurant : Kerala : Inexpensive, 293
Meneka Restaurant : South Indian Vegetarian : Moderate, 294
Palimar Restaurant : South Indian Vegetarian : Moderate, 295
Peshawri : North Indian : Expensive, 296
Raintree Restaurant : Chettinad : Expensive, 297
Saravana Bhavan : South Indian Vegetarian : Inexpensive, 299
Varandah Restaurant : North Indian, Continental : Expensive, 301
Woodlands Drive-in-Restaurant : South Indian Vegetarian : Inexpensive, 302

Nepal

Alfresco : Italian : Expensive, 306
Al Pollo E Pizzeria : Italian : Moderate, 307
Arniko Room : Chinese : Expensive, 308
Boris' Room : European : Moderate, 309
Ghar-E-Kebab : Moghlai : Expensive, 310
Helena's : Continental : Moderate, 311
Him Thai Restaurant : Thai : Expensive, 312

Mike's Breakfast : American : Moderate, 313
La Dolce Vita : Italian : Moderate, 314
Saino Restaurant And Bar : Chinese, Indian, Continental : Moderate, 315
Tashi Deleg : Tibetan : Inexpensive, 316

Pune

Abhiruchi : Maharashtrian : Inexpensive, 322
Angaraj : North Indian, Chinese : Moderate, 323
Ashoka Hotel : Gujarati Thali Vegetarian : Inexpensive, 324
Badshah Cold Drink House : Snacks : Inexpensive, 325
Blue Nile : Irani, North Indian : Inexpensive/Moderate, 326
Chandni : North Indian : Expensive, 327
China Town : Chinese : Moderate, 328
Chetana : Gujarati Thali : Inexpensive, 329
Coffee House : South Indian : Inexpensive, 330
Dorabjee & Sons : Irani, Parsi : Inexpensive, 331
Golconda : Hyderabadi, North Indian : Moderate, 332
Jaws : Fast food : Inexpensive, 333
Kabab Corner : North Indian : Moderate, 334
La Pizzeria : Italian : Moderate, 335
Mirch Masala : Goan, North Indian : Moderate, 336
Portico : North Indian : Expensive, 337
Sahare : Gujarati Vegetarian Thali : Inexpensive, 338
Sanghmitra : European Vegetarian : Moderate, 339
Shabri : Maharashtrian Thali Vegetarian : Inexpensive, 340
Shreyas : Maharashtrian Thali Vegetarian : Inexpensive, 341
Shri Upakar Griha : Maharashtrian Vegetarian : Inexpensive, 342
The Charcoal Pit : North Indian : Moderate, 343
The Coffee Shop : Snacks : Moderate, 344
The German Bakery : Continental, Health Food Vegetarian :
    Inexpensive/Moderate, 345
The Place : Continental, Indian, Sizzlers : Moderate, 346
Vaishali : South Indian : Inexpensive, 347
Zamu's Place : Sizzlers, Continental, Indian : Moderate, 348

READ MORE IN PENGUIN

In every corner of the world, on every subject under the sun, Penguin represents quality and variety – the very best in publishing today.

For complete information about books available from Penguin – including Puffins, Penguin Classics and Arkana – and how to order them, write to us at the appropriate address below. Please note that for copyright reasons the selection of books varies from country to country.

In India: Please write to *Penguin Books India Pvt Ltd, 706 Eros Apartments, 56 Nehru Place, New Delhi, 110019*

In the United Kingdom: Please write to *Dept. JC, Penguin Books Ltd, FREEPOST, West Drayton, Middlesex, UB7 OBR.*

If you have any difficulty in obtaining a title, please send your order with the correct money, plus ten per cent for postage and packaging, to *PO Box No. 11, West Drayton, Middlesex UB7 OBR*

In the United States: Please write to *Penguin USA Inc., 375 Hudson Street, New York, NY 10014*

In Canada: Please write to *Penguin Books Canada Ltd, 10 Alcorn Avenue, Suite 300, Toronto, Ontario M4V 3B2*

In Australia: Please write to *Penguin Books Australia Ltd, 487 Maroondah Highway, Ringwood, Victoria 3134*

In New Zealand: Please write to *Penguin Books (NZ) Ltd, 182–190 Wairau Road, Private Bag, Takapuna, Auckland 9*

In the Netherlands: Please write to *Penguin Books Netherlands B.V., Keizersgracht 231 NL–1016 DV Amsterdam*

In Germany : Please write to *Penguin Books Deutschland GmbH, Friedrichstrasse 10–12, W–6000 Frankfurt/Main I*

In Spain: Please write to *Penguin Books S. A.,C. San Bernardo, 117–6* *E–28015 Madrid*

In Italy: Please write to *Penguin Italia s.r.l., Via Felice Casati 20, I–20124 Milano*

In France: Please write to *Penguin France S. A., 17 rue Lejeune, F–31000 Toulouse*

In Japan: Please write to *Penguin Books Japan, Ishikiribashi Building, 2-5-4, Suido, Tokyo 112*

In Greece: Please write to *Penguin Hellas Ltd, Dimocritou 3, GR–106 71 Athens*

In South Africa: Please write to *Longman Penguin Southern Africa (Pty) Ltd, Private Bag X08, Bertsham 2013*

THE PENGUIN INDIA MOTOR-CAR HANDBOOK

Hormad Sorabjee

A comprehensive and fully illustrated guide to help you get the best out of your car, this book is packed with practical advice on the following:

- *How to choose your car*: A detailed analysis of every model available on the market should help you choose the best possible car for your needs. An exhaustive section on second-hand cars tells you what to look for and how to assess their condition and price.

- *How your car works*: A complete guide to all the important systems and components of your car, and how they function.

- *How to maintain your car*: The best and most practical ways to keep your car in good condition and save money in the long run.

- *How to tackle breakdowns*: 'First aid' for your car explained in a lucid and reader friendly manner.

- *How to improve your driving skills*: Tips on everything from basic driving procedures to advanced motoring techniques to help you tackle traffic better and drive more safely.

Written by an expert, the *Penguin India Motor-Car Handbook* should be an essential feature of your car's glove compartment.